Springer Series in Cognitive Development

Series Editor
Charles J. Brainerd

Springer Series in Cognitive Development

Series Editor: Charles J. Brainerd

Discourse Development
Progress in Cognitive Development Research

Edited by
Stan A. Kuczaj, II

Springer-Verlag
New York Berlin Heidelberg Tokyo

Stan A. Kuczaj, II
Department of Psychology
Southern Methodist University
Dallas, Texas 75275
U.S.A.

Series Editor
Charles J. Brainerd
Department of Psychology
University of Alberta
Edmonton, Alberta
Canada T6G 2E9

With 5 Figures

Library of Congress Cataloging in Publication Data
Main entry under title:
Discourse development.
  (Springer series in cognitive development)
  Bibliography: p.
  Includes index.
  1. Language acquisition. 2. Children—Communication.
I. Kuczaj, Stan A. II. Series.
P118.D57   1984   401'.9   83-20360

Typeset by MS Associates, Champaign, Illinois.
Printed and bound by R.R. Donnelley and Sons, Harrisonberg, Virginia.
Printed in the United States of America.

9 8 7 6 5 4 3 2 1

ISBN 0-387-90938-9 Springer-Verlag New York Berlin Heidelberg Tokyo
ISBN 3-540-90938-9 Springer-Verlag Berlin Heidelberg New York Tokyo

To Ann Wassel.
For all you do, this book's for you.

Series Preface

For some time now, the study of cognitive development has been far and away the most active discipline within developmental psychology. Although there would be much disagreement as to the exact proportion of papers published in developmental journals that could be considered cognitive, 50% seems like a conservative estimate. Hence, a series of scholarly books devoted to work in cognitive development is especially appropriate at this time.

The *Springer Series in Cognitive Development* contains two basic types of books, namely, edited collections of original chapters by several authors, and original volumes written by one author or a small group of authors. The flagship for the Springer Series is a serial publication of the "advances" type, carrying the subtitle *Progress in Cognitive Development Research*. Each volume in the *Progress* sequence is strongly thematic, in that it is limited to some well-defined domain of cognitive-developmental research (e.g., logical and mathematical development, development of learning). All *Progress* volumes will be edited collections. Editors of such collections, upon consultation with the Series Editor, may elect to have their books published either as contributions to the *Progress* sequence or as separate volumes. All books written by one author or a small group of authors are being published as separate volumes within the series.

A fairly broad definition of cognitive development is being used in the selection of books for this series. The classic topics of concept development, children's thinking and reasoning, the development of learning, language development, and memory development will, of course, be included. So, however, will newer areas such as social-cognitive development, educational applications, formal modeling, and philosophical implications of cognitive-developmental theory. Although it is anticipated that most books in the series will be empirical in orientation, theoretical and philosophical works are also welcome. With books of the latter sort, heterogeneity of theoretical perspective is encouraged, and no attempt will be made to foster some specific theoretical perspective at the expense of others (e.g., Piagetian versus behavioral or behavioral versus information processing).

C. J. Brainerd

Preface

The brief history of developmental psycholinguistics contains a number of zeit-geist shifts. In the 1960s and early 1970s, the field was dominated by an overriding concern with the nature of syntax and syntactic development, due largely to the seminal work of Noam Chomsky. During this period, relatively little attention was given to children's emerging communicative skills, the operative assumption being that if syntactic development could be explained, explanations of other language-related phenomenon would soon follow. For a variety of reasons (e.g., disenchantment with Chomsky's theory; the difficulty of studying syntactic development), a different operative assumption began to emerge in the early 1970s. This view held that if the development of communicative skills could be explained, then other aspects of language development would be more readily accounted for. Not only did this new assumption result in a marked increase in the amount of work being done on communicative development, it also resulted in attempts to explain phono-logical, semantic, and syntactic development in terms of children's intrinsic and extrinsic needs to be more efficient communicators.

At present, it is unclear whether any single aspect of language development can provide an explanatory basis for the whole of language development. Just as the focus on syntactic development resulted in the neglect of areas such as commu-nicative development, the focus on communicative development as *the* relevant topic for investigation has resulted in the relative neglect of important phenomena such as syntactic development. Those of us who study language development must remember that it is a multidimensional field. Children who are perfecting their communicative skills are also learning to articulate sounds, attach meanings to words, and utilize a variety of morphological and grammatical constructions. We do children an injustice if we assume that any of these skills develop in isolation.

Although the focus of this book is on the development of communicative skills in children, this focus is not intended to minimize the importance of other aspects of language development. The authors of the chapters do not argue that communication is the essence of human language, but instead point out aspects of communicative development of which scholars of language development should be aware. The topics range from a discussion of the implications of ethology for the consideration of communicative development to a consideration of communicative development in atypical language learners. Despite the range of topics, the chapters are tied together by a common concern, namely the importance of studying and eventually understanding communicative development. Recognizing that such a topic has many aspects, and that communicative development is intimately intertwined with other aspects of language development, is necessary if we are ever to explain what seems to be an unfathomable phenomenon—young children's relatively easy mastery of their native tongue. We (the authors and editor) hope that the present volume makes the mystery slightly more fathomable.

Dallas, Texas   Stan A. Kuczaj, II
February, 1984

Contents

             Development** **37**
             Michael F. McTear

             The Structure of Conversation 38
             Structure in the Conversation of Young Children 51
             Applied Discourse Analysis..................................... 66
             Appendix A... 71
             Appendix B 71
             References 72

Chapter 4 Skill in Peer Learning Discourse: What Develops? **77**
             Catherine R. Cooper and Robert G. Cooper, Jr.

             What Is a Peer?... 78
             What Is Peer Learning?.. 79
             Issues for the Study of Peer Learning Discourse 80
             Constraints on Children's Effectiveness........................ 81
             Research Evidence: Three Studies of Children's Discourse
             During Peer Learning 84
             Summary and Conclusions....................................... 92
             References 94

**Chapter 5 The Development of Narrative Skills: Explanations and
             Entertainments... **99**
             Susan Kemper

             The Content of Children's Stories 101
             The Plots of Children's Stories 103
             Causes and Consequences in Children's Stories................. 113
             Conclusions... 120
             Appendix 121
             References 123

**Chapter 6 Of Hawks and Moozes: The Fantasy Narratives Produced
             by a Young Child.. **125**
             Stan A. Kuczaj, II, and Leslie McClain

             Method 127
             Results and Discussion... 129
             Summary and Conclusions....................................... 142
             References 144

Contributors

Judith A. Becker Department of Psychology, University of South Florida, Tampa, Florida 33620, U.S.A.

Gina Conti-Ramsden Fingerpost Cottage, Norley Cheshire WA6 8LE, United Kingdom

Catherine R. Cooper Department of Home Economics, University of Texas, Austin, Texas 78712, U.S.A.

Robert G. Cooper, Jr. Department of Psychology, Southwest Texas State University, San Marcos, Texas 78666, U.S.A.

Sandy Friel-Patti Callier Center for Communication Disorders, University of Texas at Dallas, Dallas, Texas 75235, U.S.A.

Susan Kemper Department of Psychology, University of Kansas, Lawrence, Kansas 66045, U.S.A.

Stan A. Kuczaj, II Department of Psychology, Southern Methodist University, Dallas, Texas 75275, U.S.A.

Leslie McClain Department of Psychology, Southern Methodist University, Dallas, Texas 75275, U.S.A.

Laura McCloskey   Department of Psychology, Human Performance Center, University of Michigan, Ann Arbor, Michigan 48104, U.S.A.

Michael F. McTear   School of Communication Studies, Ulster Polytechnic, Newtownabbey BT37 OQB, North Ireland

Marilyn Shatz   Department of Psychology, Human Performance Center, University of Michigan, Ann Arbor, Michigan 48104, U.S.A.

Roger Wales   Department of Psychology, University of Melbourne, Parkville, Victoria, Australia, 3052

1. Implications of Ethology for the Study of Pragmatic Development

Judith A. Becker

"Hello. Yeah. This is Rosie. Yeah, I would like to bor- I would like to borrow your little 'raser. No? Why not? Uh, O.K. Bye."

"You better give me back that book! Or I'm going to really punch you in the face. I don't care if your sister protects you. I'll beat you both up. Bye."

Both of these samples come from the speech of a 10-year-old girl. In the first, she is pretending to speak on the telephone to a new male teacher in her school and is asking to borrow an eraser from him. In the second, she is pretending to talk to the 3-year-old sister of a friend and is asking the little girl to return a book she took without asking.

Any conclusions drawn about these samples must address a number of questions. Are the samples typical of 10-year-olds? Under what circumstances will children speak in this way? How did the girl acquire these abilities? What functions do the behaviors serve for the child in those contexts? Why would a child have these behaviors in her repertoire at all, that is, what adaptive significance do the behaviors have? Given the current state of knowledge about pragmatics and our current theoretical perspectives (or lack thereof), we cannot adequately address these questions. In order to answer them, it is necessary to view pragmatic behaviors in a broader context—the context of other social behaviors and the environment in which children develop. In this chapter I argue that attention to ethology, the study of the natural behavior of animals, can lead us to view pragmatic phenomena in just such a new and productive way. I first describe the basic tenets of ethology: description of behaviors observed naturalistically and analysis of the ontogeny, phylogeny, and function of these behaviors. I illustrate the implications of each point for the study of pragmatic development with examples drawn primarily from my own work on children's use of requests. Most of the emphasis is on the usefulness of a functional approach in studying pragmatics. Such an approach leads one not only to describe behaviors but to explain why these behaviors occur, that is, how they serve the individual child and the species.

Ethology

In 1877, Charles Darwin published "A Biographical Sketch of an Infant" (1877/ 1977), a paper based on a diary he kept of the cognitive development of his son. This paper was perhaps the first application of ethology to the study of child development in that Darwin observed a wide variety of behaviors and placed them in an evolutionary framework. Among the behaviors he described were early vocabulary, use of intonation, and reflexes. During this same period, theorists such as Preyer (1881/1901) and Baldwin ((1895/1925) were inspired by Darwin and published similar descriptive studies. Until the early 1970s, however, there was a virtual hiatus in work that utilized an ethological approach in studying human development. Since that time, the literature in human ethology has increased dramatically. The beginning of this renewed academic interest was marked by the inclusion of an article on ethology as the first chapter in the third edition of *Carmichael's Manual of Child Psychology* (Hess, 1970). The publication of the chapter in so prominent a volume helped legitimize the ethological approach and reinforced its relevance for the study of human development. Closely following the conceptual Hess chapter, McGrew (1972) and Blurton-Jones (1972) published detailed, empirical books and clearly demonstrated the applicability of ethology's methods and theory to developmental research. Concurrently, the more popular work of Robert Ardrey and Desmond Morris as well as the fascinating observations of Jane Goodall and Konrad Lorenz brought an ethological approach to the attention of the general public.

It is time for those of us studying language development, particularly pragmatics, to take a careful look at the ethology literature. Ethology has important and interesting implications for the ways in which we study pragmatic development and for the conclusions we draw about pragmatic behaviors. Unfortunately, ethologists do not usually concern themselves with language. This may be because the discipline has its origins in the study of nonhuman animal behavior where language is not an issue. When ethologists do describe and analyze language, they often deal with it globally in terms of "vocalizations." Conversely, psycholinguists usually do not concern themselves with ethology. Previous attempts to relate ethology to language development suffer from vagueness. For example, Mahoney (1975) used ethological concepts loosely and almost metaphorically in the context of an otherwise traditional, pragmatic approach to language delay. Similarly, Foppa (1979) construed children's ability to ascertain linguistic rules as involving unspecified "selection pressures."

A more useful application of ethology requires the precise and accurate use of ethological concepts and principles. Most ethologists share a common approach to the study of behavior. First, they begin their work by attempting to describe thoroughly the behaviors typical of a particular species in its natural habitat. This description is known as an *ethogram,* and is obtained by means of naturalistic observation. Following this lengthy descriptive process, and often more controlled experiments, ethologists organize and explain their findings in terms of the ontogeny, phylogeny, and function (or survival value) of the behaviors. In this chapter I elaborate on each of these points and suggest ways in which they are relevant for the study of pragmatic development, particularly the use of requests.

Ethological Methods and Pragmatics

According to Hess (1970, p. 2), "ethology has as its major premise the notion that the study of behavior begins through the compilation of as complete an inventory as possible of all the behaviors of the organisms in, and in relation to, its [sic] natural environment, throughout its entire life cycle." Ethologists believe that a given behavior can only be understood in relation to other behaviors and so one should not study that particular behavior in isolation. Further, they emphasize the inductive method of deriving general principles from specific facts. Researchers studying pragmatic development, as in other developmental areas, have implicitly concurred with this perspective by beginning their work with description. Good examples of such work are the longitudinal, observational studies of infants' pragmatic behaviors by Bates (1976) and Zukow, Reilly, and Greenfield (1982) and similar studies of older children and adults by Ervin-Tripp (1976, 1982). There is also an enormous amount of descriptive information about one type of pragmatic behavior: children's use and understanding of requests (see Becker, 1982, for a review of this literature). However, the literature is limited in that the studies tend to be done in classrooms (e.g., Cherry Wilkinson, Clevenger, & Dollaghan, 1981; Dore, 1977) and are typically not longitudinal.

Another aspect of ethologists' descriptive work is that behaviors are catalogued objectively without reference to their hypothetical function. That is, they are labeled morphologically. For example, a child might be described as "raising an arm with a clenched fist" rather than as "making a threatening gesture." Such molecular description is important because a given behavior may serve different functions in different contexts (Lehner, 1979). The raised arm with clenched fist may indeed serve as an aggressive signal in some situations, but have an entirely different meaning during play.

The notion that the meaning of a behavior depends on the context in which it is used is the essence of pragmatics. According to the pragmatic perspective, semantic, syntactic, and phonological analyses of an utterance are insufficient for determining the utterance's meaning. One must also consider who used that utterance with whom under what circumstances. Consider the utterance "Gee, it's cold in here." It is an assertion of fact if someome shivering in a Minneapolis bus shelter in the middle of January says it. It is sarcasm if someone says it in a crowded, un-air-conditioned car in Tampa on a humid, August afternoon. It is an indirect request to close the window if a person who is sniffling and blowing her nose says it to someone sitting next to an open window through which wind and rain are blowing. These meanings are based on an interaction between characteristics of the utterance and circumstances of its use.

While researchers and theorists in pragmatics claim to recognize the dependence of meaning on context, this is not always reflected in their writing. With relatively few exceptions (e.g., Garvey, 1975; McTear, 1980), researchers study specific pragmatic behaviors such as requests in isolation without considering sequences of behaviors or the role of requests in discourse. Rerequests and modifications of persuasive strategies should also be investigated in order to better understand this aspect of pragmatic development. For example, the utterance "Gimme that!" would be interpreted differently if it were used alone than if it were used at the end of a series of less direct requests that had been refused.

More problematically, some writers neglect to describe pragmatic behaviors objectively and instead categorize them according to supposed function.[1] One example of such imprecision is the ready classification of some utterances as "polite" rather than as specific syntactic forms. For instance, utterances such as "Would you please be so kind as to hand me that book, Miss Stanley" have been described as being polite without regard for the contexts in which they are used (e.g., James, 1978). While this request might be polite if it were directed by a younger woman to her elderly neighbor, it would not be polite at all if it were directed by that same woman to her young daughter who has just ignored several more direct requests. The meaning and function of a behavior, in this case politeness, reside not in the behavior itself, but in the use of that behavior in a particular context. Function cannot be ascertained solely on the basis of observation of the occurrence of the behavior, but only after careful consideration and experimental manipulation. I expand this argument in a later section.

The Ontogeny and Phylogeny of Pragmatic Behaviors

Once a set of behaviors has been carefully observed and described, ethologists attempt to analyze the development of the behavioral repertoire. This is done on two levels: development of the behaviors in the individual and development or evolution of the behaviors in the species. Clearly, the former is much more readily accomplished, while the latter requires comparison of the species being studied to evolutionarily related species.

Psycholinguists know a good deal about the course of development of a few pragmatic abilities, especially requests. As I mentioned earlier, this developmental progression is derived primarily from a compilation of cross-sectional studies. To

---

[1] In addition to being a conceptual error, such classification may also be an unfortunate effect of journal limitations. We seldom have the opportunity to define categories or present detailed examples. Gross functional classification may be an expedient, albeit imprecise, solution.

the extent that pragmatic skills are affected by cultural vagaries, conclusions drawn from cross-sectional studies must be qualified, given the possibility of confounding cohort effects.

While we know some things about the course of development of abilities such as the use of requests, we know far less about how these abilities are acquired. There has been considerable research on the relation between parental input ("mother-ese") and subsequent acquisition of syntactic and semantic abilities. In contrast, there has been virtually no attention to factors affecting the acquisition of prag-matic abilities, as Bates, Bretherton, Beeghly-Smith, and McNew have pointed out (1982). Most of the current evidence is anectodal. For example, Barrett (1980) and Bates (1976) noted that parents explicitly train children in the use of some request forms: "You can't have it until you say 'please.'" More systematic work has also been done. Gleason and Weintraub (1978) have investigated how parents teach language routines such as requests, thank yous, greetings, and farewells. Eisenberg (1982) has done similar research on Mexican families that have immi-grated to the United States. In my laboratory, we are currently exploring pragmatic socialization. We have begun by looking at adults' expectations about the develop-ment of pragmatic abilities and about the degree to which these abilities are manip-ulable. Preliminary results suggest, for example, that adults believe parents are the most important source of influence in the development of pragmatic skills such as saying "please" and "thank you," using the appropriate volume and tone of voice, taking turns in a conversation, and making polite requests. In addition, they believe that it is never too late for children to acquire these pragmatic abilities. Presumably, these attitudes are reflected in child-rearing practices related to pragmatics.

The second aspect of development with which ethologists deal, *phylogeny,* is considerably thornier. It would be very difficult to explore the evolution of prag-matic behaviors in primates, relative to the ease of investigating the evolution of, for example, bipedalism. Theorists have discussed the evolution of language more generally, and some argue that pragmatic aspects of language were precursers to other aspects (Jaynes, 1976). It may be premature to consider the phylogeny of pragmatics, but it is not premature to try to understand how pragmatic behaviors are similar to other social behaviors that both children and nonhuman primates exhibit. I elaborate on this point in the next section.

The Functional Significance of Pragmatic Behaviors

Ethologists, given their evolutionary orientation, believe that behaviors and physical structures typically serve important functions for the species that pos-sesses them. That is, no behavior or structure evolves arbitrarily. Theoretically, deleterious characteristics do not contribute to the survival of the individual or species and will eventually be selected against and disappear from the species. On the other hand, characteristics that are adaptive (that enable the individual to cope successfully with environmental conditions and improve fitness to survive and reproduce) are passed along genetically through the mechanisms of natural selection.[2]

The adoption of such an evolutionary perspective leads one to wonder what purpose pragmatic behaviors serve for children and for the species as well as why pragmatic behaviors have the forms they do. It is in the area of function that I believe ethology has the greatest implications. For example, we know that children use particular types of requests in certain situations and use other types in other situations. Why is there this regular relationship and not some other? What general role do requests play in the social life of the child? Is this role comparable to the role played by other communicative behaviors exhibited by children and other species?

The failure of researchers in pragmatics to consider the functional significance of requests and other behaviors may be due to their reasons for studying pragmatics in the first place. I see the current pragmatics literature as arising from a desire to demonstrate that young children are not egocentric in their communicative behaviors, but are able to adapt their messages to their listeners. Let me present an historical overview to clarify this point.

Piaget published *The Language and Thought of the Child* in 1924 (1924/1974). In it he claimed that pre-school-aged children are basically egocentric thinkers and are unable to understand other people's perspectives. This, he said, is reflected in the fact that preschoolers cannot conduct normal conversations with their peers; they cannot truly interact or mutually discuss a topic. As with Piaget's other writings, *Language and Thought* inspired an enormous amount of research. In an attempt to retain the cognitive flavor of Piaget's work but investigate the ideas more carefully, Glucksberg and Krauss and their colleagues (Glucksberg, Krauss, & Higgins, 1975) studied children's referential communication abilities during the 1960s. Their basic task involved having children describe a series of novel geometric forms to a listener on the other side of an opaque barrier. They found that preschoolers performed quite poorly, and concluded that preschoolers are egocentric communicators. Two lines of research emerged from this referential communication work. Some researchers (notably Maratsos, 1973, 1974) continued to investigate referential communication, but with simpler, more interesting tasks, and found earlier evidence of sociocentric speech. Other researchers employed more social and naturalistic methods. The most significant of these studies (Shatz & Gelman, 1973) entailed having 4-year-olds converse with 2-year-olds, peers, and adults. The children modified their speech for the listeners both syntactically and in terms of the amount of speech used.

Since the mid-1970s, there has been a plethora of demonstrations comparable to Shatz and Gelman's. Researchers have shown that young children vary their speech (particularly requests) to a variety of listeners (e.g., siblings, unfamiliar children, babies, dolls, pets, handicapped children) and in a variety of situations (e.g.,

---

[2] Not all ethologists or evolutionary theorists agree with this perspective. Some (e.g., Rajecki & Flanery, 1981) argue that neutral characteristics may survive either because they are not maladaptive or because they are genetically associated with adaptive characteristics.

borrowing something, asking someone to return something). The primary motivation for these studies is to show that Piaget was wrong about preschoolers' communicative egocentrism. That point has clearly been made. Yet, similar studies continue to be done and published as researchers continue to come up with novel listeners and situations to which children can react. Despite the importance of gathering further descriptive data about children's pragmatic abilities, it is no longer enough simply to demonstrate children's nonegocentrism. It is time for those of us studying pragmatics to consider *why* it is that children vary their speech for different listeners and *why* they vary it in the lawful and regular fashion that they do. Again, the literature on requests can be used to illustrate my points.

The Function of Modifications of Requests

What regularities have been observed in children's use of requests with different listeners and in different situations? In general, children and adults use requests that have a particular set of characteristics with listeners of higher status (e.g., who are older or more dominant) or in situations in which they are at a disadvantage with respect to power (e.g., when asking for a favor). They use another type of request with listeners of lower status (e.g., who are younger or less dominant) or in situations in which they are at an advantage with respect to power (e.g., when asking to have something returned). There are two major characteristics that differentiate request forms to higher status listeners from those to lower status listeners: syntactic directness and semantic markers. Syntactic directness, as initially described by Ervin-Tripp (1976), is a measure of how explicitly the structure of the sentence indicates that it is a request and what that request entails. Descriptions and examples of her categories of syntactic directness, arranged from most to least direct, are the following:

Imperative: normally includes a verb and, for transitive verbs, an object and sometimes a beneficiary—*Give me a book.*
Need statement: imperative stated as a need or want—*I need a book.*
Embedded imperative: actor, action, object, and often beneficiary, are as explicit as in an imperative, but are embedded in a frame with other syntactic and semantic properties, usually modals—*Could you give me a book?*
Permission directive: question form includes a modal, beneficiary, and verb (typically *have*)—*May I have a book?*
Question directive: desired act and often the agent of the act are not specified—*Have a book?*
Hint: general statement of condition—*I like to read.*

Speakers tend to use more indirect forms with higher status listeners and more direct forms with lower status listeners.

Semantic markers also help speakers differentiate requests to listeners of different status. Semantic markers are words or phrases that change the meaning of a request and that cannot be described in terms of syntactic directness. Requests to higher status listeners tend to include semantic softeners such as "please," reasons for the request, and promises such as "If you give me that, I'll give you this." Requests to lower status listeners, in contrast, tend to include semantic aggravators such as threats and profanity.

When considering these regularities, many ethologists would not take them to be an accident. Rather, they would attempt to explain why particular request forms have come to be used with particular status relationships. The different forms are not arbitrary and may serve a function in the interaction. This appears to be the case. Higher status individuals have authority to regulate the behavior of others. They can make unambiguous, coercive requests. In contrast, lower status individuals must be extremely careful in attempting to regulate the behavior of other people. If they are going to make requests at all, the requests must be as ambiguous and submissive as possible.

Speakers who are of higher status regulate their listeners' behaviors by using direct requests with semantic aggravators. Syntactically direct requests are authoritative forms in that they indicate explicitly that they are requests for action. They allow no clear alternatives to compliance except for overt refusal or ignoring. Semantic aggravators such as threats (e.g., "or else") or phrases indicating immediacy (e.g., "right now") place additional limitations on the way the listener can respond. Other aggravators such as profanity and sarcastic address terms (e.g., "Hey kid") serve to denigrate the listener. Higher status speakers are able to command obedience and assert their power.

Speakers who are of lower status than their listeners tend to use indirect requests with semantic softeners. By virtue of the power differential, these speakers cannot be assertive or threatening. Instead, they must allow the other person options for responding aside from being beneficent and complying. Indirect requests appear to be ambiguous since they are embedded within other syntactic forms. They thus allow a number of alternative responses (e.g., taking an embedded imperative as a request for information or agreeing with the assertion made in a hint.) Listeners do take advantage of these alternatives. Adults have been observed to respond to indirect requests with both compliance and an answer to the literal question (Clark, 1979; Clark & Schunk, 1980; Munro, 1979). For example, a speaker might ask "Do you close before seven tonight?" and the listener would be likely to reply, "No, we close at nine" (Clark, 1979, p. 445). People also create pragmatic jokes by treating an indirect request as a question: "Is your father there?" "Yes, he is." Garvey (1975, p. 56) has reported an interaction between two preschoolers in which one child indirectly requested another child to pick up a ringing telephone: "Why don't you answer me?" The second child, answering the literal question, replied, "I don't know." Aside from such observations, there is no systematic evidence for children's tendency to treat indirect requests as anything other than requests for action. While both children and adults seem to be predisposed to respond to indirect requests as requests for action (Labov & Fanshel, 1977; Shatz, 1978), indirectness nonetheless serves a purpose insofar as listeners are aware of it (Morgan, 1975). In general, children and adults judge indirect requests to be more polite than direct requests (Bates, 1976; Bates & Silvern, 1977 ; Clark & Schunk, 1980).

Semantic softeners in requests also enable the lower status speaker to appear properly submissive. Hesitations, errors, and fillers (e.g., "um," "shir-jacket," "and and") suggest uncertainty, weakness, and incompetence. Softeners can also degrade their speaker (e.g., "I feel stupid asking"). Phrases such as "kind of," "a small favor," or "for just a bit" minimize the request by making it seem inconsequential. Similarly, references to the listener's convenience (e.g., "if you feel like it") and vagueness about time (e.g., "no hurry") allow the listener complete leeway in determining the conditions for compliance. Unlike direct requests, indirect requests also tend to include reasons; lower status speakers must justify the presumption of their requests. In general, syntactic indirectness and semantic softeners enable lower status speakers to appease and avoid antagonizing their listeners (Brown & Levinson, 1978; Labov & Fanshel, 1977).

The Function of Requests in Social Groups

Given that the manner in which children and adults vary their requests to listeners of different status is meaningful, one might next consider another way in which this functional regularity serves a purpose. Syntactic directness and semantic markers in requests can mark or indicate status relationships because they vary so regularly and predictably in different interactions. By providing information about relative status while at the same time accomplishing other business, children can avoid more serious conflict over power, rights, and obligations.

It is certainly advantageous for children to avoid unnecessary conflict over status. In groups of social animals, peers are both partners and rivals. Individuals must find ways to resolve the conflict between natural competitiveness and the need for cooperation. This is true in virtually all social species (Chance & Jolly, 1970; Dewsbury, 1978; Immelman, 1980; Marler, 1974; Schein, 1975). One mechanism by which groups manage to balance the tension between competition and cooperation is the formation of dominance hierarchies. Individuals at the top of the hierarchy enjoy their dominant status by virtue of physical power, access to desired resources, social role, and so on. Individuals lower on the hierarchy possess fewer or none of these attributes and are thus submissive to higher members. Once a hierarchy is established, members can avoid having to reassert their position through direct aggression by signaling their relative status (Alcock, 1975; Darwin, 1872/ 1965). Signals of dominance warn of the fruitlessness of fighting and signals of submission inhibit fighting. Such signals are mutually advantageous.

The forms of signals used to indicate relative status are comparable for nonhuman animals and children (see Omark, Strayer, & Freedman, 1980, for papers on this topic). Both nonhuman primates and children use remarkably similar facial expressions to indicate threatening dominance and appeasing submission (Blurton-Jones, 1969; Camras, 1977, 1983; Chevalier-Skolnikoff, 1973; Zivin, 1977). Children and other species also use posture and gestures to indicate dominance (Eibl-Eibesfeldt, 1975; Lorenz, 1963; McGrew, 1972; Strayer & Strayer, 1976). For example, during a conflict, dominant individuals may stand erect and otherwise increase their size, while less dominant individuals tend to make themselves smaller and expose vulnerable parts of their bodies. Finally, various species mark relative status with visual attention (Chance & Larsen, 1976). Less dominant members of the hierarchy spend more time watching more dominant members than vice versa.

Requests are functionally analogous[3] to facial expressions, postures and gestures, and visual attention in signaling relative status or dominance. Solely on the basis of the way in which children use requests with different listeners, this assertion seems to be true. However, stronger evidence is needed to make such a claim with greater certainty. Experimental manipulation would be useful. It is often a second methodological step for ethologists, especially when they are investigating signals or "releasing stimuli." Among other techniques, ethologists break the hypothesized signals down into components to see which are critical in producing the previously observed responses. I have modified this strategy as a way to assess a number of possibilities. First, if requests are used as signals for status, children might be able to manipulate them deceptively by using forms they would not normally be expected to use in order to obtain social advantage. They might use a more direct request than usual in order to raise their status or use a less direct request to suppress unwanted aggression. Second, children should be able to infer the relative status of speakers by hearing requests directed toward them. Third, children should be able to convey status-related nuances such as "bossiness" by using characteristics of requests in a predictable way.

The Deceptive Use of Signals for Dominance and Submission. Nonhuman animals have been observed to deceive other animals through the use of signals for status. For example, lizards and crabs attempt to threaten predators by raising themselves up and extending parts of their bodies (Eibl-Eibesfeldt, 1975). Some animals feign injury when attacked, and thus forestall further aggression by giving the impression that they are powerless (Marler, 1974). Incubating or brooding birds often exhibit similar behavior to distract and mislead predators (Eibl-Eibesfeldt, 1975). Children can also behave deceptively, and they do so consciously.

Mitchell-Kernan and Kernan (1977), in a study of children's requests during role play, noted what they called "imperative traps." By this they meant the use of requests, not to gain compliance, but to manipulate or test status relationships.

[3] My use of the term "analogous" is purposeful. In addition to its common usage, "analogy" has a particular meaning in ethology. When ethologists look at the phylogeny of structures or behaviors, they consider similarities across species. These similarities may either represent homologies or analogies. Homologies are similarities due to genetic inheritance from common ancestors. Analogies are similarities that developed independently in species that evolved in similar environments and thus responded to similar selective pressures. Identifying homologies and analogies is notoriously difficult. Ethologists argue about the degree of similarity necessary for such identification and even about whether behaviors can represent homologies or analogies at all (see von Cranach, 1976). In light of the fact that no other animal is able to use language as humans do, I do not think I can legitimately call request usage an analogy. In this case the similarity to the behaviors of other social animals is functional rather than strictly structural. Nonetheless, I think it is useful to suggest this connection.

One illustration of such a trap involved an 8-year-old girl saying to Mitchell-Kernan, "I want that chair." This was an inappropriately direct request. When Mitchell-Kernan gave up her chair while continuing a conversation with someone else, the girl appeared smug. She had successfully used a signal for dominance to assert power she did not in fact possess. Labov (1972) has observed the same types of behavior by teenage blacks and Puerto Ricans.

The converse of the imperative trap is the ploy of forcing victims to make unusually submissive requests. This is exemplified in the ubiquitous situation in which children fight and the losers, in order to avoid further injury and be extricated, are forced to beg for release. Only a submissive request such as "Pretty please with sugar on it will you let me go?" will work. Speakers are thus tricked into demeaning themselves by acting as if they are of low status or power. Mitchell-Kernan and Kernan (1977) also described appeasement behaviors similar to these. Elementary-school-aged children who had had a falling out with peers tended to switch to requests that were less direct and contained more semantic softeners. Again, these data are only anecdotal. More conclusive evidence is necessary to support my claim about the function of requests.

Inferring Status from Requests. If requests function as signals for status, they must be interpretable as such by their receivers. That is, syntactic directness and semantic markers should serve as cues for relative dominance and submissiveness. Children who have sufficient experience with requests should be able to infer relative status from requests they hear. I have found evidence for this ability in preschoolers in my laboratory.

A group of 4- and 5-year-olds listened to pairs of requests addressed to them by two dolls. The dolls were described as being the subjects' age (i.e., peers). Each pair of requests differed solely with respect to one of the hypothesized cues for status. Some pairs differed in their levels of syntactic directness (e.g., "Gimme a penny" vs. "I really like pennies") and others differed in the number of semantic softeners they contained (e.g., "Give me a penny" vs. "Give me a penny, please"). After each pair, the children decided which doll was "asking in a bossier way." (In preschoolers' terms, being bossy means that one is or is pretending to be powerful and of higher status.) As expected, the children viewed the more syntactically direct requests and those with fewer semantic softeners as bossier. These were the requests that were more likely to have been spoken by a higher status person. Older children were able to infer status over a wide range of contrasting pairs of requests, whereas the 4-year-olds did so consistently only for the more extreme contrasts. This developmental difference probably reflects the 5-year-olds' greater experience with requests in a variety of situations as well as their greater cognitive abilities.

Children's definitions of bossiness provide an additional source of evidence that children see connections between the form of requests and status. Before children began this experiment, they were asked "what it means when someone is bossy" to ensure that they understood this term. Many children spontaneously mentioned language in their definitions. For example, one 4-year-old boy said that bossy means saying things like, "Don't come in!" A 5-year-old girl suggested that being bossy means "yelling and not letting people do what they want to do, just what they want to do." Similarly, another girl this age said, "They boss you around and they tell you what to do. They make people do things what [sic] they don't want to do." The best definition came from the 5-year-old girl who said that her father was bossy. "One day," she explained, "they went to a party and my dad said, 'Let's go home.' My mom wanted to stay, but they went home."

Conveying Status-Related Nuances by Means of Requests. I have presented evidence that children can infer relative status from requests. They also occasionally use requests strategically to present themselves as higher or lower in status than they actually are. They do so by deceptively using requests as signals for their listeners. Can children also convey more subtle messages and shades of meaning by systematically varying characteristics of their requests? Their ability to do so in a consistent, predictable, and meaningful fashion would provide more evidence that requests have signaling value with respect to status.

In another experiment in my laboratory, I asked subjects to produce requests that conveyed the nuances of bossiness and niceness. One might expect a speaker to make a bossy request of a peer by being more syntactically direct and using more semantic aggravators than usual, by asking more like a higher status speaker than a peer. On the other hand, one might expect a speaker to make a nice request of a peer by being more syntactically indirect and using more semantic softeners than usual, by asking more like a lower status speaker than a peer. The only research that has addressed a similar question was done by Bates (Bates, 1976; Bates & Silvern, 1977). She found that Italian- and English-speaking children can increase the niceness of their requests by making them increasingly indirect and adding semantic softeners.

In my experiment, 5-year-olds, 10-year-olds, and adults pretended to address requests to imaginary peers, listeners of the same status. Each subject asked the peers to return borrowed items in both a "bossy way" and a "nice way." The following six sets of responses are typical of those obtained in this experiment:

5-year-old boy
Bossy request: You give me that jacket back.
Nice request: Can you give me my book back?

5-year-old girl
Bossy request: Let me have my book back right now.
Nice request: Can you please give me my ball back?

10-year-old boy
Bossy request: I want my jacket back right now.
Nice request: I'd like to know if you're not using the ball and if I could um please have it back.

10-year-old boy
Bossy request: I want you to bring it over right now or I'll beat your face in.

Nice request: Well, could you please bring it over to me 'cause I need it really bad.

Man

Bossy request: You want I want you to bring the ball over right now 'cause we're going to be leaving in about 5 minutes.

Nice request: Um I borrowed you my jacket last night and um there's no real hurry in returning it but, as, you know, whenever it's convenient for you I'd appreciate it if you'd have somebody bring it by or if maybe I could come over and get it from you.

Woman

Bossy request: Could you please bring it back over here right now?

Nice request: I wa I was just wondering if I could get my jacket back, but if you're cold that's that's OK you know I I really don't need it back right away, but, you know, whenever you're done with it um maybe you could just bring it over or something, but only if um you don't need it any more.

In each case the speakers clearly conveyed their meanings.

As predicted, subjects' bossy requests were more syntactically direct than were their nice requests. This was true for each age group. Bossy requests were also more negative semantically than were nice requests. They contained more threats and references to immediacy and far fewer hesitations than did the nice requests. While all three age groups were able to differentiate their bossy and nice requests, there were developmental differences in the ways they did so. The 5-year-olds relied primarily on semantic markers. The 10-year-olds and adults tended to use both semantic markers and syntactic directness.[4]

The results of this experiment indicate that children and adults know how to be bossy by issuing requests that make them seem dominant and how to be nice by issuing requests that make them seem more submissive. The only way that they would be able to do so in such similar and predictable ways, and the only way that listeners could comprehend the nuances, would be if syntactic directness and semantic markers carried signaling value. Speakers and listeners must at some level understand that request structures bear a systematic relationship to social structures, particularly status.

Again children's definitions of bossiness and niceness help support this claim. The children's definitions indicated that bossy people nastily issue direct imperatives to control resources and nice people are pleasant and use more indirect question directives and semantic softeners to share resources. A 10-year-old boy described a bossy person: "All the time he tells you what to do, especially when you don't want to do it." Nice people, according to another 10-year-old boy, "Walk up to you and say, 'Hi. Would you like to come over and play and we can have some candy?'"

---

[4] The reader may note that the adults' bossy requests are less syntactically direct than the children's. This may reflect both greater socialization to be polite and the restraining effect of the presence of an adult experimenter.

Conclusions

In this chapter I have reviewed several characteristics of an ethological approach to studying behavior and drawn implications from them for the study of pragmatic development. My intention is not so much to criticize current work as it is to provoke discussion and suggest additional directions for our research and theory. I have argued that attention to ethological methods and theory can lead us both to collect different sorts of data and to reconsider our existing data from a new perspective. As Chance and Jolly (1970, p. 162) have pointed out, "Comparative studies are . . . an essential part of any attempt to build up a picture of the structure underlying the social behaviour of all mammals, including ourselves." Pragmatic behaviors are one form of social behavior. Ethology provides a broad framework in which to understand pragmatic behaviors such as children's use of requests.

Not only do my comments have implications for pragmatics, they have implications for ethology. Washburn (1978, p. 414) has facetiously stated, "Human ethology might be defined as the science that pretends humans cannot speak." Clearly, human ethologists must begin to study language along with other behaviors, and they are beginning to recognize this fact (Omark, 1980).

Given the comments I have made, what can we say about the speech samples with which I opened the chapter? As is typical of children her age, Rose varied her speech to different listeners by varying her request strategies. In speaking to an unfamiliar, higher status adult of whom she was asking a favor, she used an indirect request and several semantic softeners. That is, she presented herself as a submissive, unassuming person. Interestingly, she referred to herself with the diminutive "Rosie," which was not typical of her. In contrast, in asking a familiar, lower status child to return a borrowed item, she used a direct request and several strong semantic aggravators. That is, she presented herself to this listener as a dominant, coercive person. In addition to speaking differently, Rose probably also marked the different situations with other behaviors, much as would nonhuman primates and other animals in comparable circumstances. Her repertoire of pragmatic behaviors represents just a portion of a behavioral system that helps her effectively and strategically to regulate interactions with others. Our further attention to the ethological literature can help us better understand how and why this is the case.

References

Alcock, J. (1975). *Animal behavior.* Sunderland, MA: Sinauer Associates.
Baldwin, J. M. (1925). *Mental development in the child and the race.* New York: Macmillan. (Originally published 1895)
Barrett, M. (September 1980). *Early pragmatic development.* Paper presented at the Annual British Psychological Society Developmental Section Conference, Edinburgh.

Bates, E. (1976). *Language and context.* New York: Academic Press.

Bates, E., Bretherton, I., Beeghly-Smith, M., & McNew, S. (1982). Social bases of language development: A reassessment. In H. Reese & L. Lipsitt (Eds.), *Advances in child development and behavior* (Vol. 16). New York: Academic Press.

Bates, E., & Silvern, L. (1977). Sociolinguistic development in children: How much of it is social? *Program on Cognitive and Perceptual Factors in Human Development* (Report No. 10, Institute for the Study of Intellectual Behavior). Boulder: University of Colorado.

Becker, J. A. (1982). Children's strategic use of requests to mark and manipulate social status. In S. Kuczaj (Ed.), *Language development: Language, thought, and culture.* Hillsdale, NJ: Lawrence Erlbaum.

Blurton-Jones, N. (1969). An ethological study of some aspects of social behavior of children in nursery school. In D. Morris (Ed.), *Primate ethology.* Garden City, NY: Anchor Books.

Blurton-Jones, N. (Ed.) (1972). *Ethological studies of child behaviour.* Cambridge: Cambridge University Press.

Brown, P., & Levinson, S. (1978). Universals in language usage: Politeness phenomena. In E. Goody (Ed.), *Questions and politeness.* Cambridge: Cambridge University Press.

Camras, L. (1977). Facial expressions used by children in a conflict situation. *Child Development, 48,* 1431–1435.

Camras, L. (1983). Ethological approaches to nonverbal communication. In R. Feldman (Ed.), *Development of nonverbal behavior in children.* New York: Springer-Verlag.

Chance, M. R. A., & Jolly, C. (1970). *Social groups of monkeys, apes, and men.* London: Jonathan Cape.

Chance, M. R. A., & Larsen, R. (Eds.) (1976). *The social structure of attention.* London: Wiley.

Cherry Wilkinson, L., Clevenger, M., & Dollaghan, C. (1981). Communication in small instructional groups: A sociolinguistic approach. In W. P. Dickson (Ed.), *Children's oral communication skills.* New York: Academic Press.

Chevalier-Skolnikoff, S. (1973). Facial expressions of emotion in nonhuman primates. In P. Ekman (Ed.), *Darwin and facial expression.* New York: Academic Press.

Clark, H. (1979). Responding to indirect speech acts. *Cognitive Psychology, 11,* 430–477.

Clark, H., & Schunk, D. (1980). Polite responses to polite requests. *Cognition, 8,* 111–143.

Darwin, C. *The expression of emotions in man and animals.* Chicago: University of Chicago Press, 1965. (Originally published 1872)

Darwin, C. (1977). A biographical sketch of an infant. In P. Barrett (Ed.), *The collected papers of Charles Darwin* (Vol. II). Chicago: University of Chicago Press. (Originally published 1877)

Dewsbury, D. (1978). *Comparative animal behavior.* New York: McGraw-Hill.

Dore, J. (1977). Children's illocutionary acts. In R. Freedle (Ed.), *Discourse production and comprehension* (Vol. 1). Norwood NJ: Ablex.

Eibl-Eibesfeldt, I. (1975). *Ethology: The biology of behavior* (2nd ed.). New York: Holt, Rinehart, and Winston.

Eisenberg, A. (1982). Understanding components of a situation: Spontaneous use of politeness routines by Mexicano two-year-olds. *Papers and Reports on Child Language Development, 21,* 46–54.

Ervin-Tripp, S. (1976). Is Sybil there? The structure of some American English directives. *Language in Society, 5,* 25–66.

Ervin-Tripp, S. (1982). Structures of control. In L. Cherry Wilkinson (Ed.), *Communicating in the classroom.* New York: Academic Press.

Foppa, K. Language acquisition: A human ethological problem? In M. von Cranach, K. Foppa, W. Lepenies, & D. Ploog (Eds.), *Human ethology: Claims and limits of a new discipline.* Cambridge: Cambridge University Press.

Garvey, C. (1975). Requests and responses in children's speech. *Journal of Child Language, 2,* 41–63.

Gleason, J., & Weintraub, S. (1978). Input language and the acquisition of communicative competence. In K. E. Nelson (Ed.), *Children's language* (Vol. 1). New York: Gardner Press.

Glucksberg, S., Krauss, R., & Higgins, E. T. (1975). The development of referential communication skills. In F. Horowitz (Ed.), *Review of child development research* (Vol. 4). Chicago: Chicago University Press.

Hess, E. H. (1970). Ethology and developmental psychology. In P. Mussen (Ed.), *Carmichael's manual of child psychology* (3rd ed., Vol. 1). New York: Wiley.

Immelman, K. (1980). *Introduction to ethology.* New York: Plenum Press.

James, S. (1978). Effect of listener age and situation on the politeness of children's directives. *Journal of Psycholinguistic Research, 7,* 307–317.

Jaynes, J. (1976). *The origin of consciousness in the breakdown of the bicameral mind.* Boston: Houghton Mifflin.

Labov, W. (1972). Rules for ritual insult. In D. Sudnow (Ed.), *Studies in social interaction.* New York: Free Press.

Labov, W., & Fanshel, D. (1977). *Therapeutic discourse: Psychotherapy as conversation.* New York: Academic Press.

Lehner, P. (1979). *Handbook of ethological methods.* New York: Garland.

Lorenz, K. (1963). *On aggression.* M. K. Wilson, Trans. New York: Harcourt, Brace, and World.

Mahoney, G. (1975). Ethological approach to delayed language acquisition. *American Journal of Mental Deficiency, 80,* 139–148.

Maratsos, M. (1973). Nonegocentric communication abilities in preschool children. *Child Development, 44,* 696–700.

Maratsos, M. (1974). Preschool children's use of definite and indefinite articles. *Child Development, 45,* 446–455.

Marler, P. (1974). Animal communication. In L. Krames, P. Pliner, & T. Alloway (Eds.), *Advances in the study of communication and affect. Vol. 1. Nonverbal communication.* New York: Plenum Press.

McGrew, W. C. (1972). *An ethological study of children's behavior.* New York: Academic Press.

McTear, M. (1980). Getting it done: The development of children's abilities to negotiate request sequences in peer interaction. *Belfast Working Papers in Language and Linguistics, 4,* 1–29.

Mitchell-Kernan, C., & Kernan, K. (1977). Pragmatics of directive choice among children. In S. Ervin-Tripp & C. Mitchell-Kernan (Eds.), *Child discourse.* New York: Academic Press.

Morgan, J. (1975). Two types of convention in indirect speech acts. In P. Cole & J. Morgan (Eds.), *Syntax and semantics. Vol. 3. Speech acts.* New York: Academic Press.

Munro, A. (1979). Indirect speech acts are not strictly conventional. *Linguistic Inquiry, 10,* 353–356.

Omark, D. (1980). Human ethology: A holistic perspective. In D. Omark, F. F. Strayer, & D. Freedman (Eds.), *Dominance relations: An ethological view of human conflict and social interaction.* New York: Garland STPM Press.

Omark, D., Strayer, F. F., & Freedman, D. (Eds.) (1980). *Dominance relations: An ethological view of human conflict and social interaction.* New York: Garland STPM Press.

Piaget, J. (1974). *The language and thought of the child* (M. Gabain, Trans.). New York: New American Library, 1974. (Originally published 1924)

Preyer, W. (1901). *The mind of the child* (H. W. Brown, Trans.). New York: Appleton. (Originally published 1881)

Rajecki, D. W., & Flanery, R. (1981). Social conflict and dominance in children: A case for a primate homology. In M. Lamb & A. Brown (Eds.), *Advances in developmental psychology* (Vol. 1). Hillsdale, NJ: Lawrence Erlbaum.

Schein, M. (Ed.) (1975). *Social hierarchy and dominance.* Stroudsburg, PA: Dowden, Hutchinson, and Ross, 1975.

Shatz, M. (1978). On the development of communicative understandings: An early strategy for interpreting and responding to messages. *Cognitive Psychology, 10,* 271–301.

Shatz, M., & Gelman, R. (1973). The development of communication skills: Modifications in the speech of young children as a function of listener. *Monographs of the Society for Research in Child Development, 38* (Serial No. 152).

Strayer, F. F., & Strayer, J. (1976). An ethological analysis of social agonism and dominance relations among preschool children. *Child Development, 47,* 980–989.

von Cranach, M. (Ed.) (1976). *Methods of inference from animal to human behavior.* Chicago: Aldine.

Washburn, S. L. (1978). Human behavior and the behavior of other animals. *American Psychologist, 33,* 405–418.

Zivin, G. (1977). On becoming subtle: Age and social rank changes in the use of a facial gesture. *Child Development, 48,* 1314–1321.

Zukow, P., Reilly, J., & Greenfield, P. (1982). Making the absent present: Facilitating the transition from sensorimotor to linguistic communication. In K. E. Nelson (Ed.), *Children's language* (Vol. 3). New York: Gardner Press.

2. Answering Appropriately: A Developmental Perspective on Conversational Knowledge

Marilyn Shatz and Laura McCloskey

Conversation is a social activity by definition. The behaviors of participants are contingent on one another. This contingency is partially expressed explicity in the language, with certain forms in speaker language determining or biasing the choice of form in the respondent's language. The clearest examples of such contingency are ritualistic: "Do you take this woman to be your lawful, wedded wife?" "I do." Apart from such ritualistic cases, however, form appears to be only one factor in the selection of appropriate respondent behavior. For example, yes/no questions in some contexts can take a variety of responses. A-D are all acceptable replies to the question, "Can you go to the movies tonight?"

A: Yes.
B: Don't tempt me!
C: What time?
D: I can.

In this case, D, the elliptical repetition of the speaker form so appropriate in the ritual case, seems less natural than does the imperative or question response. Speaking appropriately, then, is not just a matter of speaking grammatically or matching forms in initiation with forms in response. Appropriate language behavior also involves knowledge of the conversational rules, conventions, and social circumstances governing linguistic interactions.

Whereas this point is recognized among language researchers, there is little understanding of the relations between such knowledge and knowledge of more formal discourse relations. Nor is much known about the factors contributing to response selection in particular situations, although several proposals have been made to explain either adult (e.g., Clark, 1979) or child behaviors (e.g., Shatz, 1978b). In this chapter we consider how it is that children begin to learn to answer appropriately. To address this question, we ask what factors govern children's earliest responses in conversation, and go on to examine what kinds of knowledge acquisitions transform those early efforts into more sophisticated ones. Then we address whether child performance sheds any light on the characteristics of the adult system. The data base for our discussion comes from a range of studies, some done in our laboratory and some culled from the literature. Our focus is primarily on responses to questions, since question-answer sequences are rich sources of contingent response data for both adults and children.

The Nature of Early Contingent Responding

Possible Knowledge Bases

In Western society, parents expend considerable effort to carry on conversations with their very young children. Even with 1-year-olds, they rehearse various routines and games that give the child an opportunity to participate in initiation-response sequences. In addition, they regularly address questions and requests for action to them. How do children respond to these early interactions and what kinds of knowledge underlie their behaviors? One possibility is that the principal basis of children's responding is the knowledge that a turn is required. In this case, one would expect to see essentially random response behavior, with little relation, other than timing, to the initiator's utterance. Another possibility is that the child attends primarily to the context in which an utterance occurs and can infer the import of an utterance on the basis of functional, nonlinguistic information in the setting. In this case, the child would be expected to produce responses reasonably appropriate in terms of function, but with little formal relation to the prior utterance. Such a possibility is consonant with arguments by Macnamara (1972) and Bruner (1975), proposing the child's dependence on nonlinguistic information as an entrée into language. A third alternative is that the child is sensitive to the formal properties in the initiating language that constrain the range of formally appropriate responses. For example, a child who answers "yes" to the telephone caller's question, "Is your mother home?," but does nothing to bring her to the phone, has recognized the formal but not the functional aspects of the caller's question. Whereas it is unlikely that children's behaviors fall precisely into these three categories, that is, responding either randomly or on the bases of purely contextual or formal information, it is worth defining these ideal types to clarify the kinds of knowledge that might underlie early response behaviors.

The nature of possible types of contextual or formal knowledge is in need of further explication. Contextual knowledge encompasses a great deal of territory, and by and large, what might constitute it has been addressed in the literature only vaguely or with a few examples (see Shatz, 1982, for a discussion of this point).

Formal knowledge can more readily be described in two different senses. The best notion of formal knowledge is one that relates characteristics of sentence form and direct readings of intention from those characteristics. The resulting interpretations of sentences are said to be "literal" (Searle, 1969). Thus, the "yes" response of the child cited above might be taken as an indication that the child interpreted the question literally, and the affirmative response is called a literal one.

However, there is an alternative notion of formal knowledge that is less directly related to the interpretation of sentences. It is best described as one that recognizes what Katz (1972) has termed the "answerhood" conditions on certain linguistic forms. For example, questions beginning with auxiliaries have a yes/no answerhood condition, *why* questions a *because* condition, and so forth. In this view, the answerhood condition is primarily a discourse continuity phenomenon. While probably grounded in semantics, it carries with it no assumptions of particular listener interpretations. That is, fulfilling an answerhood condition in response to a form does not imply that the initiation was given a literal interpretation by the responder. This approach allows for the possibility that knowledge of discourse relations may be learned independently of the interpretive knowledge required to give a literal reading of speaker intent to a sentence. As we will see, the possibility that knowledge of discourse relations is independent of notions of literal interpretations is important to an understanding of children's developing communicative competence and to an understanding of adult response performance as well.

Evidence from 1-year-olds

In examining the data on children's responses, it is important to keep in mind that there are methodological differences among studies that sometimes make comparison difficult. Some studies rely on videotape, others on audiotaped data; some researchers have examined only verbal responding, others have examined both verbal and nonverbal behavior. Definitions of contingent and appropriate speech are not always clear or consistent. Despite these difficulties, a picture of early competence emerges from a survey of the available literature. It is one that portrays the novice responder as sensitive to some formal differences in answerhood conditions but without much capacity to respond conventionally or appropriately. Rather, response behaviors seem governed by heuristics that are often idiosyncratic. Neither functional nor formal knowledge in the literal interpretation sense appropriately characterizes the understanding on which very young children base their early behavior.

Our view of the 1-year-old derives from a set of studies that have examined children in the second year of life primarily in natural interaction with their parents (Allen & Shatz, 1983; Bloom, Rocissano, & Hood, 1976; Crosby, 1976; Ervin-Tripp, 1970; Horgan, 1978; Rodgon, 1979; Shatz, 1978a; Steffenson, 1978). Each of these studies confirms that before the age of 2 children differentiate questions from nonquestions, and adjust their response behavior somewhat to accommodate that distinction. Moreover, response data from several of the studies suggest that children under 2 also already differentiate yes/no questions from wh- questions. The most interesting finding, however, is that this apparent competence at differentiating forms does not seem to be simply based on either semantic or pragmatic factors. That is, children's responses are often semantically and pragmatically inappropriate; yet, they give evidence of some early understanding of the constraints of discourse relations.

More specifically, Bloom, et al. (1976), Horgan (1978), and Steffensen (1978) all report on children under 2 who regularly respond yes or no to yes/no questions, but who do so without regard to the appropriateness of the reply. For example, one child typically said "no" as he was reaching for an offered object in response to the question, "Do you want X?" Also, in a study on responses to indirect requests (Study 1 in Shatz, 1978b), five of eight children under 2 at least once said "no" while doing the action requested by a question-directive ("Can you put the ball in the truck?"). Four of the five also used no without action to indicate refusal, and two did so in response to imperatives. However, no-plus-action never occurred following an imperative, suggesting that this sort of response indexed not a refusal and a change of heart, but compliance and marking of the yes/no question form (with a semantically inappropriate form). Further confirmation of this position comes from the fact that declaratives ("The ball can fit in the truck") did not receive no-plus-action responses, although they were met with about as many action responses generally as were questions.

Semantically empty responses are not limited to yes or no replies. Steffenson reports on a child who used the strategy of responding to yes/no questions by imitating part of the question with falling rather than rising intonation, but who did so even when he did not wish to affirm the content of the original question. (For example, "Do you want a cookie?" "Cookie," while refusing the object.) One of Steffenson's subjects apparently tried out a variety of forms from "un-huh" to "no" to "yes" over a period of time, as he tried to discover the acceptable response form. Steffenson suggests that intonation may be an early, primary cue for the child in determining that a response involving one of these forms is appropriate, but that discovering the semantics of yes/no is a considerably longer, more difficult process.

Intonation may indeed by an important cue to the child in discriminating yes/no questions not only from nonquestions but from wh- questions as well. Rodgon (1979) reports that three children under the age of 2 all used yes/no answers only in response to yes/no questions (although not all yes/no questions received such responses). All three children answered naming questions ("What is that?") with an object label, although not necessarily the correct label. Other researchers also report that children under 2 avoid yes/no responses to wh- questions, even if they do not know how to respond with labels. Wh- questions have quite different intonation patterns from yes/no questions and may be readily discriminable on that basis alone. However, there is some evidence that children may use more than just intonation cues at this level of response performance. They apparently distinguish between utterances beginning with wh- words and other sorts of utterances with nonrising final intonation, although they do not necessarily discriminate among different kinds of wh- words. For example, Allen and Shatz (1983) report that subjects aged 1;4 (1 year; 4 months) regularly interpreted "what" questions to be wh- questions of the sorts they were most used to hearing in ritual or game interactions with their mothers. They did not respond to non-wh- utterances in this way. Horgan (1978) also reports that her subject responded to all wh- words as though they were "where." These findings suggest that children may be sensitive to the kinds of words or sounds at the beginnings of utterances in addition to the intonation differences among utterances.

If young children are sensitive primarily to intonation in deciding how to respond, then one might expect that yes/no questions with similar final intonation patterns would be answered similarly regardless of speaker intent. That is, a request for action ("Can you put the ball in the truck?"), a request for confirmation ("The ball goes in the truck?"), and an informational question ("Is that a truck?") might all receive the same sort of response. Alternatively, if children are sensitive to differences in first words or in utterance function, then one would expect to see different responses to these sorts of questions. Unfortunately, most of the studies in the literature report responses to questions of particular forms (e.g., yes/no questions vs. wh- questions) or particular functions (requests for action vs. requests for information) without regard to specific form-function relations in the input speech or the relation of response form to particular form-function initiations.

To answer the question of whether children under 2 have different verbal response strategies for such questions, we returned to the data collected for studies of children's responses to indirect directives of different types (Shatz, 1978b). In one study, children heard utterances such as "Can the ball fit in the truck?" as they were playing with a set of toys. The test utterance was preceded by conversation that was irrelevant or neutral with regard to the intent of the test question, and the question was said in as neutral a way as possible. In a second study, the children heard similar sentences either preceded by a sequence of imperatives or a sequence of informational questions such as "Is that a truck?" in order to bias them toward a directive or an informational response. Thus, we can compare the children's responses in several ways. First, we can ask whether the children responded differently to the clearly informational questions ("Is that a truck?") than to the more ambiguous[1] questions ("Can the ball fit in the truck?"). Second, we can ask whether the context in which the ambiguous sentences were heard affected the kind of verbal responses the children made.

Five children under the age of 2 participated in both studies. The verbal responses the children produced were classified as imitations of the last part of the adult utterances ("Is this a fruit?" "Fruit."), a "yes" or "no" accompanied by action, or a "no" alone. Other verbalizations were idiosyncratic or related to play

---

[1] By ambiguous we mean that such utterances can be taken as expressing either of two speaker intentions: The speaker intends the utterance as a request of the listener to do the action mentioned or to give the information requested (yes/no).

with the toys and will not be considered here. No "yes only" responses were observed.

Table 2-1 shows the patterns of responses for each child to three kinds of initiations: ambiguous questions, informational questions, and imperatives. Repetitions (often accompanied by action in the ambiguous and imperative cases) were produced by the majority of the children to all three types of utterances, whereas yes/no with action and no alone were reserved primarily for ambiguous questions.

These data show that the children responded somewhat differently to the clearly informational questions than to the more ambiguous ones. However, one cannot yet conclude that the children were sensitive to differences in speaker intent per se in the two kinds of sentences. Rather, they may have been responding to differences in the first word or phrase in the clearly informational sentences (generally is) and in the more ambiguous ones (can, does, may). One piece of evidence supporting this possibility is that the one informational question receiving a yes/no plus action response was a "can" question ("Can Mommy talk on the telephone?").

Another piece of evidence available to address this issue comes from an examination of the data on possible effects of preceding linguistic context on the responses to ambiguous test questions. It concerns three of the five children previously reported to have produced no-plus-action responses to ambiguous questions in a neutral context. These three also participated in the second study, and we can examine their responses to such questions when they were preceded by clear imperatives (which never received no-plus-action responses). If the children's earlier no-plus-action responses were a consequence of confusion over intent rather than marking of form, then, in the context of a sequence of imperatives clearly marking intent, marking of the subsequent question form should have disappeared. However, two of the three children still produced at least one no-plus-action response to can questions in the directive context. These sparse data do not allow us to conclude that young children are inattentive to intentional differences in formulating

Table 2-1. Selected Types of Verbal Responses Produced by 1-Year-Olds to Three Types of Utterances

Type of Utterance	Repetition					Yes/No Plus Action[a]					No Alone[b]				
	1	2	3	4	5	1	2	3	4	5	1	2	3	4	5
Ambiguous questions	X	X	X	X		X	X	X	X		X	X	X	X	X
Informational questions	X	X	X	X		X							X		
Imperatives	X	X	X								X				

Note: X indicates the subject produced at least one such response.

[a] The vast majority of the responses were no plus action.

[b] No alone is uninterpretable with regard to a child's intention: It can be either a refusal or an informing reply.

verbal responses to yes/no questions, but they suggest that intention is not the primary determinant of verbal response choice in the 1-year-old.[2]

The data presented thus far are consistent with suggestions made by Shatz (1978b) that young children's responses are not governed by a literal interpretation strategy. Shatz argued on the basis of the frequency of children's action responses to both direct and indirect directives that the directness of an utterance was not the guiding factor in response selection. In those studies, children were as likely to respond with action to indirect requests as to imperatives, and the tendency to act persisted even in contexts facilitating literal replies. In considering the occurrence of verbal responses that accompany such action responses, we have found that even 1-year-olds exhibit some sensitivity to imperative and question form. Yet, their sensitivity does not seem dependent on literal interpretation. Whereas yes/no responses were given to yes/no questions but not to imperatives it was the ambiguous questions rather than the informational ones that were more likely to be answered by a yes or no.

In sum, the data from the studies on indirect directives as well as other studies on 1-year-olds' speech are uniform in showing an early sensitivity to question form. As the studies show, that sensitivity is not a straightforward mapping of yes/no responses to all questions or even all yes/no questions. Before their second birthday many children seem to have two different strategies for answering questions: one is to respond to wh- questions in a routine way. The other is to mark the question form expressing some action with a yes/no while performing the action. In neither case do the children conform to mature standards of semantic or pragmatic appropriateness, nor are they following a literal interpretation strategy.

Evidence from 2-year-olds

The data on 2-year-olds' responses to questions confirm the kind of picture derived from younger children, but they also indicate that the second year of life is an important time for developing semantic knowledge of various response forms. As for continuity with the earlier data, Ervin-Tripp (1970) pointed out that taking one form of wh- question as another is still common in children up to age 3. Whereas younger children typically took most wh- questions as though they were "where" questions, older 2-year-olds often mistook "why" questions to be "what" questions. For example, one response to "Why is the deer drinking?" was "Water." Ervin-Tripp suggested that the semantic features distinguishing the various wh-questions were learned gradually during the first 3 years of life, with where and what being the earliest acquisitions. Her data and those presented earlier on 1-year-olds support this picture.

---

[2] Other findings support the notion that children at this age do not have a general idea of speaker intention (although they themselves may exhibit intentional behavior). Firm evidence for the beginnings of that concept are found in the second half of the third year of life. See Shatz (1983a) for a discussion of the evidence.

Two-year-olds also continue to respond with action to yes/no questions when action is mentioned in the question (Shatz, 1978a, 1978b). Unlike 1-year-olds, they rarely respond with "no" while doing so, but frequently accompany action responses with "yes," suggesting they have unraveled the semantics of yes/no. Even children in the first half of their third year of life are much more sophisticated in this regard than children just a few months younger. Table 2-2 shows that 24–30-month-olds who participated in the indirect directive studies had learned how to use yes responses to answer informational questions, although two of the five children in this age group still occasionally used imitation in response to questions like "Is this a fruit?." Imitations generally were much less frequent than in the speech of 1-year-olds, suggesting that imitations in younger children may constitute a response strategy reserved for cases in which understanding is deficient.

The 2-year-olds were also more sensitive to the linguistic context in which they heard ambiguous questions. All five of the children produced at least one yes response without action to such a question when the question had been preceded by a sequence of informing utterances. As can be seen in Table 2-2, two children produced such responses only in informing contexts. Generally, however, yes plus action was the prevalent response to ambiguous questions regardless of context and yes alone was the prevalent response to informing questions.[3] Finally, a response that had not appeared in the 1-year-olds was noted. Four children occasionally used OK plus action to indicate willingness to do the action. Interestingly, OK appeared in response to imperatives whereas yes never did, indicating the strength of the yes/no answerhood constraint in such young children. Although several children also occasionally used yes or OK in response to declaratives, these responses were quite rare in the 24- to 30-month-olds.

In summary, the younger 2-year-olds showed more semantic sophistication than the 1-year-olds, both in terms of their understanding of wh- words and their use of yes. They were more able to vary their responses to ambiguous questions depending on the preceding linguistic context, but they were still inclined to give action responses when action was mentioned in the utterance. Yes/no responses were no longer restricted to a narrow set of yes/no questions. "Is" questions as well as occasional declaratives received such responses.

As for children in the second half of their third year, Table 2-3 shows that in the directive studies they produced a similar response pattern to the younger 2-year olds. These children produced primarily yes alone to informational questions, yes plus action to ambiguous questions, and very few imitations. They differed from the younger 2-year-olds in two ways. They were more likely to produce an OK without action to an imperative and a yes/no to a declarative. Both of these responses address the discourse demand that one answer when one is spoken to, without actually providing the response desired by the first speaker. In the case of the imperative, the children provided a response typically associated with imperative forms, but it was pragmatically inappropriate to accede to a request

---

[3] It should be noted that the children regularly responded with action but without verbalization not only to imperatives but to many of the ambiguous utterances. Since we are concerned here with verbal responses, we have not included nonverbal responses in our discussion. See Shatz (1978b) for a detailed analysis of action-only responses.

Table 2-2. Selected Types of Verbal Responses Produced by Five Younger 2-Year-Olds to Three Types of Utterances

Type of Utterance	Repetitions					Yes/No Plus Action[a]					OK Plus Action					Yes Alone					No Alone				
	1	2	3	4	5	1	2	3	4	5	1	2	3	4	5	1	2	3	4	5	1	2	3	4	5
Ambiguous questions			X			X	X	X	X	X			X[b]		X	X	X[c]	X	X	X		X	X		
Informational questions																X	X[c]	X	X	X	X				
Imperatives				X	X	X						X		X	X						X				
Declaratives	X[b]			X		X[b]							X[b]		X					X					

[a] The vast majority of these responses were yes plus action.

[b] Occurred only in the directive context.

[c] Occurred only in the informing context.

Table 2-3. Selected Types of Verbal Responses Produced by Five Older 2-Year-Olds to Three Types of Utterances

Type of Utterance	Repetitions					Yes/No Plus Action					OK Plus Action					Yes Alone					No Alone					OK Alone				
	1	2	3	4	5	1	2	3	4	5	1	2	3	4	5	1	2	3	4	5	1	2	3	4	5	1	2	3	4	5
Ambiguous questions	X					X	X	X	X	X				X	X	X	X[b]	X	X		X	X	X							X
Informational questions					X				X							X	X	X	X	X				X	X					
Imperatives											X										X	X	X			X	X	X		
Declaratives				X	X	X[a]						X[a]				X	X[b]	X			X	X	X							

[a] Occurred only in the directive context.
[b] Occurred only in the informing context.

verbally without carrying it out. In the case of yes/no responses to declaratives, three of the children were beginning to refuse or accept the assertions in declarative statements. For example, in response to "This girl goes in here," one child said, "No, this (man) have to go here." (The toys in question were small figures and a set of airplanes in which they could fit.) Thus, the older children were the first to give evidence of understanding the assertive nature of declaratives.

Finally, the older children showed a growing sensitivity to linguistic context, answering with informing responses more frequently to ambiguous questions in an informational context than in a neutral or directive context. This sensitivity is aptly illustrated in Table 2-3 by subject number 3's different responses to declaratives in three different contexts. In a neutral context he responded "no" to "The men go in the plane" (possibly either a refusal to do the act or a negation of the assertion). In a directive sequence he responded "OK" and did the action when told, "The giraffe goes on the boat." In an informing sequence, he merely responded "yes." Nevertheless, the data from the 2-year-olds is consonant with the view that children do not have a literal interpretation strategy. Whereas they did attend to the context in which ambiguous questions and declaratives were spoken, they by and large still interpreted such utterances as taking action responses.

It is worth noting that the kind of linguistic context used in the Shatz studies, namely, preceding utterances with clear, unambiguous intent, is not the only kind of linguistic context that can influence young children's understanding of and responses to utterances. Ervin-Tripp (1970) and Tyack and Ingram (1977) noted that children's responses to questions varied depending upon the nature of the verb internal to the sentence under consideration. For example, the instance cited earlier of a "why" question eliciting an answer appropriate to a "what" question contained a transitive verb ("is drinking"). Questions such as "Why is the boy crying?" were unlikely to elicit such answers, at least in children around 3. Whether the useful information is internal or external to the utterance requiring a response, then, does not seem to be important. Rather, the crucial factor seems to be whether the information guides the child toward a consideration of action relations. For example, in the ambiguous yes/no questions in Shatz's studies, action was mentioned, and the children regularly attempted action, even when they also answered. In the Tyack and Ingram and Ervin-Tripp studies, children apparently responded as though wh- questions were questions about action-object relations when an action verb was mentioned. This dependence on the mention of action as a cue to responding is more understandable if we recognize that the young child does not appear to have general notions that a declarative stands for an assertion, a question for a request for information, and so on.

Knowledge Basis of Early Responding

A review of the findings on children's responses to various kinds of language has revealed that even the youngest children studied do not simply distribute responses randomly over a range of sentence types. Nor do they seem to be able to sort out solely on the basis of nonlinguistic information what is expected of them. Their responses are often either semantically or pragmatically inappropriate and sometimes two components of a response are even contradictory. Whereas young children do seem sensitive to form information, they do not use form to derive literal interpretations and respond accordingly.

Instead, young children apparently rely on a variety of cues such as the mention of action, intonation, and first words in the utterance to select verbal responses to the language directed to them. Development occurs on several dimensions: 2-year-olds have acquired more lexical items and more of a semantic understanding of the items they use, and hence they use them more appropriately than 1-year-olds. More discourse relations between initiating words and their responses are learned. For example, "why" questions begin to get "because" responses around 3 years of age (Ervin-Tripp, 1970). Finally, children develop a range of possible acceptable responses to various forms, and they use contextual cues more regularly to select among them. The response system is a dynamic one, beginning with an action-based bias and attention to surface cues to initation-response pairs; it builds from these as knowledge of semantic, syntactic, and pragmatic constraints on language use grows.

Children's earliest appreciation of speech acts, then, depends on their ability to attend to either contextual or surface features of an utterance. Their responses grow more sophisticated as their capacity to process information selectively from additional sources develops. However, children by the age of 2 or 3 do not achieve the representation of speech act knowledge advanced in adult descriptions (Searle, 1969, 1975; Clark, 1979). In the following section, we will submit an alternative approach to describing speech act knowledge; one that we think better accommodates children's response strategies.

Toward an Understanding of Responses to Speech Acts by Both Children and Adults

Speech act theory, as propounded by Searle (1969), holds that there are essentially two meanings encompassed by any single utterance: the literal and the indirect or conveyed. Each type of meaning can under certain circumstances stand for or indicate a speaker's illocutionary intention, that is, what she intends for her listener to understand (a request, an assertion, a promise, etc.). In one case (the literal), the characteristics of sentence form are a sufficient index of intention, and the speech act is considered a direct one. In the other, additional knowledge of language use is brought to bear on the interpretation of intent, and the speech act involved is considered indirect. Context determines whether the listener is to go beyond the literal marking of intent to utilize the speech act knowledge that governs indirect meanings. Only when context suggests that a literal interpretation is inappropriate, is a second stage of interpretation for indirect acts invoked. In this sense, literal meaning is basic to indirect meaning: To interpret indirect speech acts, one first must have determined the literal meaning of the message.

Originally, a two-stage processing model was rendered to account for the two types of meaning described by Searle (Clark & Lucy, 1975). In this model, literal meanings were computed, tested against context, and returned for further processing if they were identified as implausible. Whereas early findings by Clark and Lucy (1975) lent support to a two-stage model, subsequent research has cast doubt on that approach. If perception of literal meaning were preliminary to the interpretation of indirect meaning, then we might expect both that adults would be faster at interpreting literal than conveyed meanings and that children would comprehend literal messages before indirect ones. Neither prediction has been supported by recent research. Gibbs (1979) discovered that adults processed literal and indirect meanings equally rapidly, depending on prior context. As we have demonstrated in this chapter, although children at a very young age are sensitive to answerhood conditions, they do not appear to go through a period of primarily literal interpretations. In appears, then, that literal interpretation is not preliminary to the understanding of indirect speech acts.

Clark (1979) has acknowledged that a two-stage model of speech act processing is unfeasible. Instead, he has developed another model of speech act understanding that projects simultaneous rather than sequential processing of literal and indirect meanings. The two types of meaning, literal and conveyed, are retained in the later model, although it is unclear just what roles they play in the interpretive process or whether they constitute separate listener representations of speaker intent. Clark simply says they are two parts of what a speaker means in uttering a sentence on a given occasion (1979, p. 432) and that they are computed as "parts of a single package" (1979, p. 472).

Clark (1979) also describes the factors that are apparently crucial for determining in a given situation whether a question will be interpreted literally or as an indirect request. The listener's interpretation can be predicted on the basis of the degree to which the speaker's utterance is framed conventionally, and whether the intention is transparent and obvious. Conventionality refers to those expressions that are regularly agreed to stand for certain intentions although their form does not necessarily directly denote such an intention. For example, "Can you pass the salt" is a conventional request for action. Transparency refers to the degree of clarity in a speaker's utterance. A wholly transparent request explicitly mentions three parts: the supplicant, the intended hearer, and the request itself, as in "I request you to tell me what time you close tonight" (Clark, 1979, p. 442). Finally, whenever the literal answer to a literal question is mutually obvious to both participants, the listener is less likely to interpret the utterance only literally (e.g., "Could you throw me a life preserver?" from someone who has fallen overboard). These three major criteria of conventionality, transparency, and obviousness all contribute in varying degrees to the listener's interpretation of speaker intention.

Clark further suggests that the speaker's response reflects these interpretive factors in a variety of ways. He adopts the notion of "conversational moves" (Goffman, 1976), and claims that the number and type of moves produced in a response provide insight into the various factors weighed during the interpretive process. Thus, a conventional indirect request such as "Can you pass the salt?" may receive only a single response move. An unconventionally expressed request, on the other hand, may elicit two or more moves, if the listener takes account of reasonable (under the circumstances) alternative interpretations.

In addition to conventionality, other factors also can influence the nature of the response, for example, politeness (see Clark & Schunk, 1980). A polite response to an indirect request involves at least two moves—one addressing the literal meaning, the other addressing the conveyed request. Thus, polite responses are generally "fuller" than impolite ones.

This brief description of Clark's analysis of adult response performance suggests that adults utilize considerable knowledge and information in responding to requests. To access literal meaning, one must have available adequate sentence-processing capacity and an appreciation for grammatical relations and sentence mood. Accessing conveyed meaning involves reading contextual variables simultaneously and drawing on a knowledge of what is conventional in certain circumstances. Additionally, the competent language user must integrate the response moves expected by the speaker with moves that, in a given context, fulfill politeness criteria. In sum, the adult listener is seen as going through a rather elaborate calculation to arrive at appropriate responses to various request forms.

One issue that can be raised about the foregoing analysis is a developmental one: How does the young child achieve adult status? It should be clear from our discussion of their responses to discourse, that young children do not know much, if anything, about literal meaning. Whereas literal meaning may be the foundation of the adult interpretation theories of Searle and Clark, it does not seem to hold a basic place in the early conversational development of the child. Young children do not use literal meaning to determine what response is expected of them; they may even be relatively insensitive to speaker intention, as our data also suggest. It is important, therefore, that an account of children's early participation in conversation should not rely on knowledge of either literal meaning or speaker intention as basic explanatory devices.

An Alternative to the Literal-Conveyed Meaning Distinction

We propose an account of children's early conversational behavior and development based on their ability to process surface features of language and context. We believe young children use such cues to generate adequate responses in discourse. Our account is consonant with and holds promise for an alternative view of adult performance. It is based on a theoretical proposal concerning speech act knowledge that is free of the literal-indirect meaning distinction. Instead, the proposal (first made by Shatz, 1980, 1983b), recruits notions from prototype theory to characterize speech act knowledge and to account for the ability of adults to process some speech acts more rapidly than others.

Essentially, Shatz has argued that we develop categories of speech acts organized around prototypical instances of the acts (analogous to the natural categories described by Rosch, 1978). What distinguishes prototypical instances from others is that they have more of those features commonly found among members of the category and fewer of those features rarely found. In short, they have high cue validity for their category and high discriminability from members of other categories.

The kinds of features that Shatz suggested contribute to the prototypicality organization of speech act categories are diverse and can include formal sentential features such as sentence mood and intonation as well as less formal ones, such as the marking of politeness. As an example, "Can you please pass the salt?" would rank high on the prototypicality scale for the speech act category *request for action* because it has several features typically found among instances of request forms, for example, a modal plus *you* in initial position and the explicit politeness marker, *please.* Most important for our discussion is the fact that the features we found earlier to be influencing children's responses (such as intonation and first words) are among those proposed as relevant to the adult category system.

We are not suggesting that 1-year-olds have the same category system as adults. Rather, we suggest that their earliest conversational performance indicates they are already embarked on developing a speech act category system that also may account for mature performance. Initially, they may only notice the kinds of surface features in discourse utterance pairs that regularly co-occur, without assigning intentional status to utterances. Only with time will they acquire a full understanding of the semantic and pragmatic implications of discourse relations. Yet, their early efforts indicate that at least they are attentive to relevant dimensions of the system. As children acquire the understanding that others have intentions, they will be equipped to view various utterance forms as more or less probable expressions of those intentions.

Further Considerations

In this section we clarify several issues that help illustrate the advantages of our approach. These issues involve the relation of grammatical readings of sentences to the speaker intention behind utterances, the meaning of conventionality, and the notion of "literal" response moves.

At the heart of the Searle-Clark approach is the view that a reading of a sentence based on its grammatical features can express a speaker intention, in particular, the literal one. An alternative view is expressed by Bierwisch (1980), who argues that speaker intention must be inferred for *all* utterances, on the basis of sentential information in combination with nonlinguistic information. Speaker intention is a communicative phenomenon. On the other hand, linguistic attitude (commonly referred to as *mood*) is a linguistic phenomenon. Linguistic attitude is one source of information among many in the interpretive process. The reading based on it is no longer labeled as the primary or literal meaning, nor is it given exceptional communicative status. Our approach follows that of Bierwisch, in that we recognize the importance of linguistic attitude as a feature relevant to determining the category membership of speech acts, but we do not equate grammatical readings with readings of intention.

Even young children attend to linguistic attitude, since they generally do not respond verbally to imperative forms. It is probable that imperative linguistic attitude is among the most salient and important of mood markings for the calculation of intention, since imperatives rarely serve other than directive functions. However, linguistic attitude is still only one feature contributing to prototypical speech act knowledge. Young children appear to use a variety of features beyond linguistic attitude to arrive at responses. Witness their early awareness that questions take a yes/no response, but their equally early reluctance to give yes/no responses to "is" questions. Thus, our uncoupling of literal meaning from an attention to sentence mood leaves us free to recognize children's use of cues such as mood without granting them sophisticated grammatical or intentional understanding.

Moreover, our discussion of speech act categories has clarified the notions of conventionality (Searle, 1969; Clark, 1979) and standardness (Bach & Harnish, 1979) that are always invoked to attempt to explain why some utterances ("Can you pass the salt?") are more acceptable and readily understood as requests for action than others. Previous theorists have claimed such utterances are privileged because they are conventional or standard, without giving definitions of conventionality or standardness. Shatz (1983b) has suggested that prototypical can be read for conventional or standard. Hence, this approach gives definition to constructs found central to multiple approaches to speech act knowledge.

Finally, we consider the sorts of moves in responses that Clark calls "literal." As noted earlier, Clark suggests various factors that influence whether a "literal" response (such as "yes") will accompany other moves in responses to requests expressed as yes/no questions. The degree of conventionality is one factor, with less conventional requests eliciting more such responses. Politeness is another such factor. Clark uses the occurrence of such literal responses as evidence that literal meaning has been accessed. However, he gives no explanation for why or how "literal" responses come to function as politeness markers and not as responses to intention.

As noted earlier, our children regularly included "literal" moves in their action responses to question-requests. We are loath, however, to infer (for all the reasons cited earlier) that our children represented literal meaning. Rather, we believe that our children had learned something about the discourse contingencies directly expressed in the language (see opening paragraphs). Formally contingent responses are plurifunctional: They can, in certain contexts, stand alone as appropriate responses to speaker intention. They can also, in certain circumstances, indicate politeness, deference, willingness, or agreement. Most basically, however, they are simply a way of maintaining cooperative discourse.

It is unclear why our children occasionally accompanied action responses to question-directives with a yes or no. They certainly were not very discriminating with regard to the conventionality of the various question-directives. Clark (1979) suggests more conventional requests for action will elicit fewer literal moves because the intention behind them is clear and the listener need not hedge his response. However, in our data, as many children responded with yes (or no) plus action to the most conventional request forms (can you-) as did children to the least conventional form (may you-). Thus, regardless, of context, even the oldest children discussed here did not exhibit "literal" moves as a function of level of conventionality. Nor does it seem reasonable to us that under 3-year-olds were particularly concerned with politeness.

Rather, we believe the children were concerned with taking their turn in the interaction and keeping the interaction going. This use of discourse contingencies divorced from intentional interpretations suggests at least the possibility that adults too have access to a pool of formally contingent responses even when they are not computing a "literal" intentional meaning. Again, then, there is no motivation for maintaining the literal-conveyed meaning distinction as a basis for explaining speech act understanding.

Summary

We believe the data on children's early contingent responding lend support to our view that speech act knowledge depends on the ability to identify utterance forms as more or less prototypical of particular acts. We have argued that such an approach allows us to view even 1-year-olds as embarked on the process of developing into mature speakers without having to grant them unjustified grammatical or intentional understanding. Our approach requires a suspension of belief in what has by now become a reified notion—the literal-conveyed meaning distinction. Even if new views other than our prototype approach ultimately prove more correct, we believe the arguments presented here and in Shatz (1983b), as well as by others, make that suspension inevitable. In any event, other proposals on speech act understanding would do well to account for the data on children as well as adults.

References

Allen R., & Shatz, M. (1983). "What says meow?" The role of context and linguistic experience in very young children's responses to "what" questions. *Journal of Child Language, 10,* 321–335.

Bach, K., & Harnish, R. M. (1979). *Linguistic communication and speech acts.* Cambridge, MA: MIT Press.

Bierwisch, M. (1980). Semantic structure and illocutionary force. In J. R. Searle, F. Kiefer, & M. Bierwisch (Eds.), *Speech act theory and pragmatics.* Dordrecht: D. Reidel.

Bloom, L., Rocissano, L., & Hood, L. (1976). Adult-child discourse: Developmental interaction between information processing and linguistic knowledge. *Cognitive Psychology, 8,* 521–552.

Bruner, J. (1975). The ontogenesis of speech acts. *Journal of Child Language, 2,* 1–20.

Clark, H. H. (1979). Responding to indirect speech acts. *Cognitive Psychology, 11,* 430–477.

Clark, H. H., & Lucy, P. (1975). Understanding what is meant from what is said: A study in conversationally conveyed requests. *Journal of Verbal Learning and Verbal Behavior, 14,* 56–72.

Clark, H. H., & Schunk, D. H. (1980). Polite responses to polite requests. *Cognition, 8,* 111-143.

Crosby, F. (1976). Early discourse agreement. *Journal of Child Language, 3,* 125-126.

Ervin-Tripp, S. (1970). Discourse agreement: How children answer questions. In J. Hayes (Ed.), *Cognition and the development of language.* New York: Wiley.

Gibbs, R. W. (1979). Contextual effects in understanding indirect requests. *Discourse Processes, 2,* 1-10.

Goffman, E. (1976). Replies and responses. *Language in Society, 5,* 257-313.

Horgan, D. (1978). How to answer questions when you've got nothing to say. *Journal of Child Language, 5,* 159-165.

Katz, J. J. (1972). *Semantic theory.* New York: Harper & Row.

Macnamara, J. (1972). Cognitive basis of language learning in infants. *Psychological Review, 79,* 1-14.

Rodgon, M. M. (1979). Knowing what to say and wanting to say it: Some communicative and structural aspects of single-word responses to questions. *Journal of Child Language, 6,* 81-90.

Rosch, E. (1978). Principles of categorization. In E. Rosch & B. Lloyd (Eds.), *Cognition and categorization.* Hillsdale, NJ: Lawrence Erlbaum.

Searle, J. (1969). *Speech acts.* Cambridge: Cambridge University Press.

Searle, J. (1975). Indirect speech acts. In P. Cole & J. Morgan (Eds.), *Syntax and Semantics, Vol. 3, Speech acts.* New York: Academic Press.

Shatz, M. (1978a). Children's comprehension of question directives. *Journal of Child Language, 5,* 39-46.

Shatz, M. (1978b). On the development of communicative understandings: An early strategy for interpreting and responding to messages. *Cognitive Psychology, 10,* 271-301.

Shatz, M. (October 1980). *Pragmatics from a psychologist's point of view.* Keynote address presented at the Conference on Pragmatic Development, State University of New York at Buffalo.

Shatz, M. (1982). On mechanisms of language acquisition: Can features of the communicative environment account for development? In L. Gleitman & E. Wanner (Eds.), *Language acquisition.* New York: Cambridge University Press.

Shatz, M. (1983a). On transition, continuity, and coupling: An alternative approach to communicative development. In R. M. Golinkoff (Ed.), *The transition from prelinguistic to linguistic communication.* Hillsdale, NJ: Lawrence Erlbaum.

Shatz, M. (May 1983b). *Towards a psychological theory of speech act knowledge.* Invited address presented at the Midwestern Psychological Association Annual Meeting.

Steffenson, M. (1978). Satisfying inquisitive adults: Some simple methods of answering yes/no questions. *Journal of Child Language, 5,* 221-236.

Tyack, D., & Ingram, D. (1977). Children's production and comprehension of questions. *Journal of Child Language, 4,* 211-224.

3. Structure and Process in Children's Conversational Development

Michael F. McTear

Although conversation is a universal human activity performed routinely in the course of everyday interaction with our fellow beings, the nature of conversational talk and the means by which children learn to participate in conversations are still poorly understood. Manuals abound on the "art of skilled conversation." It is a simple matter to recognize those who use talk skillfully as a means to achieve their own ends, whether in the transaction of business, as a way of creating a favorable impression, or as a device for lubricating smooth social interaction. It is also easy to recognize cases of the lack of this skill, whether in young infants who have yet to learn the art or in pathological cases such as the mentally disturbed or those suffering from some language disorder. In other words, we have some intuitions about what constitutes a well-formed and well-performed conversation, although there is little in the way of formal theoretical models of conversation. It is true that conversation has been widely studied in recent years by researchers from a variety of disciplines. Sociologists working within the ethnomethodological tradition have developed the school of *conversational analysis,* which has shed interesting light on many aspects of the structure and processes of conversation. The nature and rationale for this work has been outlined recently by Wootton (1981). In Britain, the *discourse analysis* approach has extended the traditional areas of linguistics to the investigation of units larger than the sentence and has made substantial contributions to our understanding of the structural organization of types of conversational interaction such as teacher-pupil talk. A series of papers illustrating this approach has been edited by Coulthard and Montgomery (1981). Other

I would like to thank Brendan Gunn, Margaret MacLure, Michael Stubbs, and John Wilson for their helpful comments on an earlier version of this chapter.

potentially relevant contributions have been made by psychologists (Beattie, 1980; Clarke, 1979), social psychologists (Argyle, 1980), interaction analysts (Goffman, 1981), and text linguists (Beaugrande & Dressler, 1981). In the developmental area, there are now several volumes of readings that deal with a wide range of aspects of conversational development in children (Ervin-Tripp & Mitchell-Kernan, 1977; Garnica & King, 1979; Ochs & Schieffelin, 1979).

Despite this rapidly growing literature, there is still no satisfactory account available of what is meant by basic notions such as conversational structure. Generally this is taken to describe the ways in which utterances are related to one another. It is clear that many utterances are produced with the expectation of eliciting a response, and that absent responses are noticeable for their absence and inappropriate responses for their inappropriateness. In other words, as competent conversationalists we have some intuitions about what constitutes well-formed discourse and we can recognize at least gross deviations from this. However, as will become clear, the attempt to describe the structure of conversation, using methods that have been applied in other areas of linguistic analysis such as syntax and phonology, has not been entirely successful. In any case, it is clear that any account of the ways in which conversational participants do or do not achieve coherent conversations necessitates an approach that goes beyond the exercise of descriptive analysis to an investigation of how conversations are initiated and sustained. A developmental account must also aim to trace the emergence of these processes from their earliest stages toward mature adult usage.

The present chapter is concerned with the development of the structure and processes of conversation in children. It begins with a critical analysis of approaches to the notion of conversational structure and then proceeds to review work on the development of conversation from early infancy to school age. A final section considers the potential application of this work to an understanding of some types of conversational disorder.

The Structure of Conversation

It is useful to begin with the informal observation that utterances in conversation do not occur randomly but in some sort of regular sequence: questions are usually followed by answers, offers by acceptances or rejections, and requests by compliant actions or refusals. Relations between such pairs of utterances have been explored extensively in the literature on *adjacency pairs* (Schegloff & Sacks, 1973). Observations such as these have led some analysts to explore the possibility that conversation is organized structurally in a similar way to syntax (Clarke, 1979; Clarke & Argyle, 1982). This immediately raises fundamental issues such as the nature of descriptive categories of conversation, their sequential distribution and co-occurrence constraints as well as the nature of the syntactic theory with which conversational structure is to be compared. Unfortunately, little significant progress has been made in the investigation of these issues for a number of reasons. Terminological confusion abounds in the literature. Many analyses are too data-specific and lack generalizability. Most importantly, the notion of structure in conversation has not been pursued with the same rigor as in work on syntax. In what follows, some of the issues will be explored that are raised by evoking this analogy with syntax in the hope of establishing whether such an enterprise can shed interesting light on the nature of conversational interaction.

Looking first at the nature of the descriptive units, the possibility that the relation between utterances can be accounted for solely in terms of their syntactic properties can be eliminated from the outset. Thus, while a question containing a "wh-" element such as "where" might be answered by an adverbial of place, it is often the case that no such simple grammatical relation holds between utterances:

(1)   **A:**   Where's the newspaper?
      B: Where's your glasses?

One possible paraphrase of the example is as follows:

(1a): **A:**   Where's the newspaper? (I can't see it anywhere.)
       B: Where's your glasses? (If you put on your glasses you would see it.)

This paraphrase is not intended to exhaust the complexity of (1). What it does, however, is illustrate that the analysis of conversational relations between utterances depends on something more than a description of the grammar of the utterances.

At what level then are sequences of utterances to be analyzed? The most common approach has been to appeal to utterance function rather than form. Terms such as *offer, promise, compliment, refusal* are functional labels that describe the act being performed by an utterance. This function is often only indirectly relatable to the form of the utterance, as speech act theorists have indicated (Cole & Morgan, 1975). Many analysts would thus approach the structure of conversation armed with such functional labels (though without necessarily subscribing to the analytic procedures of speech act theorists). The ultimate aim of such an analysis, if it is to proceed on analogy with work in syntax, would be to propose a finite taxonomy of functional labels and a set of rules to predict well-formed combinations of units and block ill-formed sequences. Work on adjacency pairs has produced detailed analyses of relations among several types of utterance, introducing additional structural complexities such as embedding, pre- and post-expansions as well as interesting investigations of *preference* relations between sets of alternative responses to initial utterances such as offers and compliments (Pomerantz, 1978; Schegloff, 1968). The fact that there does not yet exist a clearly defined set of functional labels for utterances should not necessarily preclude the theoretical possibility of proceeding along these lines.

There are, however, more fundamental problems, as Levinson (1981) has eloquently demonstrated. These can be summarized as follows:

1. It is not possible to set up a finite set of functional labels for discourse comparable to the finite set of categories familiar in the analysis of syntax.

2. There is no rigorous procedure for relating utterance functions to utterance forms, which means that utterance interpretation is necessarily indeterminate. This has implications for the analysis of sequential relations between utterances that again contrasts with the position in syntactic descriptions.
3. Utterances often (possibly always) can be interpreted as expressing a variety of functions simultaneously. This contrasts with the position in syntax where each item in a particular utterance can be labeled uniquely as belonging to a particular category.

These problems can be illustrated by an examination of a familiar analysis of a sequence of utterances proposed by Labov and Fanshel (1977). The sequence is a report of a conversation between R and her mother, M, as reported by R, to her therapist:

(2)   1 **R:** When do you plan t'come home?
       2 **M:** Oh, why-y?
       3 **R:** Things are a little too much.
       4 **M:** Why don't you tell Phyllis that?
       5 **R:** I haven't talked to her lately.

The first utterance in this sequence is analyzed as expressing the following speech acts simultaneously: (a) a request for information; (b) a request for action; (c) a request for help; (d) a challenge asserting that the recipient of the utterance has not fulfilled obligations; (e) an admission of inability to cope with obligations, and (f) an assertion to the therapist that a course of action recommended in previous sessions has been tried out. This list could possibly be extended further, depending on how far the analyst wishes to take the interpretation of this utterance. It can be noted that Labov and Fanshel delimit their analysis by substantiating it with evidence from the text and other reasonably accountable sources (for further details, see Labov & Fanshel, 1977, pp. 156–176). Nevertheless, the problem remains of how to relate this analysis of the first utterance in (2) to the analysis of the second utterance, which is interpreted as accomplishing four speech acts: (a) a request for information; (b) a put-off of a request for action; (c) a put-off of a request for help; and (d) a challenge to a challenge. Clearly, not all aspects of utterance 1 are answered by utterance 2. The relations between the utterances can be shown as follows (based on Labov & Fanshel's analysis, 1977, p. 176):

1		*2*
request for information	$\longrightarrow$	$\emptyset$
request for action	$\longrightarrow$	put-off
request for help	$\longrightarrow$	put-off
challenge	$\longrightarrow$	challenge
admission	$\longrightarrow$	$\emptyset$
assertion	$\longrightarrow$	$\emptyset$

Continuing further, it can be seen that the *request for information* in utterance 2 receives a response that *gives information* in utterance 3, the two *put-offs* are followed by *reinstate request,* which leads in turn to *refuse request* in utterance 4, and then *retreat from request* in 5. Similarly the *challenge* in utterance 2 receives a *defense* in utterance 3. This example should give the reader an appreciation of the type of analysis that is involved here and of its associated problems. As can be clearly seen, this is a post hoc analysis of the data that attempts to describe the complex relations between utterances in a discourse, taking into account the speaker's intentions, motives, and underlying propositions—in the words of the authors, "what the speakers are really getting at." The value of this analysis is that it shows the complexity of conversational interaction and the need to address this complexity in professional analyses of conversation such as those carried out by therapists. At the same time, it illustrates the problems of a structural analysis on analogy with syntax. Even if the issue of the nature and definition of descriptive categories such as *challenge* and *retreat* is disregarded, problems can still arise in the specification of their distributional properties. To take the most obvious example, the following structure would appear to accord with most speakers' intuitions:

(3)   request for information—give information

In the analysis presented above, however, the following is found:

(4)   request for information—∅

Is it to be assumed then that (3) is accurate or that (4) is a case of ill-formed discourse? Neither would seem to be the case in the present analysis. On the one hand, a table of possible sequences is presented that consists of a maximum of three parts along the lines of (3) (Labov & Fanshel, 1977, p. 61). This might correspond to a notion of an idealized model of combinatorial possibilities. On the other hand, however, the analysis of actual sequences proposes structures not predicted by this model. What this disparity seems to suggest is the difficulty (if not, impossibility) of predicting combinations of functionally defined units, especially if, like Labov and Fanshel, the analyst wishes to reflect the complexity of actual conversation by permitting the multifunctional interpretation of utterances. The problem still remains of accounting for the intuition that conversationalists bring certain expectations to their participation in talk and that they can recognize at least extreme deviations from these expectations. Thus, for example, speakers expect some sort of response to a request for information and notice when their partner fails to respond at all or responds with some totally irrelevant utterance. This point will be discussed more fully after a brief review of an alternative approach to the question of conversational structure.

Sinclair and Coulthard (1975) propose a more abstract categorization of utterances according to their interactional function in a discourse. Thus, utterances can be analyzed as *initiations,* in which case they predict or expect a response, and as *responses,* in which case they fulfill the expectations of a preceding utterance. In addition, they propose a third category, *feedback,* which is neither predicting nor predicted, but which reacts to a preceding utterance. The most familiar sequence of these categories can be found in teacher-pupil classroom interaction, where a teacher initiates by, for example, asking a question, the pupil responds, and the teacher follows the pupil's response with feedback that accepts and evaluates the pupil's response.

The Sinclair and Coulthard model of discourse was developed on analogy with Halliday's scale and category theory of syntax, in which items were placed hierarchically on a rank scale and the structure of an item could be related to the structure of larger and smaller items on this scale. This permits the following analogy:

Syntax	*Discourse*
sentence	lesson
clause	transaction
group	exchange
word	move
morpheme	act

The relation between items on these scales is such that the larger items consist of smaller items. Thus, words consist of morphemes but in turn combine into groups, moves consist of acts and combine into exchanges, and so on. The details of this aspect of the model are not relevant to the present discussion, although it is important to note that the model presupposes that items are identifiable as belonging uniquely to particular categories, so that, for example, "-ing" and "-en" are morphemes that occur within the structure of a nominal group. The implication of the analogy hypothesis would be that parts of the utterances are clearly identifiable as accomplishing an act such as *acknowledge,* and that these combine to form moves that can be classified as either *initiations, responses,* or *feedback.* The attempt to pursue this analogy to its limits, however, results in an atomistic view of conversation, which is only able to account for highly idealized data.

Recent work on discourse analysis that has developed out of this framework has focused mainly on exchange structure and has attempted to utilize the rigorous procedures familiar to linguists as well as concepts such as distribution and co-occurrence constraints, rather than adhering rigidly to the rank-scale hypothesis. In other words: The aim is to predict permissible combinations of items in discourse sequences and, by implication, to rule out nonpermissible combinations. In the main, this work has been concerned with exchange structure and with proposing rigorous criteria for the recognition of discourse categories (Berry, 1981a; Coulthard & Brazil, 1981; Stubbs, 1981). Two aspects are of particular interest in this work: the introduction of a category of move, labeled *R/I,* which simultaneously responds to a preceding utterance while predicting a further response, and the analysis of the discourse functions of intonation.

Although current proponents of this work differ in points of detail, they share certain basic assumptions. One of these is that they are concerned with a model of norms rather than with the analysis of particular texts. In this respect they share the aims of generative linguists and differ from analysts of conversation working within the ethnomethodological tradition (Stubbs, 1982). Ultimately, of course, this model of norms might be applied to stretches of actual discourse and indeed, given the problem of the unreliability of our intuitions about language in general and about conversational well-formedness in particular, much of this work has inevitably been data-based while linked to theory construction (Coulthard & Brazil, 1981, p. 86). This assumption leads to a second more problematic one, namely that conversational exchanges are concerned essentially with the transmission of information (Berry, 1981a; Coulthard & Brazil, 1981, p. 99). On the basis of this assumption, attempts have been made to specify the limits of exchanges by restricting the exchange to the transmission of one item of information that can occur either in the initiating or responding slot. Any new item of information will initiate a new exchange. One advantage of adopting this assumption is that it permits a rigorous account of exchange structure (see Berry, 1981a, for an elegant proposal along these lines). This is gained, however, at the expense of restricting the data for analysis to a highly idealized set (Berry's data, for example, consist of one piece of real data and a set of variants). One can better appreciate the problem by considering some of the implications of such models of idealized norms for the analysis of naturally occurring talk. For example, consider the issue of exchange boundaries, looking at the problem of certain types of response. Take the following example, discussed by Coulthard and Brazil (1981, p. 102):

(5)   **A:**   Would you like to come round for coffee tonight?
      B: Are you being serious?

Assuming that B's response is not intended as a basic realization of "yes" or "no," Coulthard and Brazil propose that an exchange boundary occurs between this pair of utterances, in that a request for "polar information" is followed by a second similar request. Such a sequence is not permitted within the limits of one exchange by this model, as the second occurrence of a same move such as a request for polar information is taken as marking a new exchange (for further details and support of this position, see Coulthard & Brazil, 1981, pp. 101ff).

One immediate question that might be asked is: How does B's utterance relate to A's if it is not related structurally in an exchange? Coulthard and Brazil do not attempt to provide an answer and the clearest statement on this issue is provided by Berry (1981b), who distinguishes among the following types of discourse: (a) well-formed discourse that transmits information; (b) deviant discourse, which breaks the rules in a permissible way; and (c) ill-formed discourse, which breaks the rules in a nonpermissible way. Which of these categories might be applied to example (5)? Berry argues that in (5) B transmits the information requested but implicates something over and above "yes." This can be related systematically to Grice's theory of conversational implicature (Grice, 1975). So a distinction is made between a response that provides more than is required by an initiating utterance [as in (5)], and one that says no more than is necessary. The latter is judged to be well-formed in terms of this discourse model while the former is deviant. The final category applies to discourse sequences that are judged to be impossible and that would be perceived as a breakdown in communication. Berry cites the following example of this type (1981b, p. 55):

(6)   **Quizmaster:**   In England, which cathedral has the tallest spire?
      Contestant: Is it?
      Quizmaster: Right.

The problem still remains of how to analyze the sequence in example (5). Clearly the intention is that it should be analyzed as follows:

(5)   **A:**   Would you like to come round for coffee tonight? Initiation Ex 1
      B: Are you being serious? Initiation Ex 2

In other words, there are two initiating utterances and no responses. Yet clearly B responds to A in a permissible way. Indeed, there is a whole range of possible responses to an initiating utterance that go beyond the minimal requirements of the initiation. For example, in response to a request for information, the next speaker might take issue with some aspect of the content of the request, query the right of the requester to make the request, assert an unwillingness to provide an answer, and so on. The complexity of such a range of responses to particular types of initiating utterances has been explored most extensively in speech act theory and developed in Labov and Fanshel (1977). Given that such responses are possible and do occur regularly in everyday conversation, it seems counterintuitive to treat these as "deviant," except in terms of a highly idealized model of discourse that is remote from and unable to account for the basic processes of conversational interaction.

As a way of illustrating the problems raised by such models of exchange structure, consider part of a conversation between two preschool children:

(6)   1 **Heather:**   Do you like his big brother?
     2 **Siobhan:**   No his br- that is his friend and he lives in a different house see?
     3 **Heather:**   He lives in the same house.
     4   That wee boy lives in the same house and the big boy lives in the same house.
     5 **Siobhan:**   No.
     6   See the one with the sort of curly hair and black hair well he lives in a different house.
     7 **Heather:**   He doesn't.

If the extract is analyzed using the criteria for exchange structure developed by Berry, Coulthard and Brazil, and others, it will be judged to be either "deviant" or structurally ill-formed. The justification for this analysis is as follows: The utterance begins with a request for polar information that does not receive a yes/no response (note that the "no" that precedes utterance 2 is not construable as a response to the polar information request but asserts disagreement with the content of the request.) So utterance 2 is not a response in a well-formed exchange initiated by utterance 1. Rather it has to be taken as initiating a new exchange. Continuing further, utterance 2 is an informing utterance to which the appropriate response in a well-formed exchange would be a minimal acknowledgment. Instead, utterance 3 occurs, which is a rejection of part of the content of 2—another initiation and thus a new exchange. There is no need to pursue this analysis further, as it is apparent where it leads. The exchanges in (6) are being analyzed as being either deviant or ill-formed when our intuitions tell us that this is a perfectly normal sample of conversation. In other words, a model of discourse that aims to predict well-formed conversation cannot be easily applied to a simple stretch of naturally occurring conversation. How then might conversation be analyzed? Is it possible to maintain the view that conversation is organized according to structural principles? Before these questions are addressed, one further related problem can be considered that will be important for the subsequent discussion.

From the discussion so far it seems that utterances that provide more than minimal expected responses create problems for the notion of the well-formed exchange. Accordingly, a response to a request for polar information, for example, which provides more than a "yes" or "no" answer (or its equivalent realization), will be judged to be outside the domain of well-formedness. In other words, anything more than the minimal response is unacceptable. Consider now the implications of this assumption for the analysis of everyday conversation. The following is a piece of invented data in which B responds minimally:

(7) A: This is a great party.
     B: Yes.
     A: Is this the first time you've been here?
     B: No.
     A: Were you here when Jane got terribly drunk?
     B: Yes.
     A: I was too.
     B: Oh?
     A: You don't say very much.
     B: No.
     A: It's hard to talk to you.
     B: Yes.
     A: You must be a discourse analyst.
     B: Yes.

In this example, B makes the minimal required responses to A's initiations. However, this conversation appears to be rather odd, and A would be justified in concluding that B was either socially inadequate in some way or else conveying something beyond the actual words spoken—for example, "giving the cold shoulder." Such data can occur and the reader is probably familiar with similar occasions when conversation lapses because of the inability or unwillingness of a conversational partner. So, from the point of view of what is socially acceptable in conversational interaction, minimal responses are either deviant or give rise to interpretations as to the speaker's motives and intentions. This example does not conform to intuitions about normal everyday conversational interaction. What is needed, then, is a model of conversation that can account for the way participants sustain talk while at the same time providing a structural framework that enables the analyst to separate permissible from nonpermissible combinations of units.

The first point to be noted in the development of such a model is that a theory of conversational structure does not necessarily have to be accommodated to already existing theories of syntactic structure in order to account for our intuitions about the structural organization of conversation. Conversation may be structured in a different way to syntax. Analogies are useful, but it is unwise to pursue them too far. In any case, given the wide variety of theories of syntactic structure in the current literature, it would be a problem deciding which particular model might be appropriate for the description of conversation and whether the analysis should account for more than the arrangement of surface strings. Although some notion of structure is important to an understanding of the complexities of conversation, too rigid an approach might inhibit further insight into the interactive nature of conversation. It is important to consider that conversations are the production of more than one speaker, unlike sentences, which are abstract units underlying the utterances produced by individual speakers (Lyons, 1968, p. 176). (For an interesting account of how utterances in a conversation are the result of a joint production between a speaker and the other parties to the talk, see Goodwin, 1981.) What this means is that a speaker cannot exert the same control over the utterance of his addressee as he can over his own utterance. Consider the following example, taken from Coulthard and Brazil (1981, p. 84):

(8)   **A:**   So the meeting's on Friday.
       B: Thanks.
       A: No I'm asking you.

Here B's "mistake" can only be recognized in light of A's response to it. In the production of an utterance, speakers can (and frequently do) recognize and correct grammatical mistakes (Schegloff, 1979). In conversation, however, such "mistakes" are not recognizable by means of a process of reflection but only as a result of intervention from the other party and sometimes only after considerable negotiation. Conversationalists frequently let such problems pass in the expectation that they will be resolved in subsequent conversation or because they feel that little is to be gained from interposing a correction at that point (Cicourel, 1973; Schegloff, 1979).

The second point follows from this, and concerns the problem of indeterminancy in conversational utterances. Because of the indirect relationship between the form and functions of an utterance, it is not possible for analysts (or conversational participants) to establish the relevance of a response in any deterministic way. Utterances that are apparent non sequiturs can be interpreted as relevant responses by appealing to the shared background of understanding of the participants. Examples abound in the literature. Coulthard and Brazil (1981, p. 84) provide the following, in which A can hear B as meaning either "yes" or "no" on the basis of knowledge shared by both participants (but not accessible to the analyst):

(9)   **A:**   So the meeting's on Friday.
       B: Tom will be back in town.

This leads to the conclusion that

> it is partly because a quality of relevance, accessible only to participants, and valid only at the time and place of utterance, can attach to any utterance regardless of its form, that no generalised judgements about well-formedness in discourse can be made. (Coulthard & Brazil, 1981, p. 85)

How does this fit in with an attempt to analyze the structure of conversation? Does this mean that such an enterprise is ill-conceived and unlikely to succeed? This depends on how the notion of structure is conceptualized. Structure can be viewed as something imposed from the outside by the analyst, in which permissible strings are separated from nonpermissible strings and the structure of the permissible ones is specified. The discussion so far has suggested that this approach confronts considerable problems. An alternative way is to analyze the ways in which participants in conversation create structure as the conversation unfolds. Obviously such an approach cannot be as rigorous as an analysis of the syntactic structure of a sentence, for the reasons that have been outlined. The only evidence that can be adduced is evidence as (and if) it arises in the text. Thus in example (8), A's third turn indicated to B that the response "thanks" was structurally unacceptable according to the intent underlying A's first utterance, although it would have been acceptable in the terms of B's interpretation. More generally, if participants reinitiate following unsatisfactory responses or failures to respond at all, then this provides fairly reliable evidence that they are seeking to repair a structure that is, from their point of view, ill-formed.

This leads to a crucial distinction in the analysis of conversation. On the one hand, it is possible to examine how a hearer interprets an utterance. It has been argued that this retrospective type of analysis is the only viable one given the impossibility of determining a speaker's intent (Goffman, 1981; Schegloff, 1977). However, it is also possible to take the complementary prospective view in which the expectations that a speaker sets up with his utterance are examined (Stubbs, 1982). Here a different notion of structure is encountered that provides a basis for interpreting what items actually occur in a conversation. This structural framework operates in the following way: An utterance sets up expectations as to what might occur as a relevant response and whatever utterance does occur is interpreted in the light of these expectations (Coulthard & Brazil, 1981, pp. 85–86). To take a simple example, if utterance 1 is a request for wh- information, the speaker of utterance 1 will inspect utterance 2 to see whether it is a candidate for interpretation as a response to a request for wh- information. Taking the previous discussion into account, such a response could range from a canonical response that fulfilled the intended perlocutionary effects of the request to other responses that recognized its illocutionary force but were otherwise noncanonical. To illustrate, the following are some possible responses to a request to wh- information by A:

(10) **A:** Where did you see him?
       B: (i) In the pub.
              (ii) Who?
             (iii) Why do you want to know?
              (iv) I didn't.
               (v) I'm busy.
              (vi) Get lost.

Response (i) is canonical—it fulfills the demand of the request for wh- (where) information with an adverbial of place. Responses (ii) and (iii) query some aspect of the request, asking for clarification of its content and the reasons for the request, respectively, while (iv) negates its presuppositions, (v) states that the addressee is presently unable or unwilling to answer, and (vi) may be seen as rejecting the rights of the requester to make the request. These can all be construed as permissible responses to a request for information. The following would be more difficult to interpret in this way:

(11) **A:** Where did you see him?
       B: (i)   It's a nice day.
                (ii) I prefer beer.
                (iii) What's on the telly tonight?

Bearing in mind the problems of determining relevance that were discussed, it can be assumed that the speaker A would inspect B's responses for their relevance and on failing to find their relevance would treat them as a nonresponse. Participants in conversations are aware of this process, which becomes particularly acute in interactions with disturbed or intoxicated conversational partners. For the analyst there is the problem of the essential indeterminancy of this process, as well as the point made earlier that speakers will often allow such apparent non sequiturs to pass either in the hope that they will be clarified later or because an immediate clarification is subordinate to their current interactional purposes. In other words, there is often insufficient evidence to substantiate an analysis of the prospective implications of utterances. It is important that this limitation should be recognized. This should not, however, preclude an analysis of those cases where the evidence is somewhat more helpful.

In light of these deliberations, a framework will now be presented that will inform the analysis of the developmental data presented later in this chapter.[1] The main concern will be to show how coherent conversations are initiated and sustained. The most obvious way to begin a conversation is to produce an utterance that expects a response. A clear example would be a request for information that has to be followed by an appropriate response for the sequence to be recognized as well-formed by the participants. Note, however, that these issues are not decided on syntactic grounds. A request for information is often realized by an interrogative. However, it is not always the case that interrogatives realize requests for information and vice versa. Rather, it is necessary to appeal to functional criteria that relate to a complex web of social rights, obligations, and conventions underlying conversational interaction. Space does not permit an extended discussion of these issues here, so a few informal observations will suffice. As far as requests for information are concerned, it can be assumed that one aspect concerns the speaker's desire to know something that prompts a request to someone who might know that information. Under normal circumstances such information is treated as "free goods" (Goffman, 1971, p. 92), and its withholding is considered to be socially deviant. Different rights and obligations obtain in other situations such as police interrogations, while conventions can also vary across cultures (Keenan, 1976). Other acts can initiate responses in similar ways. A compliment requires a recognition that expresses acceptance or thanks. This interacts with a social constraint

---

[1] The present framework is similar in many respects to that developed in Bristol by Gordon Wells and his colleagues (see, for example, Wells, Montgomery, & MacLure, 1979; Wells, MacLure, & Montgomery, 1981). Some of the approach to conversation in the analysis that follows, as well as the coding conventions that I have adopted, owe a considerable debt to this work.

by means of which participants minimize self-praise (Pomerantz, 1978). Statements referring to the other's feelings, information, and so on, can be heard as a request for confirmation (Labov & Fanshel, 1977, p. 100), while statements about the speaker's own feelings and experiences normally only require a minimal response. However, there is often a social constraint to probe further or offer additional comment in such cases. Consider the following:

(12) A: I'm feeling terrible.

One possible response would be a minimal acknowledgment such as "oh." However, there is a principle that speakers should normally show an interest in the other's welfare, so that more usually a response is expected which shows sympathy and expresses concern, such as "Oh dear, do you think you might have caught that bug that's going around?" The point of these informal observations is that utterances not only predict responses that fulfill their expectations in respect to principles of the effective exchange of information, as specified by, for example, Gricean conversational maxims (Grice, 1975). There are other socially motivated principles of politeness, tact, and sociability that have a bearing on what a speaker says (Lakoff, 1973; Leech, 1980). These principles are involved in the ways in which utterances are judged to be conversationally prospective. For example, an utterance such as (12) would set up predictions for particular types of response that are determined by and large by the nature of the social relations between the participants. Someone who was well-disposed toward the speaker would respond more elaborately than someone who was indifferent or hostile.

One class of utterances has been described that initiate by setting up the expectation of a response. Utterances that set up high expectations and following which a failure to respond would be noticeable as such can be classified as highly prospective. Other utterances set lower expectations for a response, so that it might be possible to consider viewing utterances on a scale of prospectiveness (Wells, MacLure, & Montgomery, 1981). On this scale it would be necessary to place those utterances that do not necessarily predict a response, in the sense that a failure to respond is not noticed as remarkable, but that provide for the possibility of a response. Such utterances are a means of sustaining conversation by contributing more than is required minimally by a preceding utterance. There are problems involved in distinguishing analytically between these categories. However, the theoretical significance of this distinction for an understanding of the processes of conversational interaction is beyond question. The reasons for this will become clearer when some developmental data are examined. For the present, however, it will be proposed that utterances can be highly prospective, in which case they predict a response, or minimally prospective, in which case they provide for a response and only become initiations by virtue of the fact that they do receive a response. The former type will be coded I, and the latter (I).

Moving on to utterances that respond to preceding utterances, a distinction can be made between those that respond minimally with the required information, coded R, and those that predict a further response. These utterances provide for the continuation of the dialogue by both responding to what has gone before as well as providing for further talk. Within these it is possible to maintain the same distinction introduced previously between those that predict or expect a response, coded R/I, and those that merely provide for the possibility of further talk, coded $R/(I)$. Finally, there are some utterances that reinitiate following a failure to respond or an unsatisfactory response. These will be coded as I_r. The following examples hope to illustrate these categories. In the first exchange, B provides a minimal response and so terminates the exchange. There is little or nothing that A can say in response to B and so a next utterance would have to be a new initiation by either A or B (for coding conventions, see Appendix A):

(13) **A:** But here that one . that hasn't got white. $\begin{bmatrix} I \\ R \end{bmatrix}$
     B: I know.

Such exchanges do not make for sustained dialogue as they place continuous demands on the speakers to establish new discourse topics. One way of avoiding this dilemma is to respond with an utterance that exceeds the minimally expected response either by adding further information, as in (14), or by rejecting or qualifying the preceding utterance, as in (15):

(14) **A:** But here that one . that hasn't got white. I
     B: I know. R
           Ha-has to have white.   cont (I)
     A: It should. R

(15) **A:** Father Christmas is coming today. I
     B: No we've got some presents sure already. R/I
     A: I know but he's coming the day after R/I
           tomorrow.
     B: To come and visit us so he is just? R/I

In (14), B adds something beyond a minimal acknowledgment that provides further material to which A can respond. A's response in this case is minimal and terminates the exchange. In (15), B's first response rejects some aspect of A's preceding utterance and thus provides material for a further response by A. A acknowledges and adjusts the content of her first utterance, and in so doing provides for a further response. The process continues with B's next utterance. In this way provision is made for the dialogue to continue for at least one more turn.

The following is an example of a series of reinitiations following unsuccessful attempts to elicit a response:

(16) **A:** That's what can wake you up very hard . (I)
           early in the mornings
           (0.6)
           Um it could. $(I)_r$
           (0.6)
           Couldn't it Daddy. I_r
           (1.4)
           Couldn't that one Daddy. I_r
           (0.6)
           Couldn't that sort of one wake you up I_r
           very early.
     B: Oh yes.

Other cases of reinitiations may involve responses that are not considered satisfactory by the first speaker.

There are problems in the analysis of conversation according to these categories. Why, for example, are A's first two utterances in (16) analyzed as (I)—that is, minimally prospective—rather than I? There is no definite answer to this question, as this is a reflection of the indeterminate nature of conversation that has been emphasized in this chapter. In fact, in this example it is plausible to argue that B had no reason to feel obligated to respond to A's first two utterances and that this contrasts with the subsequent more explicitly prospective utterances realized by interrogatives and accompanied by an address tag. It has been argued that intonation is a guide to whether an utterance is setting up constraints on what might follow (Coulthard & Brazil, 1981, pp. 90ff). Speakers can select the pitch level from a choice between high, mid, and low termination at the tonic syllable to constrain the particular type of response that may follow. High and mid termination place constraints on what follows, whereas low termination does not. While these distinctions play an important role for participants in conversation, as can be seen from a detailed examination of Coulthard and Brazil's examples, it is necessary to point out that speakers can exploit the intonation system to convey additional subtleties such as annoyance over and above the realization of structural relationships between utterances. In fact, as Labov and Fanshel (1977) point out, one of the strategic values of prosodic and paralinguistic features used in conversation is that they are deniable. That is, because these features are open to interpretation and are used differently by each speaker, albeit within certain specifiable, culturally determined constraints, it is not possible to use them as an explicit analytic device. As with other elements of conversation, they will be used here when there is sufficient evidence from other sources to support interpretation. Following this detailed overview of problems associated with a structural analysis of conversation the next section is concerned with a developmental account of this aspect of conversation.

Structure in the Conversation of Young Children

Although there have been no extended longitudinal studies of the development of conversational structure from the early interactions between infants and their caregivers in the prelinguistic stage to the more mature conversations of school-aged children, nevertheless a developmental program can be sketched out by piecing together findings from several sources. The next section will look at the emergence of conversation in the prelinguistic stage. Following this the development of initiations and responses in the early preschool period will be examined. This will lead to an investigation of the ways in which older preschool children sustain coherent dialogue across more extended sequences of conversation. In general, the overall impression will be of a development toward greater contingency in children's conversations during this period.

Conversational Development in the Prelinguistic Stage

The early interactions of young infants and their caregivers have been a source of rich and detailed analyses. These interactions have often been referred to as *protoconversations,* as they bear some of the markings of more mature conversations, while at the same time differing in the limited role played by the infant and the subsequently more compensatory role played by the caregiver.

Two distinct patterns of behavior have been identified in early infant-caregiver interaction. In the first, infant and caregiver time their behaviors precisely to give the impression of a closely coordinated activity. Rather than taking turns, the participants vocalize together (Stern, Jaffe, Beebe, & Bennett, 1975). The second activity, in which the participants take turns, seems a more likely precursor of conversational behavior. In many cases these turns consist of complementary behaviors that may be interpreted as elementary responses and initiations. The following are some examples of such primitive exchanges observed in a study of infant-mother dyadic interaction by Whiten (1977):

Initiation	*Response*
Baby vocalizes	Mother replies
Baby smiles	Mother talks, smiles, or laughs
Mother touches or smiles	Baby smiles or vocalizes

This is a set of infant and mother behaviors that co-occur in certain combinations to form elementary exchanges. Already two of the basic ingredients of conversation are present: turn-taking and reciprocity. The contributions of the infant to these early exchanges are limited and are compensated for by the infant's interactional partner. In order to illustrate this point, it is necessary to look separately at the contributions of each participant. The child's behaviors will be considered first.

The behavior of the child is often determined by and given meaning by what its caregiver does. However, the child's behavior can also have an influence on the caregiver. Close analysis of infant-caregiver interaction has shown that infants often attempt to take the lead in the interaction (Trevarthen, 1979). Frequently the infant sets the pace while the caregiver replies (Schaffer, Collis, & Parsons, 1977). Kaye (1977) has shown how the duration of mothers' jiggling during breastfeeding is controlled by the child, while Foster (1979) has analyzed the strategies employed by 9-month-old infants to initiate conversational topics. It is important to exercise caution, however, when attempting to ascribe communicative intentions to the behaviors of young infants. Early cries and smiles are reflex motor actions that are only used at a later stage with the intention of communicating to a conversational partner. Stern (1977) has traced the development of the smile. In the first few weeks of life, smiles are endogenous—that is, they are related to cycles of neurophysiological excitation and discharges within the brain. By about 6 weeks the baby's smile becomes exogenous—that is, it can now be elicited by external events such as gentle tickling around the area of the mouth. At this stage, babies also smile in response to the human face and voice. By 3 months the smile has become instrumental and the baby produces smiles in order to elicit similar responses from others. Lock (1978) has described a similar development from a reflex motor action to a communicative intention in relation to a child's raising of its arm while being picked up. At first the child's arm-raising is simply a response to the stimulation of the caregiver's hands. Later the child anticipates this stimulation and raises its arms. In the final stage the child uses the action of arm-raising to request being picked up. Thus there is a development from an early reflexive nonintentional behavior to a later intentional, communicative behavior. This behavior has also been described in the verbal domain, where the use of basic conversational acts such as requests and statements has been traced back to gestural performatives that develop around the age of 10 months (Bates, Camaioni, & Volterra, 1975). At around this age the child becomes able to combine schemas for interacting with objects with schemas for interacting with persons. Before this stage the child can focus only on one or the other of these types of schemas at the one time and so is unable to use an adult's help in attempts to obtain a desired object or to use objects to obtain the adult's attention. By about 10 months these behaviors become integrated and the child begins to use what Bates et al. describe as *protoimperatives* and *protodeclaratives*— that is, gestures, often accompanied by vocalizations, which have the function of getting adults to reach over a desired object and drawing an adult's attention to an object of interest, respectively.

This development takes place in the context of interaction between infants and their caregivers. The way caregivers interact with their babies can be seen as a possible source of this development. It has been shown that mothers respond selectively to their infant's gestures and vocalizations, focusing on those that are meaningful in adult communication and treating them *as if* they were intended as communicative behaviors by the child. It has been suggested that this *as if* treatment of the child's behaviors is instrumental in helping the child to appreciate the potential communicative significance of its behaviors. As Newson (1979, p. 208) puts it, "human babies become human beings because they are treated as if they were already human beings." A second aspect of caregiver's interaction with their infants concerns the ways in which they time their behaviors precisely to coordinate with what the baby is doing. Vocalizations are phased within the child's sequences of vocalizations and gestures to create the appearance of turn-taking (Schaffer, Collis, & Parsons, 1977). Caregivers also attempt to build a conversational structure around their child's behaviors by responding to and eliciting contributions from the infant that can be interpreted as if they were intentionally communicative conversational turns. Snow (1977) has analyzed this aspect of caregiver-infant interaction, showing how the child's contributions develop qualitatively over time. At 3 months these contributions consist of burps, yawns, sneezes, and vocalizations that the caregiver incorporates into an elementary conversation. The following is an example (Snow, 1977, p. 12):

(17) **Ann:**   (smiles)
     Mother: Oh, what a nice little smile.
                 Yes, isn't that nice?
                 There.
                 There's a nice little smile.
     Ann: (burps)

> **Mother:** What a nice little wind as well.
> Yes, that's better, isn't it?
> Yes.
> Yes.
> **Ann:** (vocalizes)
> **Mother:** Yes.
> There's a nice noise.

The mother responds to the child's smiles, burps, and vocalizations as if they were intentional initiations. As the child developed, the mother came to expect higher quality contributions such as vocalizations and consonantal babble by 7 months, and words by 18 months. These early conversations contain the basic elements of exchange structure: an initiation by the child and a response by the mother. However, the child's turn is limited in that it is not produced with the intention of eliciting a response. Rather the mother, by responding, defines the child's contribution retrospectively as something to which she can respond and thus constitutes it as a first pair part of an exchange. The structure of these exchanges may be represented as follows:

Exchange (child-initiated) $\longrightarrow$ $(I)R$
(I) $\longrightarrow$ burps, sneezes, vocalizations . . .

By this is meant that the child's turn, (I), is not produced with the intention of eliciting a response but can be used as an occasion for a response by the caregiver. In this way the elements of a basic conversational exchange are already present, although the child's contributions are limited.

Turning now to exchanges initiated by the caregiver, it is clear that caregivers attempt to elicit responses from the child. For example, a great proportion of interaction in early infancy consists in the adult trying to elicit a smile from the baby. Similarly, Snow (1977) reports how a mother devoted 124 utterances to an attempt to elicit a burp from her 3-month-old and only moved on to another topic after the child had burped. A special characteristic of the behavior of caregivers in these interactions is that the caregiver creates a situation in which the child's actions or anticipated next actions can be seen as relevant responses. This has been demonstrated particularly clearly in a reanalysis of Snow's examples by MacLure (1981), as in the following:

(18) (mother has been feeding Ann; she removes the bottle)
> **Mother:** Are you finished?
> Yes. (removing bottle)
> Well, was that nice?

Taking only the first line, this can be labeled as an initiation to which an appropriate response would be "yes" or "no." Whatever the child does next can be interpreted by the mother as such a response. For example, if the baby cries, then the answer is "no," but if she does nothing, then the answer is "yes." In other words, the mother structures the conversation in such a way by producing initiations to which the child's next action can be interpreted as being a relevant response (see further MacLure 1981, pp. 99-100). This structure can be represented as follows:

Exchange (caregiver-initiated) ───────────────▶ $I(R)$
(R) ──────────────────────────▶ child's next action

In this structure, the child's turn (R) differs from a mature response in that its contingency depends on the caregiver having set up a situation in which any next action can be seen as relevant. In a more mature exchange, the response results from the child's ability to interpret the interactional demands and content of the preceding initiation and then produce an utterance or action that is contingent on these. Children are assisted in this process beyond the prelinguistic stage. Söderbergh (1974) describes how at 21 months a parent provided frames into which the child could insert a suitable response, thus taking some account of formal deficiencies in the child's language. Similarly, Corsaro (1979) described how adults exert control over discourse with children by using forms that restrict the children's choice of responses such as polar interrogatives and tag questions. MacLure (1981) has investigated in detail a variety of devices used by mothers to build a complex conversational structure around their children's behaviors, compensating for their conversational deficiencies and ensuring that exchanges with young children have the appearance, at least, of being well-formed. Caregivers play such a supportive role throughout the child's conversational development. It is important to bear this process of joint-text construction (Shugar, 1978) in mind when attempting to assess the nature of the child's contribution to the exchange. For this reason, many studies of conversational development have used as data the interactions of same-aged dyads in which the relations are symmetrical as opposed to the situation in adult-child dialogue. In peer interaction the children have to be able to initiate and sustain dialogue without the assistance and intervention of a conversationally more mature and helpful partner. The following sections will be concerned with the development of children's abilities to initiate and respond, focusing mainly on the findings of studies of peer interaction.

The Development of Initiations

Keenan and Schieffelin (1976) identified four steps that have to be accomplished successfully if a discourse topic is to be initiated. Two of these are important for the present account: attention-getting and attention-directing. Attention-getting is necessary when the addressee's attention cannot be assumed. There are various attention-getting devices. Some of these are nonverbal, such as the establishment of eye contact, touching or approaching the addressee, while others are verbal, such as the use of address terms, expressive particles such as "hey," "look," or "oh," and prosodic devices such as the use of higher than usual pitch. Attention-directing involves structuring the content of the initiation in such a way that its referents—of persons, objects, and events being discussed—can be identified by the addressee. This can often be achieved nonverbally by pointing to or holding out a referent, although such nonverbal devices are inappropriate for referents outside the immediate physical context and in this case more elaborate verbal devices are required.

Various studies have illustrated the use of attention-getting devices by young children (Keenan & Schieffelin, 1976; McTear, 1984; Ochs, Schieffelin, & Platt, 1979). Verbal and nonverbal attention-getters are used by children as young as 2 years (Wellman & Lempers, 1977), and they increase in frequency of usage as a function of the child's developing communicative competence (Mueller, 1972). Similarly, Carter (1978) has shown how the use of conventional attention-directing words such as "look" in the second year has its origins in prelinguistic schemata that generally involve the coordination of gestures and vocalizations. Later, children often use common nouns as an attention-directing device (Atkinson, 1979). Reference to objects and persons not present in the immediate context can be achieved by using relative clauses, as in the following example from a 4-year-old girl:

(19) (Heather refers to plasticine that she is holding up)
    Heather: Did you bring some of this to playschool.
                  Uh things that's got wee things on . wee streety things.

Here the first reference is to plasticine that Heather is holding up for her partner's identification. However, she goes on to refer to a particular type that is not present and thus not identifiable by nonverbal means or the use of deictic pronouns such as "this." For this purpose she uses a relative clause, "that's got wee things on." Such identification can often be problematic for young children when they make false assumptions about the state of their addressee's knowledge, as in the following person reference by Siobhan (aged 4;6):

(20) **Siobhan:**   Well these are going to be for Emily instead of you then.
    Heather: Who are they going to be for?
    Siobhan: At the playschool.
    Heather: Emily?
    Siobhan: Yes.
    Heather: Who's she?
    Siobhan: The teacher at my playschool.

In this case, the identification of Emily as "the teacher at my playschool," which might have been placed appositively after the person reference in an appropriate initiation, takes place over several turns, elicited by Heather's clarification requests. This is evidence of how young children can cope with deficiencies in each other's talk. However, there is also some indication in Siobhan's response "at the playschool" to Heather's first clarification request that Siobhan, rather than directly answering the question "who are they going to be for?," is doing the work of identification. At a slightly later age, Siobhan (4;9) and Heather (5;1) were coping more efficiently with such identification problems, as the following examples illustrate:

(21) **Siobhan:**   And my wee friend Andrea doesn't let me play with her toys.

(22) **Heather:**   Guess what I was doing for Emma um Siobhan's teacher.

Here, in (21), Siobhan specifies Andrea with the appositive phrase "my wee friend," while, in (22), Heather self-corrects from the potentially inadequate identification and repairs with the appositive phrase "Siobhan's teacher."

    The question of whether children are able to elicit responses to their initiations is more difficult to resolve as it involves identifying the interactional demands of

utterances based on an assessment of their speaker's intentions. This is a basic problem in all conversational analysis as a speaker's intentions are not available to the
analyst and so it is not possible to assess whether an utterance expects a response
or not. It is possible, however, to look at cases of reinitiation as these provide fairly
reliable evidence that the speaker had expected a response and is taking steps to
secure one following its nonoccurrence. Children display an ability to reinitiate
from an early age. Halliday (1979) reports how his son at age 9 months used a
vocalization /ə̃/ meaning roughly "do that again." If this failed to elicit a response,
it was replaced with a louder, more intensified form /mn̂ŋ/. At 15 months intonation was used to distinguish a reinitiated form. For example: while reading a book
the child would say / á::dà / (midrise + midfall, no upjump), glossed by Halliday
as "what's that?" On turning to the next page, he would say / á::dá / (midrise +
upjump to high fall), which Halliday glossed as "and what's that?" The second
utterance, which reinitiated the first, differed in this special intonation pattern.

Another way of reinitiating is to repeat as a means of indicating that a response
is expected. Keenan (1974) shows how twin boys aged 2;9 used repetition in this
way when a comment was not acknowledged by the other partner. For example:

(23) **A:**   Ee moth. (repeated twice)
     B: Goosey goosey gander, where shall I wander?
     A: Ee moth. (repeated 4 times)
     B: Up, downstairs, Lady's chamber.
     A: Ee moth. (repeated 3 times)
     B: Ee (lay) moth.

Here speaker A repeats the utterance over and over again until it is acknowledged.
Similar findings have been reported by Scollon (1979). Wellman and Lempers
(1977) found that 2-year-olds reinitiated 54% of the time following no responses
and often adapted their original message by using more initiating devices such as
the establishment of eye contact, address terms, and vocatives. The following is an
example from Siobhan (3;8) and Heather (4;0) following a failure to elicit their
addressee's attention:

(24) **Heather:**   (turns to face M.McT)
                    I want a biscuit and a drink.
     Siobhan: I wanta get a drink. (turns to face M.McT)
     Heather: I want a drink and a biscuit.
     Siobhan: I want a drink and a biscuit.
     Heather: Hey.
                    I want a drink and a biscuit.
     M.McT: Okay.

At first the children repeat their request but following the failure of this strategy to
elicit a response, Heather uses the attention-getter "hey" in addition to a further
repetition. Various combinations of verbal and nonverbal devices are used by preschool children to reinitiate following failure of their partner to respond or when
the response does not meet their expectations. In addition to repeating, children
often rephrase their original utterance in a variety of ways, by, for example, isolat-
ing, reducing, expanding, or reordering sentence constituents or by making various

prosodic and paralinguistic modifications (for detailed illustration and analysis, see McTear, 1984, chap. 4). In sum, we can see how, during the preschool period, children develop the ability to get attention, identify discourse referents, taking into account their listener's state of knowledge, and secure an appropriate response. The next section will be concerned with the development of these responses.

The Development of Responses

As discussed earlier, the child's responses are determined by the nature of the adult partner's initiations in early infant-caregiver interaction. There are many limitations on the range of responses available to a young child. The present review will focus on the development of responses to requests for information, as these have been more widely researched than other responses. At the earlier stages, responses are subject to certain constraints. Halliday (1975) reported that his son, aged 18 months, was able to respond to wh- questions, but only if the answer was already known to the questioner. At this stage, the child was unable to provide responses that included information not known to the questioner—a basic aspect of mature question-answer exchanges. This ability interacts with the type of information requested. Children as young as 1;5 have been reported able to differentiate between yes/no and wh- questions (Crosby, 1976; Horgan, 1978), although Steffenson (1978) found that the responses of 2-year-olds were often inappropriate from the perspective of a mature conversationalist. It seemed that children of this age were following a rule such as if there is a question, give an answer, even if you do not understand it. In other words, the children appeared to realize when a response was required but were often unable to provide the appropriate response due to their failure to comprehend the question. Dore (1977) found that some 3-year-olds did not appear to be aware of the social obligation to respond to questions. Without more precise data, it is difficult to assess the role of comprehension of the question in Dore's study. In any case, it is well known that the ability to respond to wh-questions changes between the ages of 1 and 6 years (Cairns & Hsu, 1978; Ervin-Tripp, 1970; Tyack & Ingram, 1977). Children first learn to respond to "where" and "what" questions and later to "why," "how," and "when" questions. This is partly due to the conceptual demands of the question (for example, children acquire the concept of location before the concepts of causality and time), but is also related to the type of response required by the question. "Where" questions can often be answered nonverbally, whereas "when," "how," and "why" questions require a verbal response. Until these various factors are investigated more fully, it will not be possible to assess the precise development of children's responses to requests for information. The same applies to other initiating utterances such as requests for action and statements. Concerning responses to statements, it is necessary to distinguish between nonresponses that are due to a failure to comprehend the initiating utterance and those that result from a lack of knowledge of the social obligation to respond, even if only with a minimal indication of attention. As Dittman (1972) has shown, children as old as 7 years often fail to acknowledge statements, even though they have clearly understood the content of the utterances addressed to them.

In general, the developmental trend in children's responses is toward greater contingency—that is, they relate their utterances to those of their interlocutors. Bloom, Rocissano, and Hood (1976) found that, in a study of adult-child dialogue, children's responses at 21 months were mainly noncontingent. Responses to questions seemed easier than responses to statements. Mueller (1972), in a study of 3½- to 5½-year-olds, found that 62% of utterances received a definite response while a further 23% received at least a visual indication of attention. Moreover, contingency increased with age. Similar results have also been reported by Garvey and Hogan (1973).

How do young children realize these responses? Bloom et al. noted that, in the early stages, responses tended to be imitative of the adult utterance but that later the children added to or modified clause constituents in their responses. Keenan has explored the use of repetition as a response strategy in a series of papers (Keenan, 1974, 1975; Keenan & Klein, 1975). She found that repetition was used predominantly by the children in her study at age 2;9 but that by age 3;0 they had begun to use more mature substitution devices such as anaphoric pronouns. Ervin-Tripp (1978) has reviewed studies of this aspect of children's responses between the ages of 2;9 and 3;6 and has found similar results. In addition, she found that children increasingly used auxiliary ellipses in their responses (for example, "Bill was") as well as discourse connectives such as "then," "but," and "because." The following are some examples of similar devices from Siobhan (3;8) and Heather (4;0):

1. The use of "well" to acknowledge a preceding utterance but to indicate dissatisfaction with it.
2. The use of "sure," used in Ulster and Irish English to indicate contrastivity with a preceding utterance, with roughly the meaning of "yes but."

The following examples illustrate these points:

(25) **Siobhan:** I want to play with all the Lego.
     Heather: Well you can't have that.

(26) **Heather:** Well the rain won't get in.
     Siobhan: Sure it's not raining.

Later acquisitions included the concessive conjunct "anyway" and the inferential conjunct "otherwise." Other discourse devices such as "mind you" and expressions of attitude such as "frankly" were not produced by these children in the period under study (up to about 6 years) and it has to be assumed that these, and other more advanced discourse connectors are later acquisitions (Crystal, Fletcher, & Garman, 1976, p. 81).

In sum, then, children develop the ability to initiate and respond during the early preschool period, although more complex aspects of these elements of exchange structure develop later. More precise details of these particular aspects have been little researched as yet. Nonetheless it appears that the early exchanges of preschool children can be represented as follows:

Exchange → *I*   *R*

By this is meant that children are able to take the reciprocal roles of initiating and responding in conversational exchanges. However, mature dialogue consists of more than simple initiation-response exchanges. Exchanges can also have a three-part structure. In addition, there are various ways in which exchanges can be linked to form continuous sequences of dialogue. What evidence is there that children have the ability to produce exchanges consisting of more than two elements? It seems that the structural element F (feedback), which occurs frequently in teacher-pupil and doctor-patient talk, is rare in children's conversations. In a study of questions and responses by a sample of children aged 2;10 to 5;7. Berninger and Garvey (1981) found that only 5% of responses received explicit feedback. In casual conversation, feedback is often realized implicitly by incorporating the response in the next utterance, as in the following constructed example:

(27) **A:** Where's John?
      B: In the pub.
      A: Is he coming home soon?

Here the third utterance takes account of the response in the second turn without acknowledging it explicitly. Taking this wider view of feedback, Berninger and Garvey (1981) found that 38% of responses were acknowledged by a relevant next contribution. Similar findings for first-graders in peer discourse and adults in adult-child dialogue (52% and 72%, respectively) suggest a developmental progression in this respect (Mishler, 1978).

The type of exchange illustrated in (27) provides for continuity as the third element in the dialogue incorporates content from the preceding initiation-response pair. Thus, in contrast to a series of exchanges that are not linked topically, there is a series of exchanges linked topically by virtue of the incorporation of material from a preceding exchange into the next initiation. The difference can be represented as follows:

Exchanges (no topical links)

$$\text{Exchange 1} \rightarrow \begin{bmatrix} I \\ R \end{bmatrix}$$

$$\text{Exchange 2} \rightarrow \begin{bmatrix} I \\ R \end{bmatrix}$$

$$\text{Exchange 3} \rightarrow \begin{bmatrix} I \\ R \end{bmatrix}$$

Exchanges (linked topically)

$$\text{Exchange 1} \rightarrow \begin{bmatrix} I \\ R \end{bmatrix}\bigg)$$

$$\text{Exchange 2} \rightarrow \begin{bmatrix} I \\ R \end{bmatrix}\bigg)$$

$$\text{Exchange 3} \rightarrow \begin{bmatrix} I \\ R \end{bmatrix}$$

The structures on the right are similar to those on the left in that the elements of structure, I and R, are discrete. However, those structures on the right are more complex as topical links are provided with the preceding exchange. As will become clear, such links can extend beyond the immediately preceding exchange. In general, research evidence indicates that the types of exchange that have been illustrated so far are mastered by young children during the first 3 years of life. The next development to be considered concerns the use of utterances with a dual discourse function of responding and initiating simultaneously. This development will be illustrated with an analysis of some typical samples of dialogue from different points of development.

Sustaining Coherent Dialogue

In this section some samples of dialogue between two preschool children will be examined in order to illustrate the development of the ability to create and sustain stretches of coherent conversation. The samples are taken from a larger data base that has been analyzed extensively elsewhere (McTear, 1984). The data consist of a series of videorecorded free-play conversations between two young girls, Siobhan and her friend Heather. Siobhan was 3;8 at the time of the first recording and Heather was 4;0. Recordings were taken at regular intervals over a period of 2 years. The following samples are selected as typical examples of the discourse devices that the children were using at various stages during the course of this period of investigation. The samples are coded to illustrate the following: (a) exchange structure in terms of initiations and responses, (b) links within initiating or responding moves as well as links across turns, and (c) discourse features such as cohesive devices and connectives.

Extract (28) (Table 3-1) is an example of dialogue from session I in which the children were discussing Lego instructions. This extract exhibits many of the features of dialogue that have been discussed. The children take turns and in their turns take account of preceding talk by making relevant next contributions. They use formal markers of acknowledgment: "I know" (line 11), "it should" (line 13), "yes" (line 28). Sometimes they make more than the minimally required response. For example, in line 12 Heather adds to her acknowledgment of Siobhan's line 10, and in lines 15 and 16 Siobhan adds to her response to Heather's line 14. In this way extra material is provided that can be taken up by the next speaker. The dialogue consists mainly of either exchanges with the structure: initiation and response, that is, closed exchanges, or of incomplete exchanges consisting of initiations with no responses. There are fewer turns of the type R/I, which respond and initiate simultaneously and provide for a link between exchanges. This means that new exchanges are initiated at several points, for example, at lines 4, 10, 17, 18. There are some cases of thematic continuity, where a speaker links back across turns. The most obvious is Heather's line 14 that links back to Siobhan's line 10. This link is also marked formally by "well." Tags are used frequently as a response-eliciting device, usually accompanied by high pitch termination, as in lines 4 and 14. However, on the whole the continuity in this extract derives more from the interactive context or "overall topic" in which the children are involved rather than from discourse-based links between utterances.

This example can be contrasted with an example from session II (extract 29, Table 3-2). This extract revolved around Heather's assertion that "Father Christmas is coming today." In her response, Siobhan does not just reject this proposition but gives extra information that Heather is able to take up in her next turn. Heather does so in line 5, first by acknowledging, then qualifying her original assertion.

Agreement is apparently reached by line 7, but in line 9 Siobhan adds further information linking back to her line 6. Heather rejects this, Siobhan rejects this rejection and adds a justification (line 11). The dialogue enters a cycle of rejection/

Table 3-1. Coded Extract from Session I (Siobhan 3;8, Heather 4;0). The children are examining Lego instructions

Text		Exchanges
1. **S:**	See.	Ex 1 I-
2.	And then=	
3. **H:**	=I see.	R
4. **S:**	Do that first don't we?	I
5.	And do that.	Ex 2 cont
6.	And then=	cont
7. **H:**	=and then do the wee things on it don't we?	Ex 3 R/I
8. **S:**	Yes.	R
9. **H:**	Put all the blues on. (1.2)	Ex 4 cont:(I)
10. **S:**	But here that one . that hasn't got white.	Ex 5 I
11. **H:**	I know.	R
12.	Ha-has to have white.	cont:(I)
13. **S:**	It should. (3.6)	Ex 6 R
14. **H:**	Well that one's got white too hasn't it?	Ex 7 I
15. **S:**	Yes but it's broke.	R/(I)
16.	I brokened it.	Ex 8 cont
17.	But I . have to take it all off.	Ex 9 I
18.	I show you take the white ones off?	I
19. **H:**	(nods)	Ex 10 R
20. **S:**	I know.	
21.	You take it off at the sides don't you?	Ex 11 I
22. **H:**	(nods)	R
23. **S:**	Look.	cont: I_r 21
24. **H:**	It's very tight for me., (1.0)	Ex 12 I
25. **S:**	You do that see. (1.2)	I
26.	And put them here. (1.0)	Ex 13 cont
27. **H:**	I does the whites and you does the blues.	I
28. **S:**	Yes.	Ex 14 R
29. **H:**	You have the wee blues chairs and I have that . I have that wee chairs don't we=	
30.	=I have the wee baby . chairs don't I.	Ex 15 I
31. **S:**	Yes.	R

Table 3-2. Coded Extract (29) from Session II (Siobhan 4;3, Heather 4;7)

Text		Exchanges	
1. **H:**	Father Christmas is coming today.	Ex 1 ⌈	*I*
2. **S:**	No he's not=	⌊	*R-*
3. **H:**	=tonight.	Ex 2 ⌈	*-I*
4. **S:**	No we've got some presents sure already.	Ex 3	*R/(I)*
5. **H:**	I know but he's coming um the day after tomorrow.	Ex 4	*R/(I)*
6. **S:**	To come and visit us so he is just?	Ex 5 ⌈	*R/I*
7. **H:**	Yes.	⌊	*R*
8. **S:**	And that's all.		*I$_r$*
9.	And then he'll go back home see.	Ex 6	cont:*I*
10. **H:**	No he'll give the other children some.	Ex 7	*R:(I)*
11. **S:**	No cos there's no more children.	Ex 8	*R/(I)*
12. **H:**	There is.	Ex 9	*R/(I)*
13. **S:**	There isn't.	Ex 10	*R/(I)*
14. **H:**	There is.		*R/(I)*
15. **S:**	Cos that that that's Santa Claus there.	Ex 11	*R/(I)*
16. **H:**	It's morning time.	Ex 12 ⌈	*I*
	Time to play with things.	Ex 13	cont

counterrejection exchanges typical of earlier immature dispute sequences in the data. Siobhan adds a further justification (line 15) and then Heather changes the topic. Structurally these exchanges are linked by utterances that respond and initiate simultaneously. If the intonation patterns in this extract are examined (see Appendix B) it can be seen that each of these utterances is realized by midkey termination, which allows for the continuation of the exchange, until utterance 7, which has low termination and is accompanied by voice quality adjustment to a lowered laryngeal setting. This utterance sets no further constraints on the continuation of the exchange. Siobhan reopens the topic by looking back in her lines 8 and 9 to line 6. Line 8 terminates in midkey. In contrast, line 9 has high termination, indicating that a further response is expected. The function is also carried by the response-eliciting tag "see."

Extract (30) (Table 3-3) illustrates a different way of creating continuity in dialogue. Here the children's turns often consist of more than one act as the children continue by justifying, adding further information, or requesting additional related information. A good example is Heather's response in lines 4-6 to Siobhan's line 3. Such cases provide material that the next speaker can address in her response. This contrasts with the alternative option of terminating the exchange with a simple acknowledgment. For example, there are potential termination points at lines 2, 4, 8, 10, 13, and 15. Even where Siobhan initiates a new topic at line 12, Heather reestablishes the original topic, acknowledging Siobhan's line 11 and providing a further justification. Similarly, Heather allows the topic to close at line 10 but

Table 3-3. Coded Extract (30) from Session IV (Siobhan 4;9, Heather 5;1).
The children are traveling in the car

Text	Exchanges
1. **H:** I'm going to be out first.	Ex 1 — I
2. **S:** I know that	R
3. but I don't mind sure I don't.	cont:I
4. **H:** No I don't mind anyway	Ex 2 — $R/(I)$
5. what's the matter with not not getting out first?	cont:I
6. It's no no difference. (1.0)	Ex 3 — cont:(I)
7. Sure it's not Siobhan.	cont:I_r
8. **S:** No.	R
9. We don't have to fight.	cont:(I)
10. **H:** No.	Ex 4 — R
11. **S:** No we don't have to fight anyway.	Ex 5 — I
12. Ah oh oh ouch it's <u>burny</u>	
13. **H:** I know because Big girls like us don't fight. (0.8)	Ex 6 — I / $R/(I)$
14. Big girls like us don't fight.	Ex 7 — cont:$(I)_r$
15. **S:** Um.	R
16. But we used to fight didn't we?	Ex 8 — cont:I

Siobhan reopens it by reinitiating at line 11, linking back to line 9 (see also links between lines 14 and 16). This structure has its realization in the intonation patterns used by the children. As in the previous example, most of their utterances have midpitch termination, allowing for continuation. Lines 8 and 9 have low-level termination and the sequence almost comes to an end here, only to be revived by Siobhan's line 11, which is marked by a rise in key and has midlevel termination.

The final example is taken from session VI (extract 31, Table 3-4). Here continuity is achieved in two ways. The children use responses that provide for further responses, that is, utterances coded $R/(I)$ or R/I. This includes responses such as "they might" (line 16) realized by high key, and "no" (line 17) in midkey. As these responses reject preceding utterances, they provide for a further response by the next speaker over and above the cues provided by the intonation. The second device that the children use to achieve continuity is to link their utterances within their own turns, as in Siobhan's lines 7-9. There are also thematic links across turns. For example, Heather's line 18 links back thematically to her line 16 and expands on it. The children also use cohesive devices, for example, Heather's proform "so do I" (line 2), and her "it" in line 4 that refers back not to a preceding noun phrase but to a preceding proposition ("pity it wasn't our camera"). There are various markers of agreement and acknowledgment (lines 5, 10, 11, 14, and 20), as well as markers of disagreement or rejection (lines 13 and 17). "But" (line 15) and "well" (line 19) acknowledge but qualify preceding utterances.

Table 3-4. Coded Extract (31) from Session VI (Siobhan 5;5, Heather 5;9). The children have been playing with the video camera

Text	Exchanges
1. **S:** I like to do that.	Ex 1 ⌈ *I*
2. **H:** So do I.	*R/(I)*
3. Pity it wasn't our camera.	cont:(*I*)
4. Wouldn't it be good Siobhan.	cont:*I*
5. **S:** Yes and <u>my daddy</u>=	Ex 2 *R/(I)*-
6. **H:** * *	⌈ ?
7. **S:** =If if you had a toy one and I had a toy one and he had a real one it'd be good.	*I*
8. We'd all be taking pictures of Jason. (sings)	Ex 3 cont:*I*
9. And my daddy.	cont:*I*
10. **H:** Yes and he'd be taking lots of pictures of us instead of us taking pictures of ourselves.	*R/(I)*
11. **S:** Yes.	Ex 4 *R*
12. How could we take pictures of ourselves.	cont:*I*
13. **H:** No I could take a picture of you and you could take a picture of me.	Ex 5 *R/(I)*
14. **S:** Yea.	Ex 6 *R*
15. But they wouldn't come out like real cameras.	Ex 7 cont:(*I*)
16. **H:** They might.	*R/(I)*
17. **S:** No.	Ex 8 *R/(I)*
18. **H:** If we had a real one and your daddy had a real one it'd be good we=	Ex 9 *R/(I)*
19. **S:** =well ours would have to be small.	Ex 10 *R/(I)*
20. **H:** I know	Ex 11 *R*
21. Cos if it was big it would be far too heavy.	Ex 12 cont:(*I*)
22. **S:** Ah there's a sticker on your two feet.	Ex 13 *I*

It is now possible to summarize the main development that takes place in children's ability to structure their conversations. In the earlier stages, children can initiate and respond to simple topics. However, their exchanges are usually fairly closed and do not combine into larger topically or interactionally related sequences. One aspect of development consists in the ability to structure longer sequences of dialogue. This can be achieved in several ways. At first, children can link exchanges by incorporating material from a preceding exchange into the next exchange, for example, by continuing on a linked topic having implicitly acknowledged the response made in the preceding exchange. The major development, however, comes when children learn to respond to a preceding turn and simultaneously set up expectations or, at least, provide for the possibility of a further response. This can be combined with the device of fitting more than one utterance within a turn, which has a similar effect of providing for the possibility of further talk. These different structural possibilities can be schematized as shown in Table 3-5.

Table 3-5. Development of Exchange Structure

I	II	III	IV
A: ⌈ I	A: ⌈ I	A: ⌈ I	A: ⌈ I
B: ⌊ R	B: ⌊ R ⌉	B: ⌊ ⌉R	B: ├ R/I
A: ⌈ I	A: ⌈ I	⌈ cont (I)	A: ├ R/I
B: ⌊ R	B: ⌊ R	A: ⌊ R	B: ⌊ R

It must be emphasized that this is a preliminary account based on a fairly restricted set of data. More studies are needed of a larger sample of children engaged in a wide variety of activities. Moreover, the present account has been restricted to the most general aspect of conversational structure—how utterances are related sequentially in terms of prospective constraints and retrospective fulfillment—and has not examined the particular speech acts performed by the children within these structures nor the topical and propositional links between their utterances. Each of these aspects would need to be considered in a more extensive investigation of conversational interaction and doubtlessly developmental accounts will be forthcoming. However, the present focus has isolated the way in which children develop the ability to engage in conversation by initiating appropriate topics and by sustaining the talk once it has been initiated. In the next section it will be shown how these aspects of interaction provide an important dimension for clinical applications of discourse analysis.

Applied Discourse Analysis

In this final section, some applications of the type of discourse analysis that has been exemplified in the present chapter will be considered. Two areas are particularly important: the analysis of patterns of interaction in selected situations and the description of conversational disorders.

It was noted earlier that certain types of discourse situation give rise to a pattern of interaction that consists of three-part exchanges with the structure *IRF*. In these situations one of the participants is in a position of authority over the other and thus controls the interaction. Typical examples are teachers with pupils, doctors with patients, interviewers with interviewees. What these situations have in common is that the participant in authority initiates exchanges by requesting information and then follows the response of the lower status participant with an evaluating move. In the case of teacher-pupil interaction the control is even more rigid as the teacher's questions are aimed at eliciting displays of knowledge from the pupils rather than information. That is, many teacher questions are not concerned with information that the teacher does not have and expects that the pupils might have, but are actually about information that the teacher has and wishes to test in the pupils. Similar patterns occur in interactions between speech therapists and their patients, especially where the aim of the talk is to elicit samples of language from the patient for the purposes of assessment. The following is a typical example:

(32) **T:** Let's have a look at some pictures.
            What's this one about? $\begin{bmatrix} I \\ R \end{bmatrix}$
      P: Milk.
      T: What time is it at school? $\begin{bmatrix} I \\ R \end{bmatrix}$
      P: Break-time.
      T: And what are the children doing? $\begin{bmatrix} I \\ R \\ F \end{bmatrix}$
      P: Drinking milk.
      T: That's right.
            Why are there some empty bottles in the crate? $\begin{bmatrix} I \\ R \\ F \end{bmatrix}$
      P: Drink all.
      T: That's right.
            Those children have drunk it all up.

This discourse is made up of exchanges of the structure *IR* and *IRF,* in which the therapist has control and the patient supplies the minimally expected response. In some cases, the answer is already known to the therapist, while in others the patient has some latitude to construct his response from a range of reasonable alternatives, as in the initiation "Why are there some empty bottles in the crate?" However, if the distribution of the moves *I* and *R* is examined, it can be seen that *I* is predominantly taken by the therapist and *R* by the patient. In fact, in the 10-minute sample from which this extract is taken, there were only two cases where the patient initiated. In the first case he added to the response predicted by the therapist's preceding initiation:

(33) **T:** What's the teacher showing the children? $\begin{bmatrix} I \\ R \end{bmatrix}$
      P: Flower.
      T: And what are the children doing? $\begin{bmatrix} I \\ R \end{bmatrix}$
      P: Looking at it.
      T: It's like your nature class isn't it? $\begin{bmatrix} I \\ R \end{bmatrix}$
      P: Nature table.
            I got a nature table.   cont (*I*)
      T: What have you got on your nature table?   R/*I*
      P: A lot of things.   R
      T: What's the wee boy doing here? $\begin{bmatrix} I \\ R \end{bmatrix}$
      P: Writing.

In this example there is a slight deviation from the pattern of *IR* and *IRF* exchanges as the patient continues his turn with information that provides for the possibility of further talk. However, the therapist is, as it were, locked into the predominant discourse pattern. She responds implicitly to the patient's move by incorporating it topically into her next initiation and then moves on to another topic in the next exchange.

The second case of an initiation by the patient receives no response at all. The therapist takes out a book about a farm and the patient comments:

(34) **P:** I got that story at home.   ⌐ I
      T: Have you been on a farm?   ⌐ I
      P: (nods)   ⌊ R
      T: What did you see?   ⌐ I
      P: Cows and tractors.   ⌊ R

Consider now the implications of the analysis of such patterns of interaction. First, there is a marked contrast with casual conversation, where the privileges of discourse initiation are distributed more symmetrically and exchanges are linked by the use of moves that respond while simultaneously initiating a further response. If the aim of the interaction is to train the patient to be able to participate in normal, everyday conversation, then this type of experience will be of little use. It must be remembered, however, that the aims of the dominant participant in such interactions, whether it be a teacher, doctor, interviewer, or speech therapist, may be quite specific. For example, the aim may be to test a pupil's knowledge, to diagnose an illness, to gather information, or to elicit samples of language. These aims may be fulfilled by the types of discourse structure that have been illustrated here. What is important to consider is that such exchanges constrain the options available to the lower status participant so that his responses are controlled by the dominant participant. This may be the explicit goal of the interaction, as in the Socratic type questioning designed to lead the pupil to the discovery of new knowledge, the careful questioning by the doctor that focuses on information relevant to the diagnosis and excludes irrelevant information, or in the attempt by the speech therapist to exert control over the patient's language output by restricting it to structures and topics that the patient is known to be able to handle. The justification of these strategies is beyond the scope of the present chapter. The important point is that professionals who employ such interactional strategies should be aware of their limitations. To pursue the examples from speech therapist-patient interaction, it is obvious that the patient's responses are minimal and closely related to the therapist's initiations. Such responses would be useful as an indication of the patient's ability to respond to a particular range of questions and to use elliptical syntax in these responses, but they would be less useful as a sample of language on which an analysis of the patient's syntax could be based (as was, in fact, the aim of this particular therapy session). The patient produces elliptical responses that are entirely appropriate, but that do not permit an analysis of common clause patterns. For example, there are few responses in which a subject noun-phrase is present, and in many the verbs are also absent. Similarly, such an interaction would be an inadequate basis for the development of conversational ability. What is required here is a type of interaction in which the patient has greater opportunity to initiate topics and to exert control over the discourse. This may be difficult within the constraints that operate in clinical practice. It may be worth considering, however, the potential role of peer group activities in clinics on analogy with their use as a setting for learning in open classrooms (Allen, 1977).

Now we turn to the second concern of this section, the nature of conversational disorders that can be described within the framework presented in this chapter. Two aspects of this problem will be considered: problems associated with initiating exchanges and those associated with responses.

There are two important aspects of initiating utterances: attention-getting and attention-drawing. The use of attention-getting devices suggests an intention to communicate and seems to be acquired very early by children. Children use various attention-getting strategies even before they have developed the language to follow them up. Some children, most notably those with autistic tendencies, fail to use devices such as establishing eye contact, vocatives, and attention-getting words such as "hey," possibly because they lack communicative intent in the first place (Fay & Schuler, 1980).

Attention-drawing is more problematic as it depends on a combination of cognitive and linguistic skills. Speakers have to assess their listener's state of knowledge in order to design their utterance appropriately. In the case of higher level communicative tasks, such as those required in studies of referential communicative ability, speakers have to provide for the unique identification of referents by their listener on the basis of a comparison of the relevant referent attributes. In order to accomplish these tasks successfully, speakers need to use a variety of linguistic devices such as definite and indefinite articles, tenses, relative clauses, and other modifying expressions. Young children who have not yet developed these linguistic devices have difficulty in establishing discourse referents. A typical problem with conversationally disordered children is the inability to use these devices appropriately. For example, autistic children are often unable to distinguish old and new information so that they misuse anaphoric pronouns, definite articles, and relative pronouns (Baltaxe, 1977) or overspecify discourse referents with the result that speech is often redundant, that is, they tell the listener more than he needs or wants to know. Such children also have problems with introducing new topics that link back to previous discourse topics or which break topical continuity, using devices such as "do you remember" and "by the way" (Fay & Schuler, 1980).

Other disorders related to initiations include a tendency to initiate infrequently as well as an inappropriate use of initiations. Regarding the latter, Baltaxe (1977) reports a tendency in adolescent autistics to ask the same question over and over again, despite receiving apparently appropriate answers. Concerning reinitiations, it has been found that disordered patients have problems in using more complex devices to rephrase their reinitiations (Fay & Schuler, 1980; van Kleeck & Frankel, 1981).

Following the successful initiation of a topic, the continuation of the dialogue depends on how the speakers respond to each other's turns. Minimal responses, while fulfilling the requirements of their preceding initiations, do not carry the dialogue any further while inappropriate or irrelevant responses result in conversational breakdown. Such problems are common in the literature on conversational disorders. Greenlee (1981) reports how her subject, an 8-year-old boy diagnosed as psychotic, failed to respond to 40% of her questions and gave inappropriate or unrelated responses to 25%. Brinton and Fujiki (1982) noted how some language-disordered children, aged 5;6 to 6;0, gave responses to yes/no questions that were structurally intact but contained information that was contrary to fact. In this case, the responses seemed to indicate a recognition of the basic conversational principles of taking turns and responding to preceding initiations but problems in the processing and organization of the specific information being requested. Similar points have been made about the echolalic responses of autistic children (Prizant & Duchan, 1981).

Little is known about difficulties in the construction of continuous sequences of dialogue. Autistic children are often reported as talking ad nauseum about things of interest only to themselves and producing "pseudo-dialogues" in which they leave no room for their conversational partners to take turns (Ricks & Wing, 1975). In other cases the child's performance can be constrained by the nature of the other participant's interactional strategies. Either the interaction is so tightly controlled that the child has little scope to develop more elaborate responses, or the more competent participant makes allowances for the child's inabilities and creates the semblance of dialogue, rather as mothers do with their very young children in the early stages of language development. Further work in this area must take into account the structural, functional, and sequential properties of utterances as well as the interactional strategies of the participants.

By way of conclusion, the main points that have emerged in the course of this chapter can be summarized briefly. The chapter began by exploring the structural organization of conversation and found that there was some profit in pursuing an analogy with the notion of structure as it has been applied in other areas of linguistic analysis such as syntax. The main advantage would be a rigorous account of how utterances are related in conversations. It was found, however, that many problems were raised by this analogy, such as the question of descriptive units and their co-occurrence possibilities. The fact that conversation is jointly constructed and that speakers' intentions are essentially indeterminate also posed problems for the analogy with syntactic structure. This led to a consideration of the ways in which participants create coherent dialogue by producing utterances that can be either prospective or retrospective or that fulfill both functions simultaneously. The development of these features was traced from the early interactions of young infants and their caregivers to the more mature conversations of school-aged children. Finally, some problem areas were considered: first, the constraining effect of certain interactional styles on the conversational development of young children in classrooms and speech therapy clinics, and then some examples of conversational disorders in the areas of initiations and responses. There is still much to learn about the art of skilled conversation but it is to be hoped that the approach adopted in this chapter will inform further research in this field of inquiry, which is of vital concern to all aspects of communication between human beings.

Appendix A

Discourse Coding Conventions

Exchanges

I: initiation—an utterance that breaks continuity with the preceding discourse and predicts a response

R: response—an utterance that is predicted by and responds to a preceding utterance

R/I: response/initiation—an utterance that is predicted by and responds to a preceding utterance, and that simultaneously predicts a further response

R/(I):   response/(initiation)—an utterance that is predicted by and responds to a preceding utterance, and that simultaneously provides for the possibility of a further response

cont: continuation—an utterance that continues or adds to a previous utterance within a turn

I_r: reinitiation—an utterance that attempts to elicit a response following null or unsatisfactory responses

Symbols

[:   exchange
[:   series of linked exchanges
{ :   links between utterances within a turn
) :   thematic links between nonadjacent utterances

Appendix B

Intonation Patterns in Extract (29)

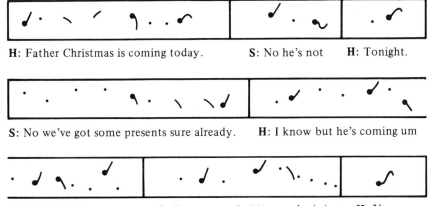

H: Father Christmas is coming today.   S: No he's not   H: Tonight.

S: No we've got some presents sure already.   H: I know but he's coming um

the day after tomorrow.   S: To come and visit us so he is just. H: Yes.
(falsetto)

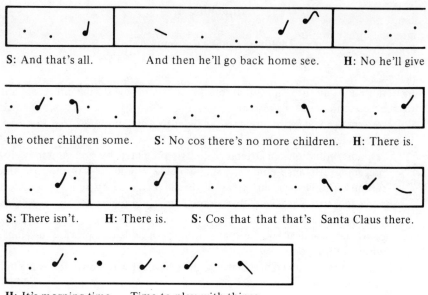

S: And that's all.   And then he'll go back home see.   H: No he'll give

the other children some.   S: No cos there's no more children.   H: There is.

S: There isn't.   H: There is.   S: Cos that that that's   Santa Claus there.

H: It's morning time.   Time to play with things.

References

Allen, V. L. (Ed.) (1976). *Children as teachers: Theory and research on tutoring.* New York: Academic Press.

Argyle, M. (1980). Interaction skills and social competence. In P. Feldman & J. Orford (Eds.), *Psychological problems: The social context.* New York: Wiley.

Atkinson, M. (1979). Prerequisites for reference. In E. Ochs & B. Schieffelin (Eds.), *Developmental pragmatics.* New York. Academic Press.

Baltaxe, C. A. M. (1977). Pragmatic deficits in the language of autistic adolescents. *Journal of Pediatric Psychology, 2,* 176–180.

Bates, E., Camaioni, L., & Volterra, V. (1975). The acquisition of performatives prior to speech. *Merrill-Palmer Quarterly, 21*(3), 205–224.

Beattie, G. W. (1980). The skilled art of conversational interaction. In W. T. Singleton, P. Spurgeon, & R. B. Stammers (Eds.), *The analysis of social skills.* New York: Plenum.

Beaugrande, R. de, & Dressler, W. (1981). *Introduction to text linguistics.* London: Longman.

Berninger, G., & Garvey, C. (1981). Relevant replies to questions: Answers versus evasions. *Journal of Psycholinguistic Research, 10*(4), 403–420.

Berry, M. (1981a). Systemic linguistics and discourse analysis: A multi-layered approach to exchange structure. In M. Coulthard & M. Montgomery (Eds.), *Studies in discourse analysis.* London: Routledge and Kegan Paul.

Berry, M. (1981b). Polarity, ellipticity, elicitation and propositional development: Their relevance to the well-formedness of an exchange. *Nottingham Linguistic Circular, 10,* 1.

Bloom, L., Rocissano, L., & Hood, L. (1976). Adult-child discourse: Developmental interaction between information processing and linguistic knowledge. *Cognitive Psychology, 8,* 521–552.

Brinton, B., & Fujiki, M. (1982). A comparison of request-response sequences in the discourse of normal and language-disordered children. *Journal of Speech and Hearing Disorders, 47,* 57–62.

Cairns, H. S., & Hsu, J. R. (1978). Who, why, when and how: A developmental study. *Journal of Child Language, 5,* 477–488.

Carter, A. (1978). From sensori-motor vocalizations to words: A case study of the evolution of attention-directing communication in the second year. In A. Lock (Ed.), *Action, gesture and symbol: The emergence of language.* New York: Academic Press.

Cicourel, A. V. (1973). *Cognitive sociology.* Harmondsworth: Penguin.

Clarke, D. D. (1979). The linguistic analogy: When is a speech act like a morpheme? In G. Ginsburg (Ed.), *Emerging strategies in social psychological research.* London: Wiley.

Clarke, D. D., & Argyle, M. (1982). Conversational sequences. In C. Fraser & K. Scherer (Eds.), *Advances in the social psychology of language.* Cambridge: Cambridge University Press.

Cole, P., & Morgan, J. L. (Eds.) (1975). *Syntax and semantics. Vol. 3: Speech acts.* New York: Academic Press.

Corsaro, W. A. (1979). Sociolinguistic patterns in adult-child interaction. In E. Ochs & B. Schieffelin (Eds.), *Developmental pragmatics.* New York: Academic Press.

Coulthard, M., & Brazil, D. (1981). Exchange structure. In M. Coulthard & M. Montgomery (Eds.), *Studies in discourse analysis.* London: Routledge and Kegan Paul.

Coulthard, M., & Montgomery, M. (Eds.) (1981). *Studies in discourse analysis.* London: Routledge and Kegan Paul.

Crosby, F. (1976). Early discourse agreement. *Journal of Child Language, 3,* 125–126.

Crystal, D., Fletcher, P., & Garman, M. (1976). *The grammatical analysis of language disability.* London: Edward Arnold.

Dittman, A. T. (1972). Developmental factors in conversational behaviour. *Journal of Communication, 22,* 404–423.

Dore, J. (1977). Oh them sheriff: A pragmatic analysis of children's responses to questions. In S. Ervin-Tripp & C. Mitchell-Kernan (Eds.), *Child discourse.* New York: Academic Press.

Ervin-Tripp, S. (1970). Discourse agreement: How children answer questions. In J. R. Hayes (Ed.), *Cognition and the development of language.* New York: Wiley.

Ervin-Tripp, S. (1978). Some features of early child-adult dialogues. *Language in Society, 7,* 357–373.

Ervin-Tripp, S., & Mitchell-Kernan, C. (1977). *Child discourse.* New York: Academic Press.

Fay, W., & Schuler, A. (1980). *Emerging language in autistic children.* London: Edward Arnold.

Foster, S. (1979). *From non-verbal to verbal communication: A study of the development of topic initiation strategies during the first two-and-a-half years.* Unpublished doctoral dissertation, University of Lancaster.

Garnica, O., & King, M. (Eds.) (1979). *Language, children and society.* Oxford: Pergamon Press.

Garvey, C., & Hogan, R. (1973). Social speech and interaction: Egocentrism revisited. *Child Development, 44,* 562–568.

Goffman, E. (1971). *Relations in public.* Harmondsworth: Penguin.

Goffman, E. (1981). *Forms of talk.* London: Blackwell.

Goodwin, C. (1981). *Conversational organization: Interaction between speakers and hearers.* New York: Academic Press.

Greenlee, M. (1981). Learning to tell the forest from the trees: Unravelling discourse features of a psychotic child. *First Language, 2,* 83–102.

Grice, H. P. (1975). Logic and conversation. In P. Cole & J. L. Morgan (Eds.), *Syntax and semantics. Vol. 3: Speech acts.* New York: Academic Press.

Halliday, M. A. K. (1975). *Learning how to mean.* London: Edward Arnold.

Halliday, M. A. K. (1979). The development of texture in child language. In T. Myers (Ed.), *The development of conversation and discourse.* Edinburgh: Edinburgh University Press.

Horgan, D. (1978). How to answer questions when you've nothing to say. *Journal of Child Language, 5,* 159–165.

Kaye, K. (1977). Toward the origin of dialogue. In H. R. Schaffer (Ed.), *Studies in mother-infant interaction.* New York: Academic Press.

Keenan, E. O. (1974). Conversational competence in children. *Journal of Child Language, 1*(2), 163–183.

Keenan, E. O. (1975). Evolving discourse—The next step. *Papers and Reports on Child Language Development,* No. 10, Stanford University.

Keenan, E. O. (1976). The universality of conversational postulates. *Language in Society, 5,* 67–80.

Keenan, E. O., & Klein, E. (1975). Coherency in children's discourse. *Journal of Psycholinguistic Research, 4,* 365–378.

Keenan, E. O., & Schieffelin, B. (1976). Topic as a discourse notion: A study of topic in the conversations of children and adults. In C. Li (Ed.), *Subject and topic.* New York: Academic Press.

Labov, W., & Fanshel, D. (1977). *Therapeutic discourse: Psychotherapy as conversation.* New York: Academic Press.

Lakoff, R. (1973). The logic of politeness: Or minding your p's and q's. In *Papers from the ninth regional meeting of the Chicago Linguistic Society.* Chicago: Chicago Linguistic Society.

Leech, G. (1980). *Explorations in semantics and pragmatics.* Amsterdam: John Benjamins.

Levinson, S. (1981). Some pre-observations on the modelling of dialogue. *Discourse Processes, 4*(2), 93–110.

Lock, A. (1978). On being picked up. In A. Lock (Ed.), *Action, gesture and symbol: The emergence of language.* New York: Academic Press.

Lyons, J. (1968). *Introduction to theoretical linguistics.* Cambridge: Cambridge University Press.

MacLure, M. (1981). *Making sense of children's talk.* Unpublished doctoral dissertation, University of York.

McTear, M. (1984). *The development of conversational ability in children.* London: Academic Press.

Mishler, E. (1978). Studies in dialogue and discourse III. Utterance structure and utterance function in interrogative sequences. *Journal of Psycholinguistic Research, 7*(4), 279–305.

Mueller, E. (1972). The maintenance of verbal exchanges between young children. *Child Development, 43,* 930–938.

Newson, J. (1979). The growth of shared understandings between infant and caregiver. In M. Bullowa (Ed.), *Before speech: The beginning of interpersonal communication.* Cambridge: Cambridge University Press.

Ochs, E., & Schieffelin, B. (Eds.) (1979). *Developmental pragmatics.* New York: Academic Press.

Ochs, E., Schieffelin, B., & Platt, M. (1979). Propositions across utterances and speakers. In E. Ochs & B. Schieffelin (Eds.), *Developmental pragmatics.* New York: Academic Press.

Pomerantz, A. (1978). Compliment responses: Notes on the co-operation of multiple constraints. In J. Schenkein (Ed.), *Studies in the organization of conversational interaction.* New York: Academic Press.

Prizant, B. M., & Duchan, J. F. (1981). The functions of immediate echolalia in autistic children. *Journal of Speech and Hearing Disorders, 46,* 241–249.

Ricks, D. M., & Wing, L. (1975). Language, communication and the use of symbols in normal and autistic children. *Journal of Autism and Child Schizophrenia, 5,* 191–220.

Schaffer, H. R., Collis, G. M., & Parsons, G. (1977). Vocal interchange and visual regard in verbal and pre-verbal children. In H. R. Schaffer (Ed.), *Studies in mother-infant interaction.* New York: Academic Press.

Schegloff, E.A. (1968). Sequencing in conversational openings. *American Anthropologist, 70,* 1075–1095.

Schegloff, E. A. (1977). On some questions and ambiguities in conversation. In W. Dressler (Ed.), *Current trends in textlinguistics.* Berlin: Walter de Gruyter.

Schegloff, E. A. (1979). The relevance of repair to syntax-for-conversation. In T. Givon (Ed.), *Syntax and semantics. Vol. 12: Discourse and syntax.* New York: Academic Press.

Schegloff, E. A., & Sacks, H. (1973). Opening up closings. *Semiotica, VIII,* 289–327.

Scollon, R. (1979). A real early stage: An unzipped condensation of a dissertation on child language. In E. Ochs & B. B. Schieffelin (Eds.), *Developmental pragmatics.* New York: Academic Press.

Shugar, G. W. (1978). Text-constructing with an adult: A form of child activity during early language acquisition. In G. Drachman (Ed.), *Salzburger beiträge zur linguistik: Akten des 1. Salzburger kolloquiums über kindersprache.* Tubingen: Verlag Gunter Narr.

Sinclair, J. M., & Coulthard, R. M. (1975). *Towards an analysis of discourse: The English used by teachers and pupils.* Oxford: Oxford University Press.

Snow, C. E. (1977). The development of conversation between mothers and babies. *Journal of Child Language, 4,* 1–22.

Söderbergh, R. (1974). *The fruitful dialogue: The child's acquisition of his first language: Implications for education at all steps.* Project Child Language Syntax, Reprint No. 2. Stockholms Universitet: Institutionen for Nordiska Sprak.

Steffenson, M. S. (1978). Satisfying inquisitive adults: Some simple methods of answering yes/no questions. *Journal of Child Language, 5,* 221–236.

Stern, D. (1977). *The first relationship: Infant and mother.* London: Fontana.

Stern, D., Jaffe, J., Beebe, B., & Bennett, S. R. (1975). Vocalising in unison and in alternation: Two modes of communication within the mother-infant dyad. In D. Aaronson & R. W. Rieber (Eds.), *Developmental psycholinguistics and communication disorders.* New York: New York Academy of Sciences.

Stubbs, M. (1981). Motivating analyses of exchange structure. In M. Coulthard & M. Montgomery (Eds.), *Studies in discourse analysis.* London: Routledge and Kegan Paul.

Stubbs, M. (1982). *Discourse analysis.* London: Blackwell.

Trevarthen, C. (1979). Communication and cooperation in early infancy: A description of primary intersubjectivity. In M. Bullowa (Ed.), *Before speech: The beginning of interpersonal communication.* Cambridge: Cambridge Univeristy Press.

Tyack, D., & Ingram, D. (1977). Children's production and comprehension of questions. *Journal of Child Language, 4,* 211–224.

Van Kleeck, A., & Frankel, T. (1981). Discourse devices used by language disordered children: A preliminary investigation. *Journal of Speech and Hearing Disorders, 46,* 250–257.

Wellman, H. M., & Lempers, J. D. (1977). The naturalistic communicative abilities of two-year-olds. *Child Development, 48,* 1052–1057.

Wells, G., MacLure, M., & Montgomery, M. (1981). Some strategies for sustaining conversation. In P. Werth (Ed.), *Conversation and discourse.* London: Croom Helm.

Wells, G., Montgomery, M., & MacLure, M. (1979). Adult-child discourse: Outline of a model of analysis. *Journal of Pragmatics, 3,* 3–4.

Whiten, A. (1977). Assessing the effects of perinatal events on the success of the mother-infant relationship. In H. R. Schaffer (Ed.), *Studies in mother-infant interaction.* New York: Academic Press.

Wootton, A. (1981). Conversation analysis. In P. French & M. MacLure (Eds.), *Adult-child conversation.* London: Croom Helm.

4. Skill in Peer Learning Discourse: What Develops?

Catherine R. Cooper and Robert G. Cooper, Jr.

In recent years, the significance of children's experiences with one another has been taken increasingly seriously by social scientists. Once focused on parent-child (especially mother-child) and teacher-child interactions as the key mode of socialization, scholars are now actively documenting the contribution children make to one another's development, not just in the traditionally studied areas of sex and aggression, but also in cognitive and moral domains of development as well (Hartup, 1983). In post-Piagetian times, it is fashionable to focus on the degree to which we have underestimated the competence of the younger child, and in the discussion of peer learning it is also tempting to make claims that children can offer one another the equivalent or at least the analogue of what adults offer. However, this chapter examines the nature of children's peer learning discourse, including the ways that it changes across development, in order to consider the changing contributions of children's peer experiences to their development. Our central argument is that understanding developmental and within-age differences in peer learning involves understanding development in several distinct categories of capacity.

To develop this argument, we shall first consider the definition of a peer, an issue that has elicited considerable discussion in the recent literature. Then we shall present a developmental sequence of peer learning forms, which will serve as the basis for a more differentiated understanding of the concept of peer learning dis-

This work was supported in part by a grant to the first author from the University Research Institute of the University of Texas at Austin. Portions of this paper were presented at a symposium entitled "Process and Outcome in Classroom Peer Interaction: Conceptual and Empirical Perspectives" at the Society for Research in Child Development meetings, Detroit, April, 1983.

course. Following this, we consider the classic developmental question, "what is the development of X the development of?" (Flavell, 1971). On the basis of this discussion, we shall examine a body of data on children's discourse during peer learning in experimental and naturalistic contexts, and trace developmental themes in this work.

In doing so, we shall also argue that our understanding of children's discourse will benefit from a deeper consideration of the multiple levels of Hinde's (1976) framework of social relationships, in which he distinguishes among interactions, relationships, and groups. Interactions, in Hinde's view, involve patterns of communication that accrue between persons, who may or may not be intimates. Relationships, on the other hand, are evidenced by enduring bonds between persons, often marked by histories of interactions, but also by commitments. Groups carry with them normative expectations about acceptable and unacceptable forms of behavior; these values, of course, influence the nature of both the interactions and the relationships of the members of the group.

What Is a Peer?

In recent literature on peer relations (e.g., Asher & Gottman, 1981; Hartup, 1983, 1982; Mueller & Cooper, in press; Rubin & Ross, 1982; Youniss, 1980), discussion of the definition of peer relations has focused on two dimensions: similarity in age, and equalitarianism in interaction style. For scholars studying peer interaction among children, requirements for peer status have typically been met when children are within a year of one another in chronological age. Age-grading in Western culture is widespread (Hartup, 1983), so this is by no means idiosyncratic to social scientists. These distinctions are also made by children themselves; for example, differences of only one year have been found to influence children's effectiveness as models (Thelan & Kirkland, 1976), and mixed-age interactions have also been seen as more characterized by dominance, expressed as both nurturance and directiveness (Hartup, 1983). However, it is pertinent to note from a life-span perspective that sameness in age is defined within a much larger span of years by older adults, who consider a person within 4–5 years as being the same age (Epstein, in press).

Many scholars, however, have been impressed enough with individual differences in interaction among children of the same chronological age (Markovits & Strayer, 1982) as well as with role reversals in mixed-age pairs (Furman, Rahe, & Hartup, 1979) to look beyond age in defining peer status. Investigators who have studied discourse have specified qualities of interaction that define peer relations. Especially from naturalistic observations in classrooms (Cooper, Marquis, & Edward, in press) as well as families (Dunn & Kendrick, 1982), children's peer relationships can be identified by their negotiated quality, constructed by their members, of equivalent status (Garvey, in press). Also significant for many children's peer relations is their sharing of lower status relative to adult authorities and their own potential maturity. For example, children may negotiate the pooling of their resources in coalitions against the influence of teachers or parents (Banks & Kahn, 1975; Mehan & Riel, 1980).

Consideration of these qualities helps us see how much our understanding of peer relations stands to benefit from its analysis at the interaction, relationship, and group levels. At the level of interaction, we can anticipate that the capacity to negotiate mutually acceptable roles in interaction will be a central developmental attainment. At the relational level, the capacity to reinvoke past agreements, resolve conflict, repair breakdowns in shared views, or renegotiate plans would be a benchmark of friendship. It is not just what is said (discourse) but who is saying what to whom, or the relationship, that will be critical in the outcome of a conversation. Finally, we are gaining an understanding, especially by studying children in naturalistic contexts, that the attitudes held by adults and other children toward a pair of friends, as well as their own perceptions of their place in the larger group, are powerful determinants of their interactions (Hallinan, 1981).

What Is Peer Learning?

How do children help one another in their learning? Many aspects of children's peer interaction have been studied, including play (Garvey, 1977), tutoring (Allen, 1976), modeling (Hartup, 1983), persuasion (Clark & Delia, 1976; Eisenberg & Garvey, 1981), and collaborative interaction (Cooper, Ayers-Lopez & Marquis, 1982). The roles children play in peer learning have often been considered in terms of two prototypic patterns: cooperative and didactic. Cooperative or "doer-doer" interactions involve children who have equivalent amounts of expertise with regard to a shared problem. Didactic or "knower-doer" interactions involve the transmission of information from a more to a less-skilled partner (Cooper, Marquis, & Edward, in press; Garvey & Baldwin, 1970).

When these two participant structures are considered developmentally, however, we can anticipate that younger and older children will differ considerably in the ways they are able to engage in cooperative and didactic roles. Among younger children, whose discourse and cognitive skills are less extensively developed, cooperative interaction might amount to turn-taking on simple tasks. Older children, in contrast, might be able to use their metacognitive skills to plan, organize, carry out, revise, and evaluate a project extending over days and involving differentiated roles.

In a similar pattern, didactic roles among younger children might be seen as they show and tell their peers, or, in the learner role, as they imitate others. Older children's cognitive development may allow them to orient and guide their partner, and to change teaching strategies in response to the learner's behavior. In later sections of this chapter, we shall examine the evidence for this developmental progression in peer learning forms.

Issues for the Study of Peer Learning Discourse

Investigators of children's peer learning discourse encounter the enduring issues common to discourse analysis in other contexts (Ochs & Schieffelin, 1979; J. Scherzer, personal communication, 1982). The discussion in this chapter addresses two of these issues: the unit of analysis in discourse and the question of what is learned.

The analysis of *speech acts,* especially directives and requests, has allowed scholars to study children's growing understanding of language as social action. For example, analyses of felicity and sincerity conditions, respectively, focus on the listener's and speaker's ability and intention to perform the indicated action. Developmental change in children's ability to fulfill such conditions is a key aspect of the development of discourse competence in peer learning. Children's use of mitigation and aggravation in communicating requests has also proved pertinent to their success in peer learning (Peterson, Wilkinson, Spinelli, & Swing, 1982). Adjacency pairs of requests and responses (Sacks, 1972) have provided the framework of much developmental analysis of peer exchanges (e.g., Dore, 1979).

A great deal of recent work in discourse analysis has been concerned with the larger linguistic unit of the *speech event,* in which sequences of adjacency pairs are contained and socially defined (Hymes, 1972). By describing patterns in such speech events as narratives during classroom show-and-tell periods (Michaels & Cook-Gumperz, 1979), disputes (Eisenberg & Garvey, 1981), play (Garvey, 1977), as well as peer learning (Cooper, Marquis, & Ayers-Lopez, 1982), sets of rules have been described that predict both order and violation in the patterning of different types of interaction. These rules may differ across different speech communities, and also are differentiated by roles within the group, yielding distinctive *participant structures.* For example, in some traditional communities, learners are expected to observe in silence (Greenfield & Lave, 1982), whereas in other cultures questions to the teacher are permitted (Mehan, 1979).

In peer learning, we shall see that the speech event is a useful unit of analysis because different events have different rules for participation, which children have the capacity but perhaps not always the opportunity to learn. In a speech community of the classroom, the appropriate setting in time and space for the speech event of peer teaching may be regulated or even prohibited (e.g., "children, no talking to your neighbors while you are working"); the participants may be specified (e.g., two children may work together for tutoring, four for a study group); and interpretive rules for use by the members of the group may be agreed upon (e.g., it is permissible to reveal that one is confused without losing face). Scholars have argued that children who succeed in school are those who have mastered such implicit rules of discourse in the classroom, thereby gaining optimal access to the resources available (Mehan, 1979; Merritt, 1982).

A second issue that all developmentalists confront concerns the question of what is learned. An adequate description of competence in discourse must include the ways that individuals come to use language in context. Some scholars have seen this task as one of separating contextual variables from individual ones (Wohlwill,

1973), whereas others see the core task as describing group or contextual norms that individuals must learn (Mehan, 1979). In this chapter, both individual and contextual dimensions are considered as necessary components to an understanding of the development of peer discourse skills.

Constraints on Children's Effectiveness

Why does the effectiveness of children's peer learning discourse change with age? Some answers to this sort of question focus on the child's ability or inability to perform in certain ways. Three types of limitations may operate: (a) the child does not have a particular behavior in his or her repertoire (a limitation of learning in the broad sense); (b) the child is unable to use a behavior in a particular setting when other demands on information processing capacity are high (a limitation in cognitive capacity or skill); and (c) the child does not know that it would be useful or appropriate to use a particular behavior (a metacognitive limitation).

A second type of answer to questions concerning changes in peer learning with age involves behaviors that are not directly related to capabilities and limitations to perform in particular ways. For example, the child may have been taught that cooperation on assignments is not allowed in school, or may be angry and not want to cooperate. These types of influences on children's behavior are usually discussed under the topic of social, emotional, or personality development. They do not directly constitute limitations on children's peer learning ability. Indirectly they have two effects: they act as a filter on the use of the abilities already described, and they also influence the kinds of peer learning experiences that children have, which in turn influences their ability to develop these abilities. In the remainder of this section we will examine the developmental and within-age-group variation in peer learning from the perspective of limitations in capabilities, and then consider other sources of influence.

The first type of limitation, the failure to have acquired certain behaviors or skills, will be labeled *skill acquisition* and can be accounted for in a variety of ways. One is lack of relevant learning opportunities. Another is lack of prerequisite skills, which can be formulated more generally in terms of developmental level (e.g. Piaget, 1967). Thus, although it is hard to draw a sharp boundary, failure to acquire behaviors can be considered in terms of two classes of explanations: those that focus on lack of experience (or on lack of sufficient experience) for learning the behaviors, and those that focus on characteristics of the child that make it difficult or impossible to learn from an experience at a particular developmental (or intellectual) level. Consider the role of explanations in peer learning. It has been demonstrated that the ability to give adequate explanations of a phenomenon is dependent upon experience with it (Ginsburg & Opper, 1980). In addition, preschoolers' ability to give explanations is flawed in many ways. Thus, both types of learning limitations have been documented for a skill that is crucial in peer learning.

The second category, the failure to use a skill that is in the child's repertoire because of processing limitations, has been the focus of much recent interest; it will be discussed in terms of *processing capacity*. Pascual-Leone (1970) has described processing limitations as limitations on "M-space," the area of working memory. He has suggested that M-space increases with age, which allows more complex cognitive processing to occur and/or more processes to occur simultaneously. Alternatively, Case (1978) has suggested that working memory is of fixed size from an early age and that newly acquired skills become more automated with development and experience. Shatz (1978) has developed a more explicit conception of the role of specific practice in decreasing the cognitive capacity required for specific "information-handling techniques," thereby increasing the child's processing efficiency. Further, Shatz has applied this analysis to children's communication processes and provided data that support capacity limitation as part of the problem in young children's communications. This approach is particularly useful in explaining the gradual emergence and generalization of skills that are initially exhibited in limited contexts and/or in primitive forms, although in Shatz's formulation it does not explain the emergence of new behaviors.

The child's ability to provide explanations can serve as an example of this second kind of limitation also. A child might be able to give adequate explanations in general, know the specific explanation relevant to the task at hand, but be unable in a peer learning situation to give the explanation because other features of the situation, such as negotiation and maintaining attention, have used up all available processing capacity.

The third category, failure to use a particular behavior because it is not understood to be useful, has been studied in the communications area primarily under the topic of role-taking (e.g., Flavell, Botkin, Fry, Wright, & Jarvis, 1968; Piaget, 1926/1955), although it has been a topic of more general interest under the rubric of metamemory, metacognition, and metapragmatics. We will use the term *metacognition* to refer to this category. Again, we can use explanations as an example. Flavell et al., (1968) asked children to explain a game to a blindfolded listener. The children understood the game, were capable of giving adequate explanations, but younger children failed because they did not take into account how an explanation had to be modified to communicate to someone who could not see. Similarly, Patterson and Roberts (1982) have used referential communication tasks to study the role of planning, a metacognitive skill, in the development of effective communication.

The fourth category concerns constraints on performance that will be referred to as *social*. Some are a product of general socialization, that is, members of a given culture can be expected to share the same choices about what is and is not appropriate. Others may be more idiosyncratic, for example, how shy an individual is, and are frequently described with such terms as personality or mood, depending on intraindividual stability. Using explanations once again, a child who was capable of giving explanations and who knew the correct explanation might fail to give it for fear of being wrong.

The first two categories, skill acquisition and processing capacity, are direct developmental constraints on performance; that is, they constitute limits on what the child can and cannot do. The second two categories, metacognitive and social, are indirect or second level since they involve the selection of behaviors from an existing repertoire. However, it is important to note that development in all four categories involves learning; what differs among the categories is what is learned.

Although factors underlying the development of discourse can be differentiated into the four categories just described, the performance we actually see in any particular situation is a product of all four. For example, consider the task of negotiation between two peers in order to build a large bridge with blocks. The successful outcome of such an episode depends on having acquired some capabilities in argument and negotiation (Eisenberg & Garvey, 1981); having acquired enough skill at negotiating so that it can be accomplished without losing sight of the ultimate goal of building the bridge (Brenneis & Lein, 1976); having acquired enough metacommunicative competence to realize that it is important to negotiate roles so tasks like planning of a structure can be carried out (Forbes & Greenberg, 1982); and being willing to participate in negotiation rather than withdrawing or attacking (Putallaz & Gottman, 1981).

In viewing the development of such a process, how can one detect which category or categories are the source of an observed limit on behavior? The strategy that will be illustrated in this chapter involves manipulating the context or task situation to try to isolate developmental patterns of each of the categories. A study by Shatz (1978) illustrates this strategy. She manipulated the set of alternatives in a task that involved selecting an appropriate gift for another person. As the discriminations among alternatives became more difficult, young children were more likely to make "egocentric" choices even though they had shown some ability to be nonegocentric. Similar findings have been demonstrated by varying task difficulty in a referential communication task (Shatz, 1983). Thus, manipulating the cognitive demands of the overall task is one way to investigate the role of skill development in communication.

Alternatively, one can manipulate the social situation as a way of investigating the role of social factors (e.g., Labov, 1970). Finally, one can manipulate the experiences of the participants. In a study comparing children from traditional and "open-space" schools, in which shared activities were common, Downing and Bothwell (1979) found that children from traditional schools chose their seats in a way that reflected their expectations that they would work without interacting with their peers. In a cooperative game situation their rate of cooperation was lower than for the "open-space" students. Although imperfect, these kinds of manipulations can be used to develop a more differentiated picture of the component parts of discourse development.

A final caveat is appropriate for this taxonomy: it does not represent an overall developmental sequence. It is true that an ability must be acquired before it can become a highly practiced skill, or that it must be acquired before it can be reflected upon at the metacognitive level, and, therefore, for any particular skill there is a developmental ordering. However, at all ages new abilities may be acquired, practiced to become fluid skills, understood so they can be deployed effectively, and integrated into a style of interaction. One might suspect that even a senior diplomat just assigned to a new country might agree.

Research Evidence: Three Studies of Children's Discourse During Peer Learning

In the following sections, three programs of work involving children's peer learning discourse will be considered in terms of the framework just described. Each will be used to highlight one of the categories of limitations already described.

Acquisition of Skill in Requests and Explanations

Wilkinson, Peterson, and their colleagues (e.g., Peterson et al., 1982; Wilkinson & Calculator, 1982) have combined sociolinguistic and process-product approaches in their studies of children's discourse in small classroom work groups, and have documented skills associated with school achievement that emerge during middle childhood.

In a recent study (Peterson et al., 1982), children in a combined second- and third-grade class were assigned to mixed-ability groups, each including one child of high ability, one of low ability, and two of medium ability, as determined by scores on a math pretest. The groups were observed as they sat together at tables in their classrooms while working on individual worksheet assignments following lessons on money and time. After their teacher had presented each lesson and assigned worksheets on the topic, the children were told that if they needed help, they should seek it from one another before asking the teacher.

Analyses of peer learning discourse focused on two key processes: requests and explanations. Children who used requests that were direct, sincere, on-task, designated a particular listener, and when necessary, were revised, were more likely to elicit an appropriate response (Wilkinson & Calculator, 1982). The use of direct requests was associated not only with achievement on the posttest of the 10-lesson series, but also with sociometric ratings and verbal ability measures (Peabody Picture Vocabulary Test). Most of the requests produced by the children in their work groups were procedural rather than for explanation (Peterson et al., 1982).

The second key process involved the giving and receiving of explanations. This process has been the subject of extensive investigation by a group of educational psychologists interested in peer learning groups (Swing & Peterson, 1982; Webb, 1982). Among older children, it has been reported that telling another child whether an answer is correct, or giving the correct answer without explaining it are negatively correlated with children's achievement scores following the peer experience, but receiving "higher-order" explanations is positively related to achievement (Webb, 1982).

With their second- and third-grade children, Peterson et al. did find a negative relation between the frequency of a child's receiving (merely) answers to questions and that child's subsequent achievement scores, but no relation between the use of higher-order explanations and achievement. What could explain this? These children were younger than Webb's junior high and high school samples, or Swing and Peterson's upper elementary students, and were probably not providing many higher-order explanations. Peterson et al. speculate that their children did not have the requisite cognitive and social skills to be able to provide effective explanations to their peers.

Within-Age Differences. The effects of a child's participation in the exchange of information during work appears to vary with the ability of the individual. Among older elementary school children, both high and low ability children who gave and received explanations, respectively, tended to perform better than children of their same ability level who did not participate in such exchanges, whereas no such pattern was observed for medium ability students (Swing & Peterson, 1982). With younger elementary school children, the same findings were obtained for high and medium ability children (Peterson et al., 1982). "Taskmasters," children who frequently paced themselves and other children to keep discussion focused on the worksheets and to guide their work, performed at a high level on posttests. However, low ability children did better if they did not participate in group interaction. The investigators noted that the low ability children who were interacting seemed only to be getting answers, which were insufficient to help them understand the principles assessed on the posttest. These children learned more when working alone.

The studies just described highlight skill acquisition in the development of peer learning. The skills that are acquired are those for requesting information and giving explanations. The characteristics of effective requests that are being acquired are the ability to express directness, sincerity, task-relatedness, and specificity. One characteristic, willingness to modify an unsuccessful request, also suggests a metacognitive component. Skill acquisition in both the development of requests and of effective explanations is suggested by their emergence before either is completely effective.

It is interesting to speculate about the synergism involved in the development of requests and explanations among peers. Children can differentiate effective requests from ineffective ones if someone provides effective explanations in response to effective requests and not to ineffective ones. Likewise, children discern effective explanations from ineffective ones if someone gives differential feedback contingent on their quality. Thus the development of the two skills is an interlocking process, and we see them emerging together. Further, this link seems to be important for effective learning of academic content, since the low ability children who apparently passively receive the correct answers learn less than when they work by themselves.

Children's Processing Capacity in Peer Teaching

Rogoff and her colleagues (Ellis & Rogoff, in press; Rogoff & Gardner, in press) have conducted a series of studies investigating differences in teaching styles of children and adults. In particular, they have been interested in the ways that child teachers distribute their limited cognitive resources while teaching complex tasks. Following Shatz (1978), they anticipated that when one child is teaching an unfamiliar task to another, this constitutes a situation of cognitive overload, and hence the experience becomes one of problem-solving for the teacher as well as the learner.

Given this focus, the methodology is interestingly different than that of Peterson, Wilkinson, and their colleagues. In a recent study (Ellis & Rogoff, in press) children 8 to 9 years old were compared to adults as each group taught 6- to 7-year-olds. The child dyads were of the same sex but were unacquainted. The task, which took place in a single session, involved learning to sort items in grocery store and school settings, for example, sorting snacks, fruits, sandwich spreads, condiments, baking goods, and dry goods for the grocery setting. Each teacher was encouraged to examine the items in a sorted array until he or she felt familiar with the category system. A cue sheet was available for the teacher's but not the learner's use so that the teacher's ability to remember the system was assisted.

As anticipated, children differed significantly in their teaching styles from adults. In general, children neglected to help their pupils understand the category system underlying the sorting task; instead, they focused more on the physical manipulation of the items. Three important teaching processes were used less often by children: orienting, explaining, and preparing the learner for the memory test. Orienting the learner to the task was done by 14 of the 16 adults, but only 7 of the 16 children. Explanation of the category system was provided by 15 of the adults but only 3 of the children. (It is notable that the pupils of these 3 child teachers each made excellent scores on their posttests.) Preparation for the memory test was given by 12 adults and 3 children, although 8 children made some reference to the test, for example, by admonishing their pupils to study. Ellis and Rogoff interpreted this finding as indicating that the children's difficulty lay in supplying strategies for studying rather than in forgetting the existence of the test.

A most interesting observation of this study concerns the changing patterns of involvement across the teaching session by adult and child teachers. Adult teachers began with intermediate levels of involvement, as seen in the frequency of their sorting the items while explaining their reasoning, or their pupil sorting the items while they explained. Across the session, adults typically became less controlling, or began to dismantle the scaffolding of adult-imposed structure on the interaction. They granted more control to the learner but reclaimed it when necessary. In revealing contrast, child teachers were more likely to display either total control, by sorting the items without explaining their behavior, or playing a guessing game with their pupils, requiring them to sort items with little guidance. Use of the latter strategy suggests that the children may not have fully understood the nature of the teaching role. However, a consequence observed by both Ellis and Rogoff (in press) and Mehan and Riel (1980) was that the pupils took a more active role in the learning process; whereas children taught by adults may simply wait to be told the correct strategy or answer.

This research provides an example of the second category of limitations involving processing capacity. It is instructive to examine why the demands on processing might be particularly high in these studies. First, teaching the solution to an unfa-

miliar problem produces a greater cognitive load; the child must use some processing capacity to keep track of the correct solution in order to teach it. Note that this
may be an additional reason why the child teachers sometimes solved the problem
themselves without comment. Second, teaching an unfamiliar child requires that
more cognitive capacity be devoted to managing the social situation. The two children do not have a history of mutually acceptable teacher-learner roles, so some
effort must be expended to establish them. Finally, reading cues for understanding
and misunderstanding from an unfamiliar child is more difficult. All of these features increase the processing load, leaving less capacity for the teaching process per
se and hence are likely to result in less mature teaching behavior.

Metacognitive and Social Issues

Cooper and her colleagues (e.g., Cooper, Ayers-Lopez, & Marquis, 1982; Cooper
et al., in press) have investigated how children help one another learn in classrooms,
and how to examine these spontaneous conversations and their consequences. Because of the basic developmental changes in discourse, cognitive, and metacognitive
skills during early and middle childhood, an account of the factors contributing
to effectiveness in peer learning needs to include different variables for different
ages during this period. Evidence for this argument is based on observations of classroom peer learning among children from kindergarten through sixth grade. In the
traditional classroom, the teacher usually assigns the tasks, ensures appropriate
pacing and attending to classroom work, calls on children to speak, and evaluates
the progress and outcome of children's efforts. Studying classrooms in which many
of these functions are delegated to the children reveals patterns of individual differences in how children learn to manage their own learning.

A basic sequence of events involved in peer learning has been related to children's effectiveness (Cooper et al., in press). The core of the sequence is derived
from work in adult discourse analysis which maps the patterns of discourse common to teaching, narratives, and other conversational forms that depend on the
collaboration of the participants for an exchange to succeed (Coulthard, 1977;
Dore, 1979). The prototypic sequence of events in spontaneous peer learning is
viewed as follows: (a) within a conducive classroom context (see Cooper et al., in
press), (b) a child selects a learning partner and (c) negotiates mutually acceptable
roles for the interaction, as well as the task itself. Within this exchange, the child
must (d) focus and retain the attention of the partner, and (e) provide instrumental
moves that accomplish the exchange of information, such as questions, commands,
explanations, or descriptive comments. The partner has the opportunity to (f) respond, argue, or ignore. Finally, (g) the exchange may also be evaluated.

In the work reported in this chapter, two questions concerning process and outcome in peer learning are addressed. The first involves how to think about the role
or *participant structure* of spontaneous peer learning exchanges. The key contrast
between peer and adult teacher-child interaction is that children helping one another learn are faced, in varying degrees, with the task of negotiating the roles,
tasks, and procedures of their working relationships. Seeing these participant struc-

tures in a more differentiated light can help in the identification of the different social and cognitive goals to which children's interactions are directed.

The second question concerns the evaluation of the effectiveness of these peer learning exchanges. Investigators of peer learning in the classroom, as well as in other contexts, are grappling with the formulation of useful dimensions and units of analysis, and with the mapping of these units to appropriate levels of outcome. This model would suggest several useful units, including the utterance, the instructional episode, the academic task, and the relationship. At the utterance level, individual statements can be classified according to the speaker's presumed intent, such as directives, or requests for information. By considering an utterance in the context of others adjacent to it, its role and effectiveness as a conversational move or response can be evaluated. Analyses of the peer learning exchanges of kindergarten and second-grade children, for example, showed that the success of peer learning exchanges involving learner-teacher or teacher-learner didactic forms could be predicted by children's use of certain discourse features, such as attention-focusing statements, directives, questions, and referential specificity (Cooper, Marquis, & Ayers-Lopez, 1982).

By middle childhood, however, children typically have mastered the fundamental conversational moves at the utterance level. They can use attention-focusing statements to obtain the acknowledgment of their listener and can repair unsuccessful messages by making the referent more specific or by softening or intensifying the force of a directive, although listener skills in comprehension-monitoring continue to improve (Beal & Flavell, 1982; Paris & Lindauer, 1982). Yet when children work together in the classroom, striking individual differences can be seen in their ability to engage their peers in sustained and productive collaboration. During middle childhood, a critical task in peer learning lies at the level of conversational and cognitive *strategy*, the capacity to be planful and selective in cognitive and linguistic behavior. Skill in selecting a behavior from a repertoire of potential approaches in accordance with situational requirements can be seen, for example, as children allocate mutually acceptable teacher and learner roles, plan an activity with a partner, and modify a strategy during an episode if, for example, another child interrupts, or if one of the partners becomes distracted. Such metacognitive variables become increasingly significant as predictors of successful peer learning as teachers grant permission to children to take on more unstructured tasks, and as children begin to master this level of planning in their interactions with peers.

Method. The following observations of elementary school children's peer learning exchanges are drawn from a larger study of 69 children, ranging in age from 5 to 12 years old. They comprised the entire enrollment of a Montessori elementary school that actively encouraged peer interaction as a means of accomplishing school learning. The children, who came from primarily white, middle-class families, were divided into two groups. The younger group was composed of 37 five- to nine-year-olds, with 22 girls and 15 boys, and the older group included 31 seven- to twelve-year-olds, with 18 girls and 13 boys. This program provided an unusual opportunity to study peer learning exchanges, since learning with other children was an explicit method and goal of the curriculum from the time the children entered the program at age three.

The children were observed in their classrooms to answer several questions concerning spontaneous peer learning. Among these were: In what forms of learning interaction do children engage? What roles do they assume in such situations? What are the discourse and cognitive features of the exchanges that succeed and fail? In other phases of the study, the children were observed in an experimental peer learning task and interviewed individually concerning sociometric and metacognitive issues. The teachers of both groups were also interviewed to obtain information about their principles of teaching that enabled the children to use their peers as resources in learning; teachers' ratings of each child's skills in helping and in academic areas were also obtained (Cooper et al., in press).

During key periods of peer learning activity in the daily schedule, audio tape recorders were placed on children's tables and rugs as they worked together. Pertinent nonverbal and contextual data were also recorded. The tapes were reviewed and indexed for the occurrence of instructional episodes, during which children interacted without teacher guidance while working on academic tasks. (Details of coding are available from the authors.)

Results and Discussion. The first analyses involved the forms and role structures of the peer learning exchanges. One of the most striking findings concerns the wide range of peer learning forms observed in the classroom, ranging from working alone to extended collaborative interactions. Besides solitary and onlooker forms (known as cheating in traditional classrooms), three prototypic forms were seen. The first we call *parallel/coordinate*, in which two or more children each work on their own projects, yet exchange comments and periodically help one another concentrate on and accomplish their individual goals. Often these interactions contain exchanges of task-relevant information within a stream of conversation about a range of academic and nonacademic topics, including birthday parties, social comparisons about classmates and parents, and other personal material:

> (A and B are sitting together while each works on a map.)
> **A**: I only have three more to go.
> **B**: (A), when am I ever going to get done with Russia?
> **A**: I don't know.
> **B**: (looking at A's work) You're almost done with your map!
> **A**: That's what I meant.
> **B**: I'm not even near the end of Russia . . . I'm going to take a break.
> **A**: You've been taking too many breaks. That's the problem.

In *didactic* forms, one child directs the other in accomplishing some activity; overall, one child is the teacher. In teacher-learner episodes, one child helps or teaches another, announces newly learned information, or provides unsolicited correction. A child teacher may engage in a sustained session with one or more learners:

> **A**: (Giving spelling words) *Father.*
> **B**: Father. F-A-T-H-E-R.

C: I've got a mother and a father . . . but I don't want my mother.
A: *Whose.*
C: W-H-O-S-E.
B: (C), our parents are alike. Our mother is mean and our father is nice.
C: Yes, and mine are divorced.
A: *Fruit.*
B: Fruit. F-R-U-I-T.

Learner-teacher episodes are marked by one child requesting information or help from another. More elaborate forms of guidance in which one child guides another in teaching a third child, which we have termed *executive guidance*, were also observed.

In *collaborative* interaction, the children share the power of directing the interaction more equally, either through alternating or sharing the teaching role or by not assuming a clear leader-follower pattern. In addition, especially in the older group, children were seen collaborating on loosely associated projects that accomplish some superordinate goal (*thematic collaboration*) or collaborating on a project but engaging in different interrelated tasks that accomplish the shared goal. To a naive observer, a group of children working on such *differentiated collaboration* might at any one time appear to be engaged in less complex peer interaction forms, such as solitary and parallel/coordiate work. The assistance of a member of the class is required to identify the ultimate purpose of some activities.

Like the results of a previous study (Cooper, Ayers-Lopez, & Marquis, 1982), in which spontaneous peer learning exchanges were observed in kindergarten and second-grade classrooms, a greater proportion of collaborative role structures were seen with each increase in age level: second-grade children exceeded kindergarteners, and the older elementary children exceeded their younger peers. In the elementary school, the teacher in the younger group set more structured tasks for the children, such as computation and other basic math skills, spelling, reading, and cursive writing as well as crafts such as knitting and ceramics. Also, this teacher made some referrals, asking children to serve as teachers for other children. In the older class, children continued to work on math, spelling, and reading skills tasks, but also engaged in the planning and executing of larger-scale projects in science, social studies, and language arts that involved not only the use of the school library, but even trips to the city library or other sources of information. Some of these projects extended over weeks, and involved quite differentiated roles. For this reason, it is difficult to estimate the proportion of peer learning episodes of each form. Among 22 episodes recorded involving children in the younger group, and 23 in the older group, 4 collaborative episodes took place among the younger children (2 of which succeeded), and 8 occurred among the older children (6 of which succeeded).

The second question concerns how to evaluate the effectiveness or consequences of peer learning exchanges. With standardized experimental tasks, process and outcome can be mapped in the most systematic way. Classrooms offer the opportunity to see children grappling with varying levels of demand on their capacity to process social and cognitive information (Shatz, 1978, 1983). In earlier work with kindergarten and second-grade children (Cooper, Ayers-Lopez, & Marquis, 1982; Cooper,

Marquis, & Ayers-Lopez, 1982), teachers assigned their students individual tasks. Within those settings, features of discourse, including the use of attention-focusing statements, directives, and questions were predictive of the success of the rather brief exchanges among children. In the elementary school classroom observed in the present study, children were more likely to need to do two things: first, their relative freedom of choice in work assignments required them to plan and negotiate mutually acceptable activities, roles, and procedures. Second, children's greater freedom of movement and diversity of activities in the classroom often made sustaining attention to their chosen task a challenge for peer partners.

The instructional episodes of younger and older children were examined to trace the factors involved in success, defined as either sustained engagement in task-relevant activity or actual completion of the indicated goal. Success cannot be fruitfully assessed in all-or-none terms; rather, engagement and completion are seen as signs or degrees of sustained collaboration. Further, children's conversations indicated that they were pursuing social goals as well as academic ones while working together, and the accomplishment of one was not always associated with success in the other.

For younger children, six of the nine failures were apparent in the planning or role negotiation phase of the exchange. For example, a pair of young children began manipulating feltboard figures without negotiating a plan for their arrangement; another child failed to persuade his partner to adopt a suggested plan. Developmental differences were indicated by the different sources of and strategies for recovery from attentional difficulty. For younger children, distractions were apparent in three of the failed episodes. It is notable that on two of these, which were teacher-learner exchanges, the teacher lost track of the goal by beginning to talk about another relationship. It is also important to note that successful pairs also make comments irrelevant to their task, but they survived these distractions, either by the speaker reformulating, repeating, or intensifying the force of a question or request to an inattentive partner, or by the momentarily distracted speaker redirecting himself or herself without prompting. The engagement of older children was also interrupted by their own irrelevant comments as well as by a number of visitors who were especially drawn to the more elaborate cooperative science and cooking projects. Again, the successful children redirected themselves, whereas failing children did not. When plans and attention were secure, children were free to explore and reflect, not only about the task, but also upon their own relative states of knowing, thus generating a context for metacognitive as well as cognitive feedback.

In summary, children's engagement in and completion of shared learning goals was helped if a plan regarding activity was shared, and if the partners could recover from self- or externally generated distractions. There was some evidence that collaboration was also enhanced among closer friends, although teachers reported that the most skilled child-helpers were those who were effective beyond their group of closest friends. The less effective partners were unable to derive from the materials or their own resources a plan for their activity, and showed limited responsiveness to the efforts of their partner to sustain task-relevant behavior.

Throughout this work, the increasing significance of metacognitive factors with increasing age has been prominent. After some of the basic skills of peer learning have been acquired and practiced so they impose less of a cognitive processing demand, children use them in more complex ways, such as in pursuing projects that extend over several days. These complex tasks require more planning and monitoring during their execution (Beal & Flavell, 1982).

Comparison of the monitoring function provides an interesting point of contrast between younger and older children. In earlier work, Cooper (1980) found that preschool children's success in collaboration with peers depended on their remaining focused on the task; an important peer discourse skill was the use of attention-focusing statements. In the present study with elementary school children, refocusing attention back to the task after distractions was important, but effective children could tolerate distractions of much longer duration. Apparently, the cognitive monitoring system of older competent children allowed them to digress with little disruption, whereas that of younger children did not.

Summary and Conclusions

In this chapter we have provided a framework for examining the development of peer learning discourse and then used this framework to examine three programs of research. In drawing conclusions from this body of work, several dimensions across the studies are important: the age of the children observed, the relationships among them; the means of selection and type of task, and the setting. Wilkinson and Peterson's group observed children 7 to 9 years old working in same-age groups of four on individual work sheets, a learner-teacher structure, in a classroom setting. The 8- and 9-year-olds observed by Rogoff and her colleagues taught unfamiliar 6- and 7-year-olds an unfamiliar task in a laboratory setting. Cooper et al. observed 6- to 12-year-olds who could select their work partners (frequently leading to mixed-age dyads) who then negotiated the task that was undertaken within the classroom setting. These differences among the studies provide an opportunity to examine components of peer learning discourse because the children are in situations that vary with respect to the types of limitations that influence their performance.

In all of the studies children demonstrated some basic competence with the relevant speech acts of directives and requests. However, developmental change in speech acts and even more dramatic change at the level of speech events can be observed, and these changes have important consequences for the effectiveness of the communication. The research by Wilkinson, Peterson and their colleagues highlights the acquisition of these individual discourse skills. Although some directives and requests used by young children are expressed in the most effective form, only 50% were successful in eliciting an appropriate response (Peterson et al., 1982). Their work with older children shows that effectiveness improves over a fairly broad age range. In trying to trace this development, it is revealing that directives that are direct are more effective with younger children whereas directives that are mitigated or indirect are more effective with older children (Cooper, Marquis, & Ayers-Lopez, 1982; Peterson et al., 1982). It would be particularly valuable in future work to assess the relationship between effectiveness with peers and time of initial emergence of a variety of discourse skills, including mitigation.

The research by Rogoff's group demonstrates that teaching is a complex task, involving continuing adjustments of strategy by the teacher in directing the learning of the pupil. Children's effectiveness in teaching is likely to be influenced by task and setting variations that may overload their cognitive capacity. It would be useful to identify the characteristics of contexts in which children were more and less effective in their guidance of peers. This work suggests that with complex and abstract tasks, teaching an unfamiliar child constitutes a situation in which children fail to utilize skills we know that they have.

The work of Cooper's group emphasizes the role of negotiating, planning, and monitoring. In addition to these metacognitive factors, the advantage of collaboration among close friends and the general high level of performance among these self-selected learning groups suggests the significance of children's relationships in peer learning. In this work the developmental differences can be seen more clearly at the level of speech events than speech acts. It is the sensitive coordination of discourse that leads to a successful peer learning episode.

In tracing the development of peer discourse, it is important to keep in mind the context in which these discourse skills are being learned, that is, one peer talking to another. In particular, it is important to remember that the peer of a 4-year-old is different from that of a 12-year-old in age, cognitive capabilities, and social development. It is reasonable to assume that one of the primary features of discourse development is learning to do what works, that is, the feedback one gets from peers is central to the process of skill acquisition. In fact, as Shatz and Gelman (1973) have demonstrated, preschool children learn that they must talk differently to very young children than to their peers. Reflecting on the skills one has allows one to learn *about* what works, that is, the feedback system is also central to the process of metacognitive development. However, as children grow older so do their peers, and hence the feedback contingencies change. Instructions that would have exceeded their processing capacity at one age do not at a later age. Hence the peer discourse system develops in a "bootstrap" manner; a little development leads to new feedback contingencies, which lead to more development. The immediate target for the development of peer discourse in a 4-year-old is not the adult discourse system, but rather the most efficient peer discourse system for 4-year-olds.

In closing, it is appropriate to consider what the study of peer learning interaction reveals about basic developmental issues, and what peer interaction might contribute to individual development. In classrooms that allow or foster peer learning, young children help one another by telling, showing, correcting, and asking how and what questions. Older children, with greater linguistic, cognitive, and metacognitive skill, can also guide, hint, argue, and explain. In these settings, children take on the planning, directing, and evaluation of their learning in the context of shared tasks. Peer interaction thus provides both a context for children's learning and a natural laboratory for observing this form of social cognition.

We might also consider that by helping one another assume increasing responsibility for their own learning, these children are learning to think as adults.

References

Allen, V. L. (1976). *Children as teachers*. New York: Academic Press.
Asher, S. R., & Gottman, J. M. (1981). *The development of children's friendships*. Cambridge: Cambridge University Press.
Banks, S., & Kahn, M. (1975). Sisterhood-brotherhood is powerful: Sibling subsystems and family therapy. *Family Process, 14*, 311–337.
Beal, C. R., & Flavell, J. H. (1982). The effect of increasing the salience of message ambiguities on kindergarteners' evaluation of communicative success and message adequacy. *Developmental Psychology, 18*, 43–48.
Brenneis, D., & Lein, L. (1976). "You fruithead": A sociolinguistic approach to children's dispute settlement. In S. Ervin-Tripp & C. Mitchell-Kernan (Eds.), *Child discourse*. New York: Academic Press.
Case, R. (1978). Intellectual development from birth to adulthood: A neo-Piagetian interpretation. In R. Siegler (Ed.), *Children's thinking: What develops?* Hillsdale, NJ: Lawrence Erlbaum.
Clark, R. A., & Delia, J. G. (1976). The development of functional persuasive skills in childhood and early adolescence. *Child Development, 47*, 1008–1014.
Cooper, C. R. (1980). Development of collaborative problem solving among preschool children. *Developmental Psychology, 16*, 433–440.
Cooper, C. R., Ayers-Lopez, S., & Marquis, A. (1982). Children's discourse during peer learning in experimental and naturalistic situations. *Discourse Processes, 5*, 177–191.
Cooper, C. R., Marquis, A., & Ayers-Lopez, S. (1982). Peer learning in the classroom: Tracing developmental patterns and consequences of children's spontaneous interactions. In L. C. Wilkinson (Ed.), *Communicating in the classroom*. New York: Academic Press.
Cooper, C. R., Marquis, A., & Edward, D. (in press). Four perspectives on peer learning among elementary school children. In E. C. Mueller & C. R. Cooper (Eds.), *Process and outcome in peer relations*. New York: Academic Press.
Coulthard, M. (1977). *An introduction to discourse analysis*. Essex: Longman House.
Dore, J. (1979). Conversational acts and the acquisition of language. In E. Ochs & B. B. Schieffelin (Eds.), *Developmental pragmatics*. New York: Academic Press.
Downing, L. L., & Bothwell, K. H. (1979). Open-space schools: Anticipation of peer interaction and development of cooperative independence. *Journal of Educational Psychology, 4*, 478–484.
Dunn, J., & Kendrick, A. (1982). *Siblings: love, envy, and understanding*. Cambridge: Cambridge University Press.
Eisenberg, A. R., & Garvey, C. (1981). Children's use of verbal strategies in resolving conflicts. *Discourse Processes, 4*, 149–170.
Ellis, S., & Rogoff, B. (in press). Problem solving and children's management of

instruction. In E. C. Mueller & C. R. Cooper (Eds.), *Process and outcome in peer relations.* New York: Academic Press.

Epstein, J. A. (in press). Friendship selection: Developmental and environmental influences. In E. C. Mueller & C. R. Cooper (Eds.), *Process and outcome in peer relations.* New York: Academic Press.

Flavell, J. H. (1971). First discussant's comments: what is memory development the development of? *Human Development, 14,* 272–278.

Flavell, J. H., Botkin, P. T., Fry, C. L., Wright, J. W., & Jarvis, P. E. (1968). *The development of role-taking and communication skills in children.* New York: Wiley.

Forbes, D. L., & Greenberg, M. T. (1982). *Children's planning strategies: New directions in child development.* San Francisco: Jossey-Bass.

Furman, W., Rahe, D. F., & Hartup, W. W. (1979). Rehabilitation of socially-withdrawn preschool children through mixed age and same-age socialization. *Child Development, 50,* 915–922.

Garvey, C. (1977). *Play.* Cambridge, MA: Cambridge University Press.

Garvey, C. (in press). Peer relations and the growth of communication. In E. C. Mueller & C. R. Cooper (Eds.), *Process and outcome in peer relations.* New York: Academic Press.

Garvey, C., & Baldwin, T. (1970). *Studies in convergent communication: I. Analysis of verbal interaction.* (Report No. 88). Baltimore, MD: Center for the Study of Social Organization of Schools, Johns Hopkins University.

Ginsburg, H., & Opper, S. (1980). *Piaget's theory of intellectual development: An introduction.* Englewood Cliffs, NJ: Prentice-Hall.

Greenfield, P., & Lave, J. (1982). Cognitive aspects of informal education. In D. A. Wagner & H. W. Stevenson (Eds.), *Cultural perspectives on child development.* San Francisco: Freeman.

Hallinan, M. T. (1981). Recent advances in sociometry. In S. R. Asher & J. M. Gottman (Eds.), *The development of children's friendships.* Cambridge, MA: Cambridge University Press.

Hartup, W. W. (1983). The peer system. In E. M. Hetherington (Ed.), *Social development.* In P. H. Mussen (Gen. Ed.), *Handbook of child psychology.* New York: Wiley.

Hinde, R. A. (1976). On describing relationships. *Journal of Child Psychology and Psychiatry, 17,* 1–19.

Hymes, D. (1972). On communicative competence. In J. B. Pride & J. Holmes (Eds.), *Sociolinguistics.* Harmondworth: Penguin.

Labov, W. (1970). The logic of non-standard English. In F. Williams (Ed.), *Language and poverty.* Chicago: Markham.

Markovits, H., & Strayer, F. F. (1982). Toward an applied social ethology: A case study of social skills among blind children. In K. H. Rubin & H. S. Ross (Eds.), *Peer relationships and social skills in childhood.* New York: Springer-Verlag.

Mehan, H. (1979). *Learning lessons.* Cambridge, MA: Harvard University Press.

Mehan, H., & Riel, M. M. (1980). Students' instructional strategies. In L. L. Adler (Ed.), *Issues in cross-cultural research.* New York: Academic Press.

Merritt, M. (1982). Distributing and directing attention in primary classrooms. In L. C. Wilkinson (Ed.), *Communication in the classroom.* New York: Academic Press.

Michaels, S., & Cook-Gumperz, J. (1979). A study of sharing time with first grade students: Discourse narratives in the classroom. *Proceedings of the Fifth Annual Meeting of the Berkeley Linguistics Society.* Berkeley: University of California.

Mueller, E. C., & Cooper, C. R. (in press). *Process and outcome in peer relations.* New York: Academic Press.

Ochs, E., & Schiefflin, B. B. (1979). *Developmental pragmatics.* New York: Academic Press.

Paris, S. G., & Lindauer, B. K. (1982). The development of cognitive skills during childhood. In B. B. Wolman (Ed.), *Handbook of developmental psychology.* Englewood Cliffs, NJ: Prentice-Hall.

Pascual-Leone, J. (1970). A mathematical model for the transition rule in Piaget's developmental stage. *Acta Psychologica, 32,* 301–345.

Patterson, C. J., & Roberts, R. J. (1982). Planning and the development of communication skills. In D. L. Forbes & M. T. Greenberg, (Eds.), *Children's planning strategies: New directions for child development.* San Francisco: Jossey-Bass.

Peterson, P. L., Wilkinson, L. C., Spinelli, F., & Swing, S. R. (1982). *Merging the progress-product and the sociolinguistic paradigms: Research on small-group processes.* Paper presented at conference on "Student Diversity and the Organization, Processes, and Use of Instructional Groups in the Classroom," Wisconsin Center for Educational Research, Madison, Wisconsin.

Piaget, J. (1955). *The language and thought of the child.* New York: Meridian. (Originally published, 1926)

Piaget, J. (1967). *Six psychological studies.* New York: Random House.

Putallaz, M. & Gottman, J. M. (1981). Social skills and group acceptance. In S. R. Asher & J. M. Gottman (Eds.), *The development of children's friendships.* Cambridge: Cambridge University Press.

Rogoff, B., & Gardner, W. P. (in press). Developing cognitive skills in social interaction. In B. Rogoff & J. Lave (Eds.), *Everyday cognition: Its development in social context.* Cambridge, MA: Harvard University Press.

Rubin, K. H., & Ross, H. S. (1982). *Peer relationships and social skills in childhood.* New York: Springer-Verlag.

Sacks, H. (1972). An initial investigation of the usability of conversational data for doing sociology. In D. Sudnow (Ed.), *Studies in social interaction.* New York: Free Press.

Shantz, C. U. (1983). Social cognition. In J. H. Flavell & E. M. Markman (Eds.), *Cognitive development.* In P. H. Mussen (Gen. Ed.), *Handbook of child psychology.* New York: Wiley.

Shatz, M. (1978). The relation between cognitive processes and the development of communication skills. In C. B. Keasey (Ed.), *Nebraska symposium on motivation, 1977.* Lincoln, NE: University of Nebraska Press, 1978.

Shatz, M. (1983). Communication. In J. H. Flavell & E. Markman (Eds.), *Cognitive development.* In P. H. Mussen (Gen. Ed.), *Handbook of child psychology.* New York: Wiley.

Shatz, M., & Gelman, R. (1973). The development of communication skills: modifications in the speech of young children as a function of listener. *Monographs of the Society for Research in Child Development, 38,* No. 152.

Swing, S. R., & Peterson, P. L. (1982). The relation of student ability and small-group interaction to student achievement. *American Educational Research Journal, 19,* 259–274.

Thelan, M. H., & Kirkland, K. D. (1976). On status and being imitated: Effects on reciprocal imitation and attraction. *Journal of Personality and Social Psychology, 33,* 691–697.

Webb, N. M. (1982). Group composition, group interaction, and achievement in cooperative small groups. *Journal of Educational Psychology, 74,* 475–484.

Wilkinson, L. C., & Calculator, S. (1982). Effective speakers: Students' use of language to request and obtain information and action in the classroom. In L. C. Wilkinson (Ed.), *Communicating in the classroom.* New York: Academic Press.

Wohlwill, J. F. (1973). *The study of behavioral development.* New York: Academic Press.

Youniss, J. (1980). *Parents and peers in social development: A Sullivan-Piaget perspective.* Chicago: University of Chicago Press.

5. The Development of Narrative Skills: Explanations and Entertainments

Susan Kemper

We tell stories to entertain our audience and to explain our actions. Stories transmit cultural and individual traditions, values, and moral codes. They explicate observable actions and events in terms of unobservable goals and motives, thoughts and emotions. Stories manipulate place and time to present temporal and causal sequences that are extraordinary. Storytelling is one of the first uses of language (Halliday, 1975; Keenan, 1974; Weir, 1960) and one of the most skilled (Lord, 1960; Watson-Gegeo & Boggs, 1977). Storytelling and understanding are verbal arts that children gradually master between 2 and 10 years of age. In developing narrative competence, children learn to produce and comprehend causally and temporally structured plots that are organized around a variety of themes and involve a myriad of characters.

(1) Froggie goes crash in the water, bumps his head. And he fell in dirt. He cried. Then he bumped his head off. (2-year-old boy, Pitcher & Prelinger, 1963, p. 34)
(2) Once there was an alligator who lived in New York City and all the children were his friends and he wouldn't hurt anybody. And one day he got a note

Preparation of this chapter was supported by grant IST-81110439 from the National Science Foundation. I would like to thank Mabel Rice and Margaret Schadler for their advice and encouragement and Robert Estill, Roseanne Marney-Hay, David Gleue, and Nelson Otalvaro for their assistance with developing the causal event chain analysis. Thanks also to the members of my class who willingly read and reread the children's stories looking for structure and organization.

saying, "Mr. Alligator, I hate you." And Mr. Alligator always kept feeling bad because everybody liked him. But while he was walking through the grocery store he saw little girl writing a note. The note said, "Mr. Alligator, I hate you." And he asked the little girl why she hated him. The girl said, "Because you're taking my friends away from me. They always want to play with you." Mr. Alligator said, "Why don't you play with me too?" And she said, "My mother doesn't like alligators and won't let me. She thinks they'll bite." So Mr. Alligator went to the little girl's house and said to her mother, "I'm not going to bite anybody." And the little girl's mother said, "All right, I can see that." The alligator said, "Good, so everybody else can play with me." (10-year-old boy, Sutton-Smith, 1981, p. 290)

The stories above differ on the three dimensions that characterize different approaches to the analysis of children's stories. (a) The content of children's stories changes and expands, particularly between the ages of 2 and 5 years. The themes, characters, and psychosocial symbolism that children incorporate in their stories are influenced by their own experiences and developing personality. As children's horizons broaden, so does the scope of their stories. (b) Children's stories become increasingly patterned as plot structure develops. Children gradually learn to use formal openings and closings as well as settings, outcomes, and episodic structure to construct stories. While their first stories are but "heaps" of unrelated actions, by 10 years of age, children have mastered the complexities of plot structure. (c) The stories of 2-year-olds consist of actions that are without apparent cause or consequence. Children gradually acquire the ability to explain events in terms of internal motives and external causes. The causal structure of children's narratives, like their plot structure, is gradually mastered. Thus, narrative competence involves mastering the interaction of content, plot, and causal structure. This chapter examines these three aspects of narrative competence using stories told by children between 2 and 10 years of age.

Several researchers have extensively analyzed the content, plot, and causal structure of children's stories. These analyses are based on stories elicited from children between the ages of 2 and 10. Hence the data are limited in three ways: (a) Wide individual variation is reported in children's willingness to tell stories (Gardner, 1978). An unwillingness to tell a story may arise from an inability to construct one. Hence, primitive stages in the development of narrative competence may be underrepresented in the data. (b) Stories are commonly "jointly constructed" by the teller and the audience (Cuff & Hustler, 1981; Sachs, 1974). The storyteller must monitor the reaction of the audience, responding to explicit and implicit questions about the setting, focus, or outcome of the story. Thus, the available corpora do not reflect spontaneous, interpersonal aspects of children's narrative competence. (c) The topics of children's stories may be influenced by the prompts used to elicit the stories (Ames, 1966) or by stories the children have recently heard, read, or watched on television. Consequently, the content of children's stories may be more transient than the structure of their stories because it is directly influenced by external models.

The Content of Children's Stories

The content of children's stories can be described in terms of themes, characters, and psychosocial symbolism. A story may be about violence, nurturance, eating, or rivalry. Characters may be human or animal, familiar or novel, good or bad. Stories may illustrate mistrust, guilt, shame, or inferiority. Pitcher and Prelinger (1963), Ames (1966), and Abrahms (1977) have analyzed the content of children's stories. The analyses of Pitcher and Prelinger (1963) and Ames (1966) are based on stories collected from children between 2 and 5 years of age. Abrahms (1977) included stories from children between 5 and 10, as well. Pitcher and Prelinger assumed that there are no age differences in the content of children's stories while both Ames and Abrahms took note of both age and sex differences in the stories children tell.

Themes

At all ages, violence is the predominate theme of children's stories. While boys' stories more often involve violence than do girls', children typically tell stories involving harm to human or animal characters (Ames, 1966; Pitcher & Prelinger, 1963). Spanking and falling down are typical violent events in the stories of 2- and 3-year-olds, while death and dismemberment are common themes in the stories of older children (Ames, 1966). Sibling rivalry, as a special case of violence, is common in the stories of young children but is much less common in stories by children 5 and older (Ames, 1966). Story examples (3) and (4) illustrate the kinds of violent stories young children tell.

The violence of children's stories is offset by a concern with friendly acts, sleeping, eating, and other ordinary events. Girls are more concerned with sleeping than boys; however, the reverse is true for eating. During the school years, children begin to tell stories about travel, sports competition, school experiences, and adventures (Ames, 1966; Abrahms, 1977). Thus there is an expansion of the themes of children's stories although they remain focused on familiar, everyday occurrences.

(3)   Boy fell out of car. He went in car again. He fell in water. (2-year-old boy, Pitcher & Prelinger, 1963, p. 30)

(4)   Once there was a little bear. He got pushed into some water. He didn't know how to swim. He drowned. And his father came. His father looked all around for him and then he got pushed in. Then his mommy came and seed what was the matter. She looked all around, too, and she got pushed in, and drownded. Then the little girl came. She looked all around, too, and she got pushed in, and drownded. Then the little girl came. She looked all around for her mommy and daddy. And she got pushed in. Then the little boy came and he got pushed in. Then their friends came. They got pushed down a hall. And then their head got broke off. (4-year-old girl, Pitcher & Prelinger, 1963, p. 99)

Characters

The characters in children's stories are more consistent than their themes. The incidence of children, parental figures, and animals are relatively stable from 2 to 5 years of age. Male characters predominate in the stories of both boys and girls although girls are more likely than boys to use female characters. This preference for male characters appears to increase throughout the school years (Ames, 1966). Mother figures both nurture and punish and father figures provide friendly companionship. Girls, more so than boys, use parental figures, especially nurturant ones, in their stories (Ames, 1966). In stories of children from 2 to 10, father figures become increasingly hostile in girls' stories while they become increasingly friendly in boys' stories. Mythical and fictional characters such as fairies, witches, and superheros become increasingly frequent in the stories of older children (Abrahms, 1977; Ames, 1966; Pitcher & Prelinger, 1963). Thus, while the characters of 2- to 5-year-olds are drawn from their own experience, those of older children show external influences as they borrow characters from stories they have heard or read, from cartoons, television shows, and movies.

Psychosocial Symbolism

Erickson (1950) argued that children pass through five stages characterized by different concerns or crises: (a) Infants are concerned with trust as a result of their attachment to their mothers. (b) From 1½ to 3 years of age, children are concerned with autonomy as they begin to master themselves and their environment. (c) Around 3, children become concerned with initiative as they come to act independently. (d) During the school years, awareness of industry and competence emerge as children learn essential skills. (e) Identity and intimacy appear as psychosocial concerns in early and late adolescence as the transition to adulthood is made.

Pitcher and Prelinger (1963) and Abrahms (1977) have examined children's stories for the emergence of psychosocial concerns. Perhaps because the youngest storytellers have passed through these stages, there are no apparent age trends in the incidence of stories focusing on trust or mistrust. However, girls are more concerned with trust than are boys. This, perhaps, reflects their concern with mother figures and nurturance. For boys, there are clear age trends in the emergence of the Eriksonian concerns of autonomy, initiative, and industry. Presumably, the concerns of identity and intimacy would begin to emerge in the stories of adolescents. Thus, there is a progression in the emergence of the Eriksonian psychosocial concerns in children's stories that mirrors their development as storytellers.

Similar attempts to apply aspects of Freudian theory to the analysis of chronological change in children's stories have been less successful. No clear-cut age trends have emerged in the Freudian symbols or defense mechanisms children employ in their stories (Pitcher & Prelinger, 1963; Sutton-Smith & Abrahms, 1978). Nonetheless, the interpretation of children's stories remains a useful technique for individual psychotherapy (see, for example, Gardner, 1971).

Children's stories present a wealth of information regarding their views of social and sex-role stereotypes. At all ages, children portray male characters as being more adventurous than girls and female characters as being less active and more nurturant (Abrahms, 1977; Ames, 1966). Sex-typing of toys, activities, and occupations is apparent even in the stories of 2-year-olds. For example, see stories (5) and (6).

(5) Monkey jumps in water. He walks. He jumps. He goes home and sees his mommy make cookies. Then he goes to school. He plays. He goes home again. He goes to his office to work. He goes away to his home again. He goes out when it's not raining. Then he goes home to his mother again. (2-year-old girl, Pitcher & Prelinger, 1963, p. 35)

(6) This is going to be about a little child. She went walking to her house and she missed her house. Then she went for a walk. Then she missed another house. That was her friend's house. And then she missed another house that was her boy friend's house. Then she went to a farm. Then she went home. Then she went back into bed. That's all the story. (3-year-old girl, Pitcher & Prelinger, 1963, p. 56)

Summary

The content of children's stories is drawn from their own experiences. Characters are modeled after familiar people and animals and engage in familiar activities like falling down and eating. Children's stories illustrate their own psychosocial concerns; chronological changes in these concerns appear to precede their appearance in stories. As children's experiences broaden and they become acquainted with cartoons, storybooks, and movies, they begin to incorporate elements from these sources into their own stories. As a result, the stories of children become increasingly diverse. While 5-year-olds are able to tell stories about many different types of themes with a variety of character types, their stories are, nonetheless, ill-formed. The mastery of story structure is not yet complete.

The Plots of Children's Stories

Three different approaches have been taken to the analysis of children's plot structure: (a) Applebee (1978) has applied Vygotsky's (1962) stages of concept development to the analysis of children's stories. (b) Botvin and Sutton-Smith (1977), following the work of Maranda and Maranda (1971) and Propp (1968), have demonstrated chronological changes in the structural components of children's stories. A similar analysis, also based on the work of Propp (1968), by Stein and Glenn (1977), has identified chronological changes in the episodic structure of children's stories. To directly compare these analyses, each was applied to a set of 40 stories selected from the Sutton-Smith (1981) corpus. Further, these systems were compared to the "high point" analysis system developed by Labov and Waletzky (1967). These analyses reveal two stages in the development of narrative competence.

Early Stages

Six different story structures have been identified by Applebee (1978) in the stories told by children beteen the ages of 2 and 5. Each story structure is characterized by a different pattern to the interrelationship of story elements. Resembling Vygotsky's (1962) stages in the development of category structure, Applebee calls these stages heaps, associative sequences, primitive narratives, unfocused chains, focused chains, and true narratives. Heaps consist of collections of virtually unrelated characters, actions, or events, as in story (7). The events of associated sequences are linked by arbitrary commonalities but there is no common characteristic to them all, as in story (8). In primitive narratives, there is a concrete core to the set of events described, as in story (9). Unfocused chains present an actual sequence of events yet there is no consistency of character or theme, as in story (10). Focused chains describe such a chain of events that take the form of a series of "adventures," as in story (11). Finally, true narratives adopt a consistent perspective focused on an incident, as in story (12).

(7)   Dog fell in the fence. I got a big fence. Daddy broke my fence. I hurt my knee. I go bang on the big rock. I got back home again. (2-year-old boy, Pitcher & Prelinger, 1963, p. 31)

(8)   Little boy played. He cried. He's all right. He went home. He went to bed. When he wakes up you're gonna say good-night to him. (2-year-old boy, Pitcher & Prelinger, 1963, p. 30)

(9)   A little girl drawed her mommy. Then the mommy got mad at her and she cried. She lost her mommy's cookies. She got mad at her again. And she drawed her mommy again. And her mommy got mad at her again. And her daddy got home. That was Judy. (3-year-old girl, Pitcher & Prelinger, 1963, p. 62)

(10) Once there was a fish named Flower. She went down in the water and said, "Oh, my gosh, where's my lover?" She went down in the cellar where my house is. She saw a big father fish which had a sword in his nose. She ran away from the house and hid in another house. She ran up the water and flapped out. She ran away. She went to another house in a deep, deep river. She saw her own home which had her lover in it. They kissed each other. That's the end. (4-year-old girl, Pitcher & Prelinger, 1963, p. 101)

(11) Davy Crockett he was walking in the woods, then he swimmed in the water to get to the other side. Then there was a boat that picked him up. Then he got to the other side. He went into the woods. He was in the place where Indians made. The Indians came and got him. Then pretty soon he got loose. The Indians let him loose. (4-year-old boy, Pitcher & Prelinger, 1963, p. 83)

(12) Once upon a time there was a little pussycat that wanted to be a Christmas present. He went to Mr. Rabbit's house and said, "I want to be a Christmas present." And he said, "Let's go ask Mr. Squirrel." And then he said, "We shall go to the bear's house; they probably will know." The bear said, "Today's not Christmas—tomorrow will be Christmas." In a minute Santa Claus came dashing through the sky and the kitty called up, "I want to be a Christ-

mas present." And then Santa said, "I think I know where to put you." So the next morning, he wasn't in Santa's sleigh any more, he was in a little girl's house. And then the little girl said when she saw him, "I guess Santa knew what I wanted for Christmas." (5-year-old girl, Pitcher & Prelinger, 1963, p. 135)

Between the ages of 2 and 5, children pass from telling stories that are primarily heaps of unrelated events to telling true narratives that are focused around a climax. Most of the stories by 2-year-olds are heaps or associated chains (60%). In contrast, most of the stories of 5-year-olds are focused chains of adventures and true narratives (53%). However, the development of narrative structure is not complete by age 5. Children gradually expand on the dyadic and episodic structure of the basic narrative.

Dyads and Episodes

The analysis of plot structure is derived from methods developed to analyze cultural variation in folk myths and tales. It owes much to the pioneering work by Propp (1968), Dundes (1964), and Maranda and Maranda (1971). Sutton-Smith and his colleagues have examined two different aspects of the plots children create. First, stories are dyadic, consisting of conflict and resolution pairs. Second, stories conform to grammatical principles governing the necessary structural components and their organization. Both the dyadic structure of children's stories and their grammatical organization have been examined for chronological changes.

Dyadic Structure. Stories, at one level of analysis, are dyadic: an act of villainy occurs and the villain is vanquished; a threat is made and nullified; something is lost and then regained. Older children incorporate significantly more such actions in their stories than do younger children (Sutton-Smith, 1975). Stories of young children frequently lack dyadic organization in that an attack will occur without a response or a state of deprivation will not be resolved. Gradually dyadic structure develops to include stories with multiply embedded subplots interrupting the primary action and its resolution.

Using a scoring system derived from Maranda and Maranda (1971), Sutton-Smith (1975) has shown that children's stories progress through four stages in the development of dyadic plot structure. This progression has been independently documented by Leondar (1977). The earliest stage is that of stories in which the protagonist is attacked or threatened yet does not respond. Story (13) is typical of this type of primitive story. At a more advanced stage, the protagonist does in fact respond to the attack or threat but is not successful; the protagonist merely escapes or the villain suddenly becomes benevolent. Story (14) involves such an unsuccessful response. The protagonists in level 3 stories succeed in vanquishing their foes or in improving their material states; however, the attacker only withdraws and the improvement is transitory, as in story (15). At the final stage of development, the protagonists completely transform the story world so that a permanent improvement results, as in story (12).

(13) A big big monster and a big big crocodile came with fire in his mouth and
      poison in his fire and he killed me and then he took a bite of me and he
      swallowed me. (3-year-old boy, Sutton-Smith, 1981, p. 89)

(14) Once there were two dogs and their names were Mimi and Tasha and one
      day Mimi and Tasha went into the forest with Tanya and they played in the
      trees and when they were playing in the trees Tasha got stuck in one and
      Mimi and Tanya got her out. The end. (6-year-old girl, Sutton-Smith, 1981,
      p. 171)

(15) Once upon a time there were two kittens who lived with their mother, father,
      brother, and sister. And one was a boy and one was a girl. Once one of the
      kittens went out in the fields and found thousands of mice there. So he went
      back home and told his brother about all the mice. Then they both came out
      because the brother did not believe there were that many mice. And he saw
      that there were that many mice. So they went back and told their sister and
      then they all came out because the sister did not believe there were that
      many mice. And she saw that there were that many mice. And then they
      started to catch all the mice. All the cats started to chase the mice except the
      sisters. And the sisters went home and told the mother and father about the
      mice and took them over. After about a week they chased off all the mice
      except for two. Then the two mice went home and told their parents, friends
      and friends' parents about the cats, but they didn't believe it. So the mice
      took them out to see the cats and the cats started to chase them. Then when
      the mice saw the cats were chasing them they ran into their houses, and never
      came out again. The end. (8-year-old girl, Sutton-Smith, 1981, p. 231–2)

The stories of 5-year-olds have simple, level 1 and level 2 dyadic structure. By age
10, girls have mastered the ability to tell level 4 stories. This mastery of dyadic
structure does not seem to be complete in 10-year-old boys (Sutton-Smith, 1975).
Further, there are sex differences in the types of dyads used. Girls rely on resolution through alliances while boys use domination to resolve conflicts.

The dyadic action components of stories are hierarchically organized and Botvin
and Sutton-Smith (1977) have looked at the development of this organization.
Seven types of stories were identified: Level 1 stories consist of a concatenation of
unorganized events; level 2 stories contain but a single, uninterrupted dyadic event;
level 3 stories interpose a secondary dyadic event between the initial and final elements of the primary dyad; level 4 stories have a conjunction of two or more primary dyadic events; level 5 stories include both concatenated primary dyads and
interposed secondary ones; level 6 stories have one primary dyad embedded within
another; and level 7 stories have multiply embedded primary dyads. Four chronological trends are apparent: First, the earliest organization is the repetitive
concatenation of dyads in level 1 stories, for example, story (16). Next, stories are
structured about a single, primary dyad in level 2 and 3 stories, for example, story
(17). Then, coordinate dyadic structure develops in level 4 and 5 stories, for example, story (18). And, finally, subordinate dyads are embedded within a primary,
superordinate in level 6 and 7 stories, for example, story (19). Botvin and Sutton-
Smith suggest that the primary dyadic organization of stories is mastered around

age 5, that coordinate structure appears around age 7, and that superordinate structure emerges around age 11.

(16) The little duck went swimming. Then the crab came. A lobster came. And a popsicle was playing by itself. (Botvin & Sutton-Smith, 1977, p. 379)

(17) Once upon a time there was a little bear. And he wanted to go to a place to eat. And he didn't find any place to eat. So he went to his friend's house and his friend's house said he could. So he ate, and when he was finished then he started to make another bowl, and he ate the second bowl and he stopped eating porridge. And he got full, very full. Then he decided to go outside, and when he got outside it was raining. And then he went back inside. The end. (5-year-old girl, Sutton-Smith, 1981, p. 130)

(18) One day this little boy was walking to school. Someone said something. He looked around and then he couldn't find anything who said that. Then he just walked on. He was at school. Well, then he started to play. It was lunch time. Then he opened his lunchbox and something said, "Ouch." Then he saw the lunchbox's mouth open. It said, "Ouch." It jumped down. It bit the leg and it ran away. And then it went home, destroyed the buildings. Then he went to the room. The end. (5-year-old boy, Sutton-Smith, 1981, p. 120)

(19) Once upon a time there was a man and he had a brother. And the man who had a brother was very greedy. And one day, the brother found a cave and it contained pearls, gold, and silver, and jewels. And the brother picked a big huge bag of gold. And when he got home the man said, "Tell me how to get to the cave where you found the gold." Then he said, "Okay," and he told him the magic words, which were: "Open Sassafras." And then the mean man went to the cave but that day there was a guard there. And he cut off the man's head. And then the brother came to see what took so long for the man to come home. And then he brought a pistol with him. When he got to the cave he saw the guard and shot him. And this time he didn't only take one bag of something. Then he took a cart and a donkey and he put a lot of sacks in it. And when he came back home he told his mother that he hit the jackpot. And he lived happily ever after. The end. (7-year-old boy, Sutton-Smith, 1981, p. 180)

Episodic Structure. Prescriptive grammars have also been devised for the characterization of story structure. These grammars originate in the work of Propp (1968) for analyzing folktales. However, they have been most extensively employed to characterize what is remembered or inferred from stories (Mandler & Johnson, 1977; Rumelhart, 1975; Stein & Glenn, 1979). Typically, these grammars decompose stories into hierarchically organized components; the components in (20) are typical:

(20) Setting: introduces the protagonist and the physical context
     Initiating event: an action that brings about a response from the protagonist
     Internal response: the protagonist's emotional or cognitive response
     Attempt: the protagonist's action
     Consequence: the outcome of the protagonist's action
     Reaction: the protagonist's emotional or cognitive response

Research on children's comprehension and memory for stories has shown that manipulations of story structure can affect accuracy of recall and recognition of story components (Mandler & Johnson, 1977; Stein & Glenn, 1979). For example, shifting the protagonist's internal response to the end of the story will impair recall of the entire story. Such disruptions affect younger children more than older children because the older children are better able to reorder the story components. If components are deleted, children will attempt to repair the story's structure by inferring some missing components or omitting others. Again, older children are more likely to restore story structure than younger children. Thus, it appears that the rules of the story grammar are gradually acquired and used to understand and remember stories.

Stein and Glenn (1977) have applied the story grammar analysis to a set of stories elicited from children in elementary school. They asked the children to complete story fragments. Seven types of stories were identified. Level 1 stories were no more than descriptive sequences or inventories of setting information. Level 2 stories consisted of temporally, but not causally ordered action sequences. Level 3 stories were reactive sequences; an initiating event occurred and the protagonist attempted to respond. Level 4 stories involve an abbreviated sequence; a brief internal response is interposed between initiating event and attempt. Level 5 stories are complete episodes with all necessary story components present. Level 6 stories involve more complex episodes with embedded sequences or repeated attempts by the protagonist. Finally, level 7 stories involve the interaction and coordination of two or more perspectives. Stein and Glenn's data indicate that episodic structure (an initiating event plus attempt) has been mastered by age 6, that internal responses are added around age 8, and that complex and interactive episodes appear after age 10.

Comparisons. As discussed above, different theoretical analyses have identified chronological changes in the structure and organization of children's stories. In order to compare these analyses directly, a sample of 40 stories was selected from the Sutton-Smith (1981) corpus. Five stories were selected from each age group between 2 and 10 years. Four judges independently classified these stories according to the six categories of Applebee (1978), the four levels of plot development of Maranda and Maranda (1971), the seven levels of dyadic structure from Botvin and Sutton-Smith (1977), or, finally, the seven levels of episodic structure from Stein and Glenn (1977). Each judge scored the stories on only a single structural dimension. Finally, a fifth judge scored the stories on all four dimensions as a check on the reliability of the primary coders. Reliability averaged 91% for these analyses. Due to the small sample size, only two stories were classified as heaps in the Applebee system and only a single interactive story, using the Stein and Glenn system, was identified. This latter story was classified as a level 6 story using the Botvin and Sutton-Smith system.

Figure 5-1 presents the results of using the results of using the Applebee, the Maranda and Maranda, and the Botvin and Sutton-Smith systems. To facilitate comparisons, four categories were used for the Applebee system, heaps and associative sequences, primitive narratives and unfocused chains, focused chains, and true narratives, and for the Botvin and Sutton-Smith system, stories with no dyadic structure, single primary or secondary dyadic structure, conjoined or coordinate dyadic structure, or embedded dyads. The seven levels of episodic structure from Stein and Glenn are virtually coextensive with the seven levels of plot structure from Botvin and Sutton-Smith. Only a single story was categorized differently by the two systems. This finding is not surprising since both the dyadic and the story grammar analyses are derived from the earlier work by Propp (1968). Each system treats the use, coordination, and embedding of story constituents as primarily characteristics of story structure. Levels 1 through 6 in the two systems are isomorphic. However, level 7 stories in the Stein and Glenn system do not correspond to level 7 stories in the Botvin and Sutton-Smith system. In the first case, level 7 stories are identified on the basis of interacting story perspectives; in the latter case, level 7 stories are required to have multiple embedded episodes.

The comparison of the four ways of analyzing story structure yielded four results: (a) On all four dimensions, the development of story structure appears to be essentially complete by age 10. (b) The Botvin and Sutton-Smith system and the Stein and Glenn system do not discriminate well among the stories produced by 2- to 4-year-old children. In terms of Applebee's system, there is a rapid progression, during this age range, from heaps to true narratives. The Maranda level of children's stories also does not show much change during the 2 to 4 year range. (c) Both the Botvin and Sutton-Smith system and the Stein and Glenn system do, however, capture the change in the structure of stories produced by children between 5 and 10. During this period, both the sophistication of their plots, as measured by the Maranda level, and the complexity of their plots, in terms of dyadic and episodic structure, expand. (d) The Maranda level of children's stories is not independent of plot structure. The stories from 6- to 10-year-olds with Maranda level 3 or 4 conclusions all possessed at least level 4 structure in either the Botvin and Sutton-Smith system or the Stein and Glenn system. Thus, it appears that the development of control over coordinate and embedded dyadic structures is concomitant with the development of successful responses and effective actions.

High Points

One aspect of the development of plot structure has been relatively ignored by the preceding analyses of children's stories: Stories, particularly personal narratives, are typically centered about an emotional "high point" (Labov & Waletzky, 1967). The critical events leading up to this high point may be repeated and the importance of this high point may be stressed. The story thus tells not only what happened but also provides an explanation and an evaluation of this event (Cuff & Hustler, 1981; Linde, in press; Sachs, 1974). Stories that have no point are ones in which no one event is singled out as important and relevant to the ongoing social interaction.

High points were identified in the 40 stories used for the preceding comparisons of plot structure. The judges indicated whether or not each story had a focus or

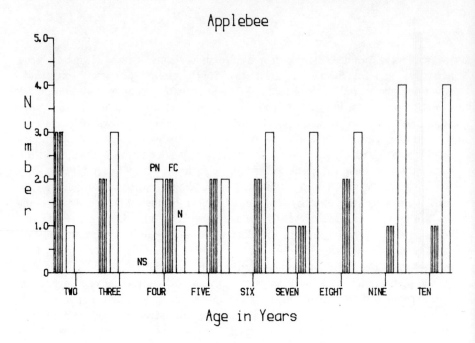

Applebee

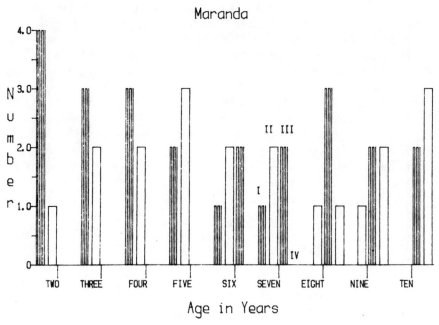

Maranda

Figure 5-1. Interrelationship of Applebee, Maranda, Botvin, and Sutton-Smith, and High Point Analyses of the Children's Stories.[a]

[a]The number of stories in each scoring category is shown for the four systems. The categories were: for the Applebee system, heaps and sequences (H & S), primitive narratives and unfocused chains (PN), focused chains (FC), and true narratives (N); for the Maranda system, stories with no response (I), those with unsuccessful responses (II), those with transitory successes (III), and those with successful transformations (IV); for the Botvin and Sutton-Smith

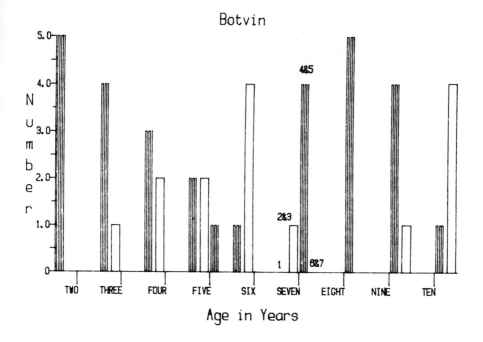

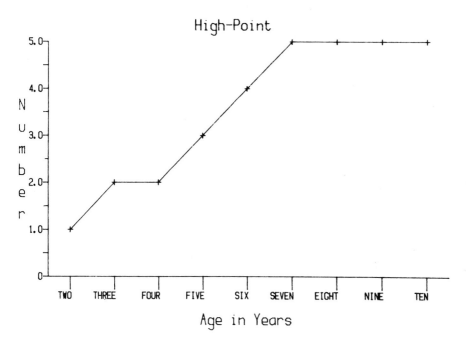

system, stories with no dyadic structure (1), those with a single, primary dyad or with a single secondary dyad (2 & 3), those with a conjunction of primary dyads or with both coordinate and secondary dyads (4 & 5), and those with an embedded primary dyad or with multiply enbedded dyads (6 & 7). Finally, the number of stories with high points recognized by three of the four judges is also plotted.

high point and, if so, what that point was. Figure 5-1 presents the summary of this data. The stories of 2-, 3-, and 4-year-olds do not have identifiable high points; only 33% were judged to have such a point. In contrast, for older children, 93% of the stories have a central focus, or high point. All stories with level 3 or above structure in terms of the Botvin and Sutton-Smith system were judged to have identifiable high points. Thus, the emergence of high points seems to co-occur with the emergence of dyadic, episodic structure.

Umiker-Sebeok (1978) and Kernan (1977) have applied a more detailed high point analysis to stories told by children as part of ongoing conversational interactions. The stories were scored for the incidence of six types of components: introductions, abstracts, background orientations, complications to the main point of the story, evaluations of the main point, and resolutions of the story. These components are derived from those of Labov and Waletzky (1967). Introductions are stylized ways of marking the beginning of a story; "Once upon a time . . . " is the prototypic introduction to a story. An abstract provides a brief summary of the significance or central event of the upcoming story. Orientations provide information about the people and places involved in the story. The story's complication is the central focus of the story. The importance of this complication is indicated by an evaluation that repeats or elaborates on the story's central event. The resolution of the story provides a summary of the story's outcome.

Umiker-Sebeok (1978) studied conversational stories told by children from 3 to 5 years of age. At age 3, children's stories contain, on the average, 1.7 such components. By age 5, 2.8 components are included. The stories of 3-year-olds typically consist of an introduction and a complication; those of 4-year-olds contain an introduction, an orientation, and a complication. Abstracts, evaluations, or resolutions are equally likely to be added in the stories by 5-year-olds.

Kernan (1977) examined conversational stories told by girls between the ages of 7 and 14 years. The stories by the youngest girls (7- and 8-year-olds) contrasted with those in the middle age group (10- and 11-year-olds) in three ways. First, the stories by the younger girls contained more abstracts and introductions than did those by the older girls. Second, the 7- and 8-year-olds' narratives provided less background information as to the characters and setting than did those of the older girls. Finally, the older girls provided paraphrases and repetitions of the narratives' complications so as to emphasize them. Thus older children frame their narratives in such a way that the audience can identify and appreciate the importance of a central focus.

Summary

There appear to be two stages in the development of plot structure. Stage 1, completed by age 6, is characterized by the mastery of simple stories focused on a dyadic event—something happens and the protagonist responds. This event is judged to be important and its importance is emphasized by the storyteller. Stage 2 involves the elaboration of this dyadic event to include coordinate and embedded events. The elaboration serves to center the narrative about its high point and to provide the background information necessary to understand and appreciate the story. Basic plot structures have been mastered by age 10, although 10-year-olds may be limited in terms of the number of embedded or interactive episodes that they can handle at one time.

These two stages of the development of plot structure appear to be independent of other aspects of narrative competence. For example, both the length and the number of thematic units in children's stories are significantly correlated with the age of the storyteller and with the structural complexity of the stories' plots. However, both Applebee (1978) and Botvin and Sutton-Smith (1977) have found that the increase in plot complexity is responsible for the increases in story length and the number of thematic units. Thus, control over coordinate and embedded dyadic episodes permits children to tell longer stories about many different happenings.

This work on the development of plot structure is primarily concerned with the mastery of hierarchical story structure. Consequently, it is not surprising that children first learn an inventory of plot constituents, then learn to coordinate them, and finally learn to embed plot constituents recursively. These are general steps in the mastery of any hierarchical structure. However, stories also have a linear, heterologus structure. Stories describe causally related sequences of actions. Children must also master the ability to construct coherent causal sequences.

Causes and Consequences in Children's Stories

Storytellers must not only master the construction of hierarchically organized plots but they must also master the construction of causally ordered sequences of events. In order to tell a story, a child must be able to describe the events in such a way that the listener can follow the chain of causality. Not only must the storyteller describe the protagonist's actions, but the storyteller must explain the character's motives, the circumstances that make some actions possible and render others impossible, and the results of the character's actions. A storyteller can explicitly state the causal connections between the states and actions described in the story or require the listener to infer them. By age 10, children have mastered the ability to tell causally well-formed stories.

The Causal Structure of Stories

Stories consist of causally connected events, states, and actions (Graesser, 1981; Kemper, 1982, 1983; Kemper, Otalvaro, Estill, & Schadler, in press; Omanson, Warren, & Trabasso, 1978; Schank & Abelson, 1977; Warren, Nicholas, & Trabasso, 1979). Research on story comprehension has demonstrated that readers actually infer the causal connections between the elements of text. They will spontaneously infer missing causal connections and restore them to stories. When asked to recall stories, readers will recall unstated causal connections and distort stated ones in order to preserve the causal structure of the story. Further, the reading difficulty of stories, in terms of their grade-level suitability, is a function of the stories' causal structure. Stories are difficult to understand when readers must infer many causal connections to explain characters' actions.

A three-step process has been developed to analyze the causal structure of stories (Kemper, 1981). Initially, a story is parsed into a sequence of clauses using syntactic criteria. Main and subordinate clauses, participial, infinitival, and noun phrase complements are distinguished. Both tensed and untensed clauses are located. Once the sequence of clauses has been identified, each clause is classified as an action, a physical state, or a mental state. Actions include both the actions of human or other animate beings as well as natural or social processes. Actions are distinguished from states because they can be expressed by verbs in the present tense, answer questions such as "What's happening?", and can be used in imperative constructions. Physical states are enduring, observable properties and characteristics of objects, places, and events. They include states of possession, attribution, and specification. Mental states are enduring, unobservable properties of human or other sentient beings. Mental states include emotions, cognitions, and dispositions. The third step is the construction of the causal event chain underlying the story. This step is based on the causal event taxonomy in (21).

(21) Resultant causation: action → physical state
      Initiation causation: action → mental state
                                  physical state → mental state
      Enablement causation: physical state → action
      Motivation causation: mental state → action

In the underlying event chain, new physical states result from agent's actions or from natural or social processes. Agent's actions are caused by internal mental states that provide reasons for the actions. These mental states are causally initiated by prior actions or physical states. While new physical states result from actions, they, in turn, enable other actions to occur. Thus, the causal taxonomy proscribes four types of causal connections among the actions, physical states, and mental states that make up a story. It assumes that actions cannot directly cause new actions; mental or physical states must intervene. One mental state cannot initiate another without an intervening action. Nor can one physical state cause a new one; an action, by an agent or by a natural or social process, is required. Finally, mental states cannot directly cause new physical states; an intervening action is needed.

To determine the event chain underlying a story, violations of the causal event taxonomy are recognized. These violations arise when action-action, physical state-physical state, mental state-mental state, or mental state-physical state sequences are found in the story. In order to repair the violation, an intervening action, physical state, or mental state is inferred. The event chain analysis of stories involves determining the minimum number of inferred actions, physical states, and mental states necessary to interconnect the stated ones. This parsimony rule is required since contemporaneous actions and states are possible; a single event may cause multiple new actions or states or a single action or state may arise from many different causes. Within a story, a chain of actions and states may dead-end; the story may continue by returning to an earlier action or state.

For example, the event chain analysis of two stories from the Sutton-Smith (1981) corpus are presented in the Appendix. Following the original story, the sequence of stated actions, physical states, and mental states, and the underlying event chain with inferred causal links is presented.

The first story consists of four clauses: three actions and one physical state. However, three inferences are required to repair violations of the event taxonomy: First, in order for the pilot to be attacked by the monster, he must be in space. Second, the monster's attack initiated an inferred mental state. Third, this inferred mental state then motivated the pilot's action of reentering his spaceship. Finally, this action resulted in the physical state expressed by the periphrastic causative construction "He got in his spaceship." The second story is longer—with 27 clauses —but it requires 12 inferences: that an act of christening occurred, that Josh was actually at the fair, that the fish were restrained after their capture, that the fishers had a ship, that the fish remained in the ship's hole, that the shark would have to catch the stingray in order to eat it, that the ray was afraid of the shark, that there was a confrontation between the shark and ray, that the second shark was content with eating Josh's family, that the ship was at sea when the storm occurred, that Josh was free to return home, and finally, that Josh remained at home.

The Development of Causal Structure

In order to examine the development of causal structure in children's stories, a sample of stories from the Pitcher and Prelinger (1963) and Sutton-Smith (1981) corpora were analyzed. Initially 54 stories were selected from the Sutton-Smith collection so that 6 stories told by different children were chosen from each age group. The number of stories contributed by girls and boys was balanced for each age group. A second sample of 20 stories was drawn from the Pitcher and Prelinger corpus. From each age group 4 stories were selected. Each of these 74 stories was analyzed using the event chain analysis. Two judges parsed each story into a sequence of clauses using syntactic criteria. Then each clause was categorized as an action, a physical state, or a mental state. Finally, the judges constructed the event chains underlying each narrative. The judges used the actions and states mentioned in the stories as well as ones required to repair violations of the taxonomy to construct the underlying event chains.

In order to check the reliability of the two judges' analyses, three measures of interjudge reliability were determined. First, the total number of stated and inferred actions, physical states, and mental states was tallied for each judge for 15 of the 40 stories. Then their percent agreement was determined using the following formula: $100 - $ (number judge A $-$ number judge B)/(total number judges A and B). For stated causal links, the two judges agreed, on the average, 94% of the time. For inferred causal links, the judges agreed, on the average, 86% of the time. Agreement was lowest for stated mental states (87%) and inferred mental states (78%).

A second check on the reliability of the judges' analyses was done. Here, an analysis of variance was used to estimate the reliability of the six different types of causal links (Winer, 1971). From this analysis, the between-category and within-category variance were used to compute $r(5)$, an estimate of the reliability of the six categories. These reliability coefficients were $r(5) = .93$, $r(5) = .95$, $r(5) = .91$ for stated actions, physical states, and mental states, respectively, and $r(5) = .87$, $r(5) = .88$, $r(5) = .82$ for the inferred actions, physical states, and mental states, respectively. Finally, a different procedure was used to compare the judges on inferred causal links. In this analysis, all sequences of three causal links in which the medial link was an inference were identified for each judge. Then the percentage of identical three-link sequences was determined for each type of inferred link. Agreement was best for inferred physical states (93%), slightly less good for inferred actions (89%), and worst for inferred mental states (84%). One explanation for the low reliability of stated and inferred mental states is their low incidence in the children's stories. Both the storytellers and the judges appear to be biased away from the use of mental states in the production or analysis of stories. The children rarely mentioned the characters' mental states and the judges rarely required that mental states be inferred to repair violations of the event chain taxonomy. A similar situation arises in the analysis of stories written for children across different grade levels (Kemper, 1983).

Two aspects of the event chain analysis of children's stories show marked developmental progressions: First, the composition of children's stories in terms of the distribution of stated and inferred causal links changes with age; second, the types of causal connections used to interconnect the stated and inferred causal links varies with the age of the storyteller. Figure 5-2 presents the distribution of stated and inferred causal links in the stories. Figure 5-3 presents the distribution of enablement, resultant, motivational, and initiation causal links in the stories.

In order to examine these age trends in the composition of children's stories more carefully, a matrix of the correlations among seven variables was obtained. The variables were: the age of the storyteller, and the density (incidence per 100 words) of stated and inferred actions, physical states, and mental states. The results of the combined analysis of the stories from the Sutton-Smith and Pitcher and Prelinger are here reported. A preliminary analysis revealed no curvilinear effects; consequently, only the linear correlations are reported. All are significant at $p < .05$ or better.

Stated actions are negatively correlated with stated physical states ($r(70) = -.48$) and positively correlated with inferred actions ($r(70) = +.58$) and inferred physical states ($r(70) = +.55$). Stated physical states are negatively correlated with inferred mental states ($r(70) = -.28$). Inferred actions increase with inferred physical states ($r(70) = +.87$) and inferred mental states ($r(70) = +.63$). Inferred physical and mental states are positively correlated ($r(70) = +.71$). Thus the storytellers appear to trade-off stated actions and stated physical states with inferred mental states. Stories that have a high density of stated actions also require many inferences, particularly of actions and physical states.

The age of the storyteller is positively correlated ($r(70) = +.71$) with the length

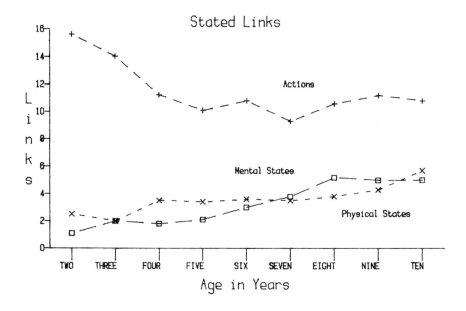

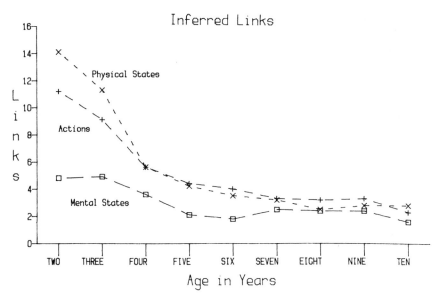

Figure 5-2. The number of stated and inferred causal links per 100 words in stories by 2- to 10-year-old children.

of the story. Thus older children told longer stories. However, with the length of the stories held constant, significant negative correlations were obtained between the age of the storyteller and the density of inferred actions ($r(70) = -.44$), inferred physical states ($r(70) = -.66$), and inferred mental states ($r(70) = -.38$).

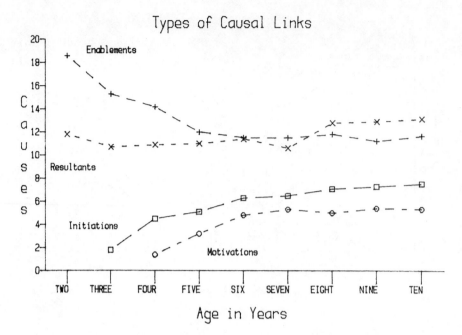

Figure 5-3. The number of enablement, resultant, motivation, and initiation causes per 100 words in the stories told by children between the ages of 2 and 10 years.

Age was positively correlated with the density of stated mental states ($r(70) = +.55$). Thus, the older children told stories that required fewer inferences than those told by the younger children. The stories of the 10-year-olds were longer but contained, proportionally, more stated actions, inferred actions, inferred physical states, and inferred mental states per 100 words than did those of the 2-year-olds.

The types of causal links children use also change with their age. Initially, children's stories are tied together with weak enablement links; a physical state (stated or inferred) merely enables an action to occur. Very few initiation or motivation links are used, reflecting the low incidence of mental states in the stories. Initiation links between physical states or actions and mental states begin to appear in the stories of 4-year-olds and motivation links between mental states and actions emerge around 5 years of age.

The incidence of all four types of causal links are relatively stable in the stories of children between 8 and 10 years of age. During this age range the densities of all six types of causal links are also relatively stable. In contrast, between ages 2 and 5 there is a marked decrease in the use of enablement causal links that is only partially offset by an increase in the use of motivation, and initiation causation. This corresponds to the rapid decrease, during this age range, in the incidence of stated actions. Thus, there is a net decrease in the density of causal links per 100 words in stories told by children between the ages of 2 and 8. This decrease arises from the increased use of descriptive words that do not introduce additional causal links.

Summary

The causal event structure of children's stories changes chronologically. Between the ages of 2 and 8, children gradually master the ability to tell stories that describe causally connected sequences of events. The stories told by 2-year-olds are primarily lists of characters' actions; these actions are without cause or consequence. Gradually, children's stories change to include the actions and physical states that initiate thoughts, emotions, and cognitions and the mental states that initiate actions. In particular, the stories of 10-year-olds include more physical states and mental states and fewer actions than those of 2-year-olds.

The inferential complexity of children's stories changes as a result of these chronological changes in the composition of their stories. Young children do not adequately describe the causes and consequences of characters' actions. Hence, the listener must infer these causal links to interpret the stories as causally connected event chains. As children's stories come to include more stated causes and consequences, particularly more motivation and initiation causal links, the stories become easier to understand as fewer inferences are required.

Finally, changes in the causal structure of children's stories co-occur with changes in their plot structure. The 40 stories previously coded in terms of the Botvin and Sutton-Smith system for analyzing plot structure were recoded using the event chain analysis. Then, the incidence of each type of causal connection was determined for four types of stories: (a) stories that were classified as level 1 stories with no dyadic structure, (b) level 2 and level 3 stories that have a single, primary dyadic event, (c) level 4 and level 5 stories with two or more coordinate event dyads, and finally (d) level 6 and level 7 stories with embedded, subordinate dyadic events. This analysis is summarized in Table 5-1.

Primitive stories that do not have dyadic or episodic structure consist mostly of enablement causes. The development of simple episodic structure appears with the emergence of initiation causal links. Coordinate dyadic structures appear to be linked to the use of motivating mental states. Finally, the most complex types of plot structures are associated with the most frequent use of resultant causation. The first episodic structures used by children, thus, appear to consist of actions or

Table 5-1. Percentage of Enablement, Resultant, Motivation, and Initiation Causal Links in Children's Stories Classified According to the Botvin and Sutton-Smith Analysis of Dyadic Structure

	Level 1	Levels 2 & 3	Levels 4 & 5	Levels 6 & 7
Enablements	73%	62%	28%	24%
Resultants	26	27	36	41
Motivations	<1	<1	10	11
Initiations	<1	9	26	23

physical states that initiate mental states; Stein and Glenn (1979) identify this sort of story constituent as an initiating event plus internal response. Somewhat latter, mental states that motivate actions are incorporated in children's stories leading to the emergence of level 4 and 5 stories with coordinate action sequences. Finally, embedded episodes are created as children come to describe the results of characters' actions in terms of the new physical states that arise.

Conclusions

While 2-year-olds' stories are limited in terms of the content, plot, and causality, 10-year-olds can tell novel and complex stories about a wide variety of topics. Mastering the art of storytelling involves three separate processes. First, there is the gradual accretion of characters, roles, themes, and symbols from which stories are created. Models, provided by ordinary experiences or by stories read, heard, or viewed, are increasingly incorporated in children's stories. Second, there is the differentiation of complex plot structure as children learn to create well-structured, dyadic episodes, to coordinate these episodes, and to embed subordinate episodes within superordinate ones. Finally, there is the substitution of initiation, motivation, and resultant causes for simple enablements. The causal structure of children's stories gradually conforms to the adult causal taxonomy as children learn to explain how and why characters act as they do.

Whereas the development of story content seems highly dependent on available models, the processes of differentiating plot structures and substituting other causes of enablement links seem independent of the types of stories children experience. General cognitive constraints on the development of hierarchical structure and linear, causal structure seem to govern the development of both sentence structure and story structure (Johnson, 1982). As Botvin and Sutton-Smith (1977) pointed out, parallel principles of structural development apply to the mastery of complex sentence structures and complex story structures. In each case, four stages are apparent: (a) the use of discrete fragments (e.g., single words, single dyadic units), (b) the production of simple structures (e.g., sentences, episodes), (c) the emergence of coordinate structures, and (d) the appearance of embedded subordinate structures. The mastery of lexical connectives and the mastery of causal structure are also governed by similar constraints. Hood and Bloom (1979) and Bloom, Lahey, Hood, Lifter, and Fiess (1980) have carefully documented the acquisition of lexical connectives. At the sentence level, there is a progression from utterances about the simple co-occurrence of events, to ones that describe temporally successive events, to ones describing motivational causation, and finally ones about the results of prior events. This progression corresponds to the observed progression in the use of causal links in children's stories: enablements $<$ initiations $<$ motivations $<$ resultants. Thus, the development of plot and causal structure in children's stories parallels the development of syntactic structure and lexical connectives.

Appendix

Event chain analyses of two sample stories are given. For each story, the numbered sequence of stated actions (A), physical states (PS), and mental states (MS) is given. The underlying event chain of stated and inferred causal links follows. Inferred actions (IA), inferred physical states (IPS), and inferred mental states (IMS) are in parentheses. The stories are taken from Botvin and Sutton-Smith (1977).

Story 1

An astronaut went into space (A1). He was was attacked by a monster (A2). The astronaut got in his spaceship (PS3) and flew away (A4).

Event Chain

A1 ─────────→ (he was in space) ──→ A2 ─────────→ (he was afraid) ─────────→
IA1   IMS2

(IMS3) ─────────→ (he re-entered his spaceship) ───→ PS3 ───→ A4 ─────────→
IA4

Story 2

Once upon a time there was a little fish (PS1) named Josh (PS2) and he was going to a fish fair (A3) and there were fishers over the fish fair (PS4) and the fishermen caught everyone (A5) including Josh (PS6). Then they put all the fish in the fishers' hole (A7) and there were sharks and stingrays (PS8) and a stingray was going after Josh (A9) and then a shark chased the stingray (A10) because he wanted (MS11) to eat the stingray (A12). So the stingray stopped chasing Josh (A13) and ran away from the shark (A14). So the shark and the stingray got into a big fight (A15). But then another shark gobbled up his mother and father and sister (A16). And then he left (A17). And then the boat was sailing (A18) and sailing (A19) and sailing (A20). There was a big storm that night (PS21). And it hit against the rocks (A22) and made a big hole in the fishers' hole (PS23) and Josh escaped (A24) and went back to his house (A25) and he stayed (A26) there until he was big (PS27).

Event Chain

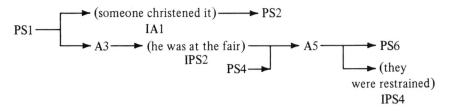

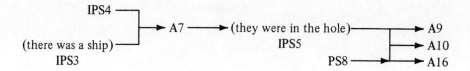

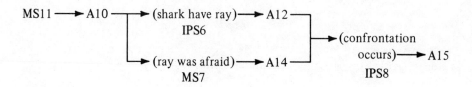

A16 ⟶ (it was satisfied) ⟶ A17
        IMS9

(IPS3) ⟶ A18
      ⟶ A19
      ⟶ A20 ⟶ (the ship was still at sea)
                            IPS10

(IPS10) ⟶ A22 ⟶ PS23 ⟶ A24 ⟶ (Josh was free) ⟶ A25
PS21 ⟶   IPS11

A25 ⟶ (Josh was at home) ⟶ A26 ⟶ PS27
       IPS12

References

Abrahms, D. M. (1977). *Conflict resolution in children's storytelling: An application of Erikson's theory and the conflict enculturation model.* Doctoral dissertation, Columbia University.

Ames, L. B. (1966). Children's stories. *Genetic Psychology Monographs, 73,* 337–396.

Applebee, A. N. (1978). *The child's concept of story: Ages two to seventeen.* Chicago: University of Chicago Press.

Bloom, L., Lahey, M., Hood, L., Lifter, K., & Fiess, K. (1980). Complex sentences: Acquisition of syntactic connectives and the semantic relations they encode. *Journal of Child Language, 7,* 235-261.

Botvin, G. J., & Sutton-Smith, B. (1977). The development of structural complexity in children's fantasy narratives. *Developmental Psychology, 13,* 377-388.

Cuff, E. C., & Hustler, D. (1981). Stories and story time in the infant classroom. In P. French & M. MacLure, *Adult-child conversation.* New York: St. Martins.

Dundes, A. (1964). *The morphology of North American Indian folktales.* Helsinki: FF Communications.

Erikson, E. (1951). *Childhood and society.* New York: Norton.

Gardner, H. (1978). From Melvin to Melville: On the relevance to aesthetics of recent research on story comprehension. In S. S. Madeja (Ed.), *The arts, cognition, and basic skills.* St. Louis: CEMREL.

Gardner, R. A. (1971). *Therapeutic communication with children: The mutual storytelling technique.* New York: Science House.

Graesser, A. C. (1981). *Prose Comprehension Beyond the Word.* New York: Springer-Verlag.

Halliday, M. A. K. (1975). *Learning how to mean: Explorations in the development of language.* New York: Elsevier.

Hood, L., & Bloom, L. (1979). What, when, and how about why: A longitudinal study of expressions of causality in the language development of two-year-old children. *Monographs of the Society for Research in Child Development,* No. 181.

Johnson, J. R. (1982). Narratives: A new look at communication problems in older language-disordered children. *Language, Speech, and Hearing Services in the Schools, 13,* 144-155.

Keenan, E. (1974). Conversational competence in children. *Journal of Child Language, 1,* 163-183.

Kemper, S. (1981). *The event chain analysis of texts* (Tech. Rep. No. 81-12). Lawrence: The University of Kansas.

Kemper, S. (1982). Filling in the missing links. *Journal of Verbal Learning and Verbal Behavior, 21,* 99-107.

Kemper, S. (1983). Measuring the inference load of a text. *Journal of Educational Psychology, 75,* 391-401.

Kemper, S., Otalvaro, N., Estill, R. B., & Schadler, M. (in press). Questions and facts and inferences. In A. C. Graesser & J. B. Black (Eds.). *The Psychology of Questions.* Hillsdale, N.J.: Erlbaum.

Kernan, K. (1977). Semantic and expressive elaboration in children's narratives. In S. Ervin-Tripp & C. Mitchell-Kernan (Eds.), *Child discourse.* New York: Academic.

Labov, W., & Waletzky, J. (1967). Narrative analysis: Oral versions of personal experience. In J. Helan (Ed.), *Essays on the verbal and visual arts.* Seattle: University of Washington Press.

Leondar, B. (1977). Hatching plots: Gensis of storymaking. In D. Perkins & B. Leondar (Eds.), *The arts and cognition.* Baltimore: Johns Hopkins University Press.

Linde, C. (in press). The life story: A temporally discontinuous discourse type. In H. W. Dechert & M. Raupach (Eds.), *Discourse production.* Norwood: Ablex.

Lord, A. B. (1973). *The singer of tales.* New York: Altheneum.

Mandler, J. M., & Johnson, N. J. (1977). Remembrance of things parsed: Story structure and recall. *Cognitive Psychology, 9,* 111-151.

Maranda, E., & Maranda, K. (1971). *Structural models in folklore and transformational essays.* The Hague: Mouton.

Omanson, R. C., Warren, W. H., & Trabasso, T. (1978). Goals, inferential comprehension, and recall of stories by children. *Discourse Processes, 1,* 355-372.

Pitcher, E. G., & Prelinger, E. (1963). *Children tell stories: An analysis of fantasy.* New York: International University Press.

Propp, V. (1968). *The morphology of the folktale.* Bloomington: Indiana University Research Center in Anthropology, Folklore, and Linguistics.

Rumelhart, D. E. (1975). Notes on a schema for stories. In D. G. Bobrow & A. Collins (Eds.), *Representation and understanding: Studies in cognitive science.* New York: Academic.

Sachs, H. (1974). On the analysability of stories by children. In R. Turner (Ed.), *Ethnomethodology.* Harmondsworth: Penguin.

Schank, R., & Abelson, R. (1977). *Scripts, plans, goals, and understanding: An inquiry into human knowledge structures.* Hillsdale, NJ: Lawrence Erlbaum.

Stein, N. L., & Glenn, C. G. (1977). *A developmental study of children's construction of stories.* Paper presented at the meeting of the Society for Research in Child Development, New Orleans.

Stein, N. L., & Glenn, C. G. (1979). An analysis of story comprehension in elementary school children. In R. O. Freedle (Ed.), *New directions in discourse processing* (Vol. 2). Norwood: Ablex.

Sutton-Smith, B. (1975). The importance of the storytaker: An investigation of the imaginative life. *Urban Review, 8,* 82-95.

Sutton-Smith, B. (1981). *The folkstories of children.* Philadelphia: University of Pennsylvania Press.

Sutton-Smith, B., & Abrahms, D. M. (1978). Psychosexual material in the stories told by children. *Archives of Sexual Behavior, 7,* 521-43.

Umiker-Sebeok, D. J. (1979). Preschool children's intraconversational narratives. *Journal of Child Language, 6,* 91-109.

Vygotsky, L. S. (1962). *Thought and language.* Cambridge, MA: MIT Press.

Warren, W. H., Nicholas, P. W., & Trabasso, T. (1979). Event chains and inferences in understanding narratives. In R. O. Freedle (Ed.), *New directions in discourse processing* (Vol. 2). Norwood: Ablex.

Watson-Gegeo, K. A., & Boggs, S. T. (1977). From verbal play to talk story: The role of routines in speech events among Hawaiian children. In S. Ervin-Tripp & C. Mitchell-Kernan (Eds.), *Child discourse.* New York: Academic.

Weir, R. (1960). *Language in the crib.* The Hague: Mouton.

Winer, B. J. (1971). *Statistical principles in experimental design.* New York: McGraw-Hill.

6. Of Hawks and Moozes: The Fantasy Narratives Produced by a Young Child

Stan A. Kuczaj, II, and Leslie McClain

The ability to tell stories is valued in many, perhaps all, human societies. The exceptional storytellers of each era are remembered and even revered by later generations (e.g., consider the works of Homer and Shakespeare). Although literary scholars have long debated the essential characteristics of great stories and their creators, until recently, relatively little attention has been paid to the development of storytelling skills in children. This recent concern with the development of children's productive narrative skills has occurred along with parallel concerns with the development of the concept of a story (Applebee, 1978; Stein, 1982; Stein & Policastro, 1983) and with the development of the comprehension skills necessary to best understand stories (Applebee, 1978; Mandler & Johnson, 1977; Miller, 1979; Stein, 1979; Stein & Glenn, 1979; Trabasso, Stein, & Johnson, 1981). Although the development of the concept of a story and the development of the abilities necessary to comprehend stories are undoubtedly related to the development of the abilities necessary to produce stories, the remainder of this chapter will be concerned only with children's developing ability to produce stories.

Previous work on this topic has yielded a number of facts and insights about the manner in which children learn to tell stories. Given that the child considered in the case study to be reported in this chapter was 5 years old when the systematic sampling of his spontaneous speech ceased, we shall mainly consider studies that deal with children 5 years of age and younger. (Chapter 5 considers the development of storytelling skills in children older than 5.)

Applebee (1978) has pointed out that by the age of 2½, and perhaps as soon as they begin to acquire their first language, children begin to employ spectator-role language, that is, "language used for looking on (an event) rather than participating in (the event) (Applebee, 1978, p. 35)." This sort of language use seems to be more common when young children play with language than when they are attempting to communicate with others (Applebee, 1978; Weir, 1962; see Garvey, 1977; Kuczaj, 1983 for detailed considerations of language play). Spectator-role language, to use Applebee's terminology, may also depend on the capacity for representing the nonpresent, and perhaps even the capability for fantasy representation on the part of the children who employ it. The capability of separating the present from the nonpresent occurs in early infancy and eventually results in the ability to distinguish the past, the present, and the future (Kuczaj & Boston, 1982). Separating reality from fantasy occurs somewhat later (see Kuczaj, 1981; Kuczaj & Daly, 1979; Scarlett & Wolf, 1979). The ability to separate the present from the nonpresent and the ability to distinguish reality and fantasy are necessary but not sufficient components of the ability to tell stories, at least insofar as fictional creations are concerned. In this chapter, we are concerned only with fictional, or make-believe, stories.

Another obvious component necessary for telling a story is the *intention* to tell a story. Although it is possible that one could tell a story without intending to do so, it seems reasonable to assume that storytelling involves the intention to engage in the storytelling act. Admittedly, it is difficult to specify the exact nature of this intention. Attempting to do so may be more the province of philosophers than psychologists at present, but psychologists should nonetheless remember that such intention is a necessary component of the storytelling process. This is particularly important for those of us who study young children, for we must attempt to ascertain when and how the intention to produce an act develops as well as when and how the actual behaviors that comprise the act develop. Not surprisingly, we know very little about this aspect of development. A reasonable first step in the study of the development of the intentions underlying behavior is to determine the age at which certain behaviors first occur. Doing so provides information about the age at which the intention to produce the behavior must have been acquired. For example, determining that children first begin to produce fantasy narratives before their third birthday means that the intention to do so has also developed before their third birthday. Such information, although of the grossest nature, does set limits on accounts of the development of the intention(s) of concern.

In addition to the three cognitive prerequisites (the ability to distinguish present and nonpresent, the ability to distinguish reality and fantasy, and the ability to intend to tell a story), in the process of learning to create and tell stories, children must learn *how* to tell a story. Studies concerned with this aspect of storytelling development have typically focused on the content of children's stories (Abrahms, 1977; Ames, 1966; Applebee, 1978; Pitcher & Prelinger, 1963) or on the structure of children's stories (Applebee, 1978; Botvin & Sutton-Smith, 1977; Menig-Peterson & McCabe, 1978; Sutton-Smith, 1979; Sutton-Smith, Botvin, & Mahoney, 1976; Umiker-Sebeok, 1979). These two aspects of how to tell a story are not easily distinguished. As the content of children's stories develops, so does the structure of their stories. An increasingly complex structure does enable children to expand the content of their stories, but a need to increase the meaningful information of their stories may lead children to acquire the structural capacity to do so. In this case, as in that of many things, it is difficult to decide what came (or comes) first.

In the following, we present data concerning the spontaneous stories produced by a child between the ages of 2;5 (years; months) and 5;0. The data have to deal with the issue of children learning *how* to tell stories. Although the data come from a single child, the child seems to have been fairly typical, if precocious, in his acquisition of his first language, at least insofar as firstborns are concerned (Kuczaj, 1977; Kuczaj & Daly, 1979). Therefore, we hope that the findings from this case study are at least somewhat generalizable. However, even if this turns out to be false, the data are sufficiently rich in a developmental sense (given the longitudinal nature of the sampling procedure) to both supplement those obtained by other investigators and to allow us to hazard some guesses about the developmental processes involved in learning to tell stories.

We present the data in a manner that reflects our three main concerns. First, we discuss aspects of the stories' content, specifically the temporal framework within with the stories occurred. Second, we consider one aspect of story structure, namely the manner in which the characters interacted with one another (or failed to do so). Finally, we attempt to ascertain the extent to which listeners contributed to the child's stories. Within each of these concerns, of course, is the overriding concern of determining (to the best of our ability) the nature and effects of developmental change.

Method

Subject

Abe, the oldest son of the first author, provided longitudinal information for this case study.

Spontaneous Speech Sampling

Approximately 1 hour of Abe's spontaneous speech in his home environment was recorded each week (two 0.5-hour sessions per week) from 2;4 to 4;1, with 0.5 hour of spontaneous speech being recorded each week from 4;1 to 5;1. Each hour of speech was transcribed the same week it was recorded. To ensure that the transcribing of the speech samples was accurate, reliability scores were obtained by having another rater transcribe randomly selected 250-morpheme-long segments (child's speech) of randomly selected transcripts. Reliability scores ranged from 90.4% to 100% agreement.

Story Sampling

From the written transcripts of Abe's spontaneous speech, we were able to cull 58 stories. Each of these stories involved the use of fantasy and so may truly be said to be Abe's creations. Although other investigators have included narratives that depict actual or expected events in their study of children's narratives (e.g., Kernan, 1977), we elected to focus solely on fantasy narratives. In the production of such stories, the child controls both the content and the structure of the fantasy narratives. However, children do not necessarily control either the content or the structure of narratives based on actual (or expected) events. In such narratives, children must faithfully reproduce (as best as they can) the actual or expected event(s), a successful reproduction usually entailing the use of particular types of linguistic forms and structures. It seemed to us that fantasy narratives provided a more accurate indicator of children's ability to tell stories, particularly in terms of creating content, but also in terms of learning how to communicate one's fantasies to others (an important aspect of the creation of fiction).

Scoring

Each of the 58 stories was scored in five ways. First, we assessed the temporal framework that Abe used—past, present, future, or some combination of the three. Second, we assessed the manner in which Abe used characters in his fantasy narratives. Based (somewhat loosely, we admit) on the work of Sutton-Smith, Botvin, and Mahoney (1976), we divided Abe's fantasy narratives into six types:

Category 1: The story is fragmentary, without any consistent theme or sequential organization. The story is best characterized as involving free association or "heaps" of ideas. (See Applebee, 1978; as well as Chapter 5 in this volume, for discussions of this notion in regard to the development of storytelling skills, and Vygotsky, 1962, for a discussion of the broader implications of the notion of "heaps.")

Category 2: The story involves the same character from start to finish, but no other character(s).

Category 3: The story involves a main character and other characters, but the only function of the other characters is to act upon the main character.

Category 4: The story involves a main character and other characters, but the only function of the other characters is to be acted upon by the main character. Sutton-Smith et al. (1976) combined categories 3 and 4. We elected to separate the two because they seem qualitatively different. In one, the secondary characters are acted upon by the main character. In the other, they act upon the main character.

Category 5: The story involves a main character and other characters, but the other characters do not interact with the main character (although they may do so among themselves).

Category 6: The main characters and the secondary character(s) are both acted upon by and act on one another.

Third, we assessed the characters that Abe used in his fantasy narratives. The narratives could involve real people or objects, but not actual events in which they had engaged. We distinguished five types of characters: (a) actual toys, (b) actual objects, (c) actual animals, (d) actual people, and (e) fantasy characters. Fourth, we assessed the extent to which each of Abe's stories contained a beginning and/or an ending. Finally, we assessed the extent to which others contributed to Abe's fantasy narratives by initiating Abe's stories, by asking questions, prodding him to provide additional information or to continue, and so on.

Results and Discussion

Table 6-1 shows the number of fantasy narratives produced by Abe during each six-month period. Other than the finding that the first age period yielded the fewest number of stories (relative to the amount of spontaneous speech collected) there were no other significant developmental trends. Table 6-2 summarizes the analyses concerned with the temporal framework within which Abe cast his stories. Stories were much more likely to be told in a past framework than in a present or future framework. The first story to be obtained from Abe's spontaneous speech samples was a "past" story at age 2;5, 4 months before he produced a "present" story, and 15 months before he produced a future story. Moreover, of the stories that in-

Table 6-1. Number of Fantasy Narratives Found in Each Age Period in Abe's Spontaneous Speech Samples

Age Period	Number of Fantasy Narratives
2;5–3;0	9
3;1–3;6	17
3;7–4;0	13
4;1–4;6[a]	13
4;7–5;0[a]	6

[a] One-half hour rather than one hour per week.

Table 6-2. Summary of the Temporal Frameworks Within Which Abe Cast His Fantasy Narratives

Temporal Framework	Number of Stories	Age at Which Temporal Framework First Appeared
Past	27	2;5
Present	12	2;9
Future	5	3;8
Past/present combination	4	3;1
Past/future combination	2	3;2
Past/present/future combination	5	2;8
Present/future combination	3	3;1

volved some combination of past, present, and future, all but three involved the past. The following are examples of each type of story from Abe's repertoire. Abe's verbalizations are on the right-hand side, and those of his parents are on the left-hand side.

Past (3;3)

(Abe attempting to tell his father, D, a story that he had told his mother, M, earlier in the day.)

> Once there was a man and he had a crocodile. There was a crocodile. I don't know the rest. I can't 'member.

D: That's all right. Just tell me the parts that you remember.

M: Go ahead and try.

> This crocodile was standing around waiting for someone to drop around. And what did he see when he saw it? He saw a mammoth elephant and some other animals and some others. And the crocodile was so happy, he jumped in the air and he thought someone was gonna be a ___ and was, was, someone was gonna have a party. And, and it was. And so they ___ and then they wanted to go join the party. So off they went, goed to it. And skunk had a party.

D: Who had a party?

> Skunk, like I said.

D: Oh.

> Remember? It had a skunk in the story. (Talking to Mother)

M: Uh huh.

> So the elephant eated a cake with his trunk. Daddy, a elephant eated a cake with his trunk. Wasn't that silly?

D: It really was.

> (Laughs) And then the party was over. And then, then something strange smelled in the sky. They, they heard something strange coming. (Makes noise of something coming)

D: What was it?

> It was a dangerous fox. And it was so long. And it was this feet tall. (Shows with hands)

D: Wow. How many feet tall is that?

It was this big and this big and this big. (Shows with hands)

D: Wow. That's big.

M: I'd hate to meet up with him in the forest.

It's in a different forest. Don't worry.

D: Then what happened?

And then he catched a big dangerous mooze and killed him by accident. Then he said "I'm sorry, Mr. Mooze." And the snake didn't say anything. He just died. The fox just killed him.

M: What did the mooze say?

He didn't say anything, I said. He didn't say anything.

D: Then what happened, Abe?

The fox went back to his home and got all that dinner to his mommy and his baby snake. And then they, and then they . . . It's really a long story.

D: Well go ahead. Keep telling me. I'm listening.

And someone else was gonna have a party. And they found out that the alligator was.

D: The alligator was gonna have a party?

He was this long. He was the biggest alligator. And so they started to eat it too. And (Interrupted)

M: What did they start to eat?

A cake. For a cake was so many. One cake. One cake. One chocolate cake.

M: Whose favorite was that?

It was, um, um, strawberry, so it was the skunk had a party like that at his. 'Cept the alligator had that kind. He liked that.

M: What kind of presents did he get?

He gotted lots of stuff. He got a toy fire engine just to work in, in the river. Know how it would work?

M: How?

Like this. (Shows with hands) And he got a piano just like me.

M: How long did the party last?

It lasted longest. The party lasted 25.

M: Twenty-five?

Yeah.

M: Minutes? Hours?

Yeah. So when that party was over, the elephant got so tired that he decided to lay down. And he did. And so when, uh, what did the hunter do the dangerous, uh, the other dangerous animal?

M: I thought that when the elephant was laying down, he heard a strange noise.

When the elephant was laying down, he heard something bad coming.

D: What was it?

Maybe it was, maybe it would be a dinosaur.

D: What was it? Tell me the rest of the story.

And then it was a dinosaur. And then the elephant got so scared, he got up and seed what did the dinosaur do?

M: What did the dinosaur do?

He eated up the meat, not him.

M: He ate who?

The meat.

M: The meat?

Uh huh.

M: Where did the meat come from?

It comed from the elephant. The elephant just had some. It was Easter in that jungle.

D: It was Easter, so the elephant had some meat? Is that right?

Yeah.

D: O.K. I just wanted to keep the story straight.

And so the dinosaur got some meat. (Makes chewing sounds) That's how he chewed. And, and he started chewing that and chewing and chewing and he got so hungry, he started jumping up and down. Up and down. Up and down. Up and down. Up and down.

M: While he was eating? Or after he was through eating?

		When he was eating. He was eating so much, he jumped up and down. Up and down. Up and down.
M:	What did that sound like?	
		It sounded like the elephant was trumpeting. And so when the dinosaur left, he goed back to sleep.
D:	Who went back to sleep?	
		The elephant. And after that, something else strange was coming. A giant bird was coming. The biggest bird. He frightened the elephant. Then the hunter comed and, and I think the hunter killed the big bad bird.
M:	Why did the hunter kill him?	
		He killed the giant bird, not the elephant.
M:	What did the elephant say?	
		He said "thanks". . . . Look. My hole is starting to get big.
M:	Uh huh. I have to repair that shirt. Did the elephant have any dreams while he was laying down?	
		Yeah. He dreamed about jumping up and down. Up and down. Like the dinosaur did.
M:	Was he able to do it?	
		No. He didn't have any more food.
M:	Who ate all the food? Gosh, I have to go.	
		Where?
M:	I have to go to my class tonight.	
D:	Tell me the story.	
		That was the end.

Present (3;3)

(Abe is discussing hawks, a fantasy character that he created)

		Daddy, did you know that hawks hadded bones and black fur?
D:	Black fur?	
		Yeah. Hawks have three feet. Web feet. Like ducks. And they have trunks.
D:	Trunks too?	

Yeah. Like elephants. And they have funny ears. And they have those kind of ears. (Points at elephant mask)

D: Elephant ears?

Yeah. They're really tall animals. They're really tall animals like elephants.

(Pause)

They don't cry and they don't have blood like people. And fish hawks are like trees. They have bark.

D: Bark?

Uh huh.

D: Wow!

Daddy, some hawks are dinosaurs.

D: There's a whole lot of types of hawks, aren't there?

Yeah. Chew hawks are really strange. They chew elephants up. They have really sharp teeth. And one more kind of hawk.

D: What type is that?

Honey hawk brontosaurus hawk.

D: Honey hawk brontosaurus hawks!

Yeah. That's a kind of hawk. Honey dinosaurs eat honey.

D: They do?

Yeah. From honey trees that don't have bees.

D: Do all the different hawks look alike?

Some don't.

D: How could I tell a nice hawk from a mean hawk?

Maybe from they, hawks eat sea shells. Some hawks eat sea shells. If you see a hawk eating a sea shell, you know he's mean.

Future (4;10)

D: What would you have done if the pumpkin said "ouch" when you were carving it?

I'd go "Yikes! I'm getting out of here."

M: Why would you get out of there?

'Cause the pumpkin would chase me. He would be running after us. And I'd get on the storage box where the pumpkin can't get me. I could kick it off if it tried to climb up and get me.

Combination (3;1)

M: I don't know. Take the other animals out and see what they are.

Here's a rhinoceros. 'Cept a rhinoceros tried to get 'em and they all ran away. . . . And this one. How come?

Here. Look at this. See? These are, these are two camels and are ___ go. Let's go. These bears are gonna go also. . . . This one could go. Where's the hippo at? I had a hippo. Here he is. And, and the boy is watching them.

M: Uh huh. The boy could get inside one of the cages and the animals could watch him.

Then, then the other animals will get in it and they will chase him.

M: Oh. If he gets in a cage?

Yeah. So animals have go to in their cages. . . . Now it's Christmas. Now it's Christmas. (Has toy Christmas tree)

Because they have Christmas trees. Boys, where's the, uh, it had two, uh, three boys a minute ago.

M: How can you tell?

Where?

M: I see 'em all.

M: Look.

Oh. . . . A boy is watching a polar bear. Another boy is watching a rhinoceros. And another boy is watching a, a, a bear. Zoom! Zoom! And then a loud noise came ___. And all of the animals were watching and watching and hiding. Zoom! Zoom! Then it got right here. And then it frightened all the animals. Then it came and all the animals got real scared. Zoom! Zoom! I have a good idea, Mom!

M: What?

When I'm through playing with this, maybe we can go ice skating.

M: Maybe, but I have to go to the co-op first.

Look. I have, I have, I have two hands.

M: That's right.

And I have two hands.

M: Two hands for what?

For these cars 'cept, 'cept I can't hold another car.

M: You can hold one car in each hand.

Yeah. Two cars. . . . And, and so, so you, I can, uh, this one goes on a ride. And Zoom! The earth shook. And all the animals were hiding and hiding in their cages. And the earth shook again. . . . And the giraffe was, uh, the giraffe was right next to a elephant. And the mountain goat was right next to the buffalo. And then, then, then the mommy walked and she was next to the giraffe and the elephant. And then Zoom! (In this example, Abe did refer to some present toys and some that were not present. He also referred to both actual activities in which he made the toys engage and to activities that were purely fictitious.)

These examples illustrate several general patterns in regard to Abe's use of temporal frameworks in his fantasy narratives. As previously noted, he was much more likely to cast such narratives in a past framework than in a present or future one. This is in direct opposition to his development of hypothetical reference skills, in which future hypotheticals emerged prior to past hypotheticals (Kuczaj & Daly, 1979; see also Kuczaj, 1981). Hypothetical reference involves the comparison of actual (or expected) events with possible ones, and as such would seem to be related to the use of fantasy narratives. However, there is one important difference between hypothetical reference and fantasy narratives. Hypothetical reference involves a contrast between an actual (or expected) event and the hypothetical event. Young children seem to find such contrasts more difficult for past events than for future ones (Kuczaj, 1981; Kuczaj & Daly, 1979). These contrasts are also easier for young children when they involve fantasy characters than when they involve familiar others such as parents (Kuczaj, 1981). Fantasy narratives require no such explicit contrasts between the real and the imagined, although we assume that Abe realized that his fantasy narratives were in fact that. Nonetheless, fantasy narratives do not necessarily involve a contrast between an actual event and a supposed one, but instead a more general recognition of the difference between reality and fantasy. In other words, hypothetical reference involves an explicit contrast between an actual event and the hypothetical one, whereas fantasy narratives do not. This difference probably accounts for the difference in developmental patterns observed in Abe's hypothetical reference and his fantasy narratives. Of course, his preference for the past temporal framework may also have been influenced by the fact that Abe was read and told hundreds of stories, the overwhelming majority using the past temporal framework. Still, the developmental differences between his hypothetical reference skills and his fantasy narratives support the notion that the two types of reference involve different cognitive skills, in particular the nature of the necessary contrast between the actual and the unactual.

Abe's tendency to cast his fantasy narratives in the past temporal framework remained strong throughout the age range in which his spontaneous speech was sampled. Moreover, when he began to use other temporal frameworks, he often switched between the present and the past, or the future and the past, in the course of telling the story (as in the example given above). The instances of his fantasy narratives that involved either the present or the future (and in which the past temporal framework was absent) served unique functions. The present tense fantasy narratives served more of a generic or "timeless" function than truly a present one, as in the above example. Of the twelve present tense fantasy narratives, there is only one exception to this tendency. Abe's future fantasy narratives served a different function, always occurring in response to some query from a parent (as in the above example). To sum up, Abe's preference for the past temporal framework in regard to his fantasy narratives did not diminish with age. He did learn to use other temporal frameworks in his fantasy narrative, but also seemed to use these other temporal frameworks to serve at least slightly different functions than the past temporal framework.

We shall next consider the findings concerning the interactions of the characters in Abe's fantasy narratives. As is shown in Table 6-3, the proportion (determined by dividing the number of each story type observed during each age range by the total number of stories produced during that age range) of Abe's stories that were characterized by free association (category 1) remained fairly constant from age 2;5 to age 4;6 (with a range from 22% to 31%), but were completely absent in the narratives produced after 4;6.

Table 6-3 also shows the extent to which Abe's stories were characterized by the presence of a main character but in which there were no other characters (Category 2). The proportion of such stories comprised a U-shaped curve, with no stories of this type being produced during the age range of 3;7 to 4;0.

Table 6-3 also shows the extent to which Abe's stories were comprised of those in which there were both main and peripheral characters (at least one) but in which the only interaction involved the peripheral character(s) acting upon the main character (category 3). This story type was not found in three of the age periods

Table 6-3. Percentage (and number in parentheses) of Abe's Fantasy Narratives That Fell into Each of the Six Categories During Each Age Period

Age Period	Category					
	1	2	3	4	5	6
2;5–3;0	22(2)	33(3)	0	0	0	44(4)
3;1–3;6	29(5)	18(3)	18(3)	0	0	35(6)
3;7–4;0	31(4)	0	0	38(5)	0	31(4)
4;1–4;6	23(3)	23(3)	15(2)	23(3)	0	15(2)
4;7–5;0	0	33(2)	0	0	0	67(4)
Overall	24(14)	19(11)	9(5)	14(8)	0	34(20)

shown in Table 6-3. It was found with almost equal relative frequency in the two other age periods (3;1 to 3;6 and 4;1 to 4;6).

Table 6-3 also shows the extent to which Abe's stories consisted of those that had both a main character and at least one peripheral character, and in which the only interaction involved the main character acting upon the peripheral character(s) (category 4). This type of story was found in only two of the age periods shown in Table 6-3, and were more common in the age period 3;7 to 4;0 than in the age period 4;1 to 4;7. Interestingly, this type of story appeared at a later age than did category 3 story types.

Surprisingly (at least to us), stories that contained main and secondary characters and in which the characters both acted upon and were acted upon by one another (category 6) comprised a fair proportion of Abe's fantasy narratives even at the earliest ages. Although such stories comprised the highest proportion of Abe's stories during the last age range sampled, they comprised the lowest proportion in the immediately preceding age period. There were no instances of category 5 story types in Abe's speech samples. These results are also shown in Table 6-3.

The above results have been concerned with the relative proportion of each type of story for each age range. The overall relative proportion of each story type (collapsing across age) is also shown in Table 6-3. These results, which ignore age effects, reveal that the most common story type was category 6, but that the next most frequent type was category 1. Category 2 was the third most frequent, followed by category 4 and then category 3.

The data summarized in Table 6-3 may also be considered in terms of the relative frequency of each story type during each age period. At the youngest age range (2;5 to 3;0), category 6 was the most frequent story type, category 2 the next most frequent, and category 1 the next most frequent. No instances of categories 3 and 4 were found in this age range.

Category 6 was also the most common story type during the next age range (3;1 to 3;6), followed by category 1, and then by categories 2 and 3 (which were equally frequent). There were no instances of category 4.

The most common story type from 3;7 to 4;0 was category 4 (which had not occurred at all prior to this time period). Categories 1 and 6 were equally frequent. There were no instances of categories 2 and 3.

Each of the story types (with the exception of category 5, which was never observed) was produced by Abe during the age period 4;1 to 4;6. Categories 1, 2, and 4 were equally frequent, and more frequent than categories 3 and 6 (which were equally frequent). Categories 2 and 6 were the only story types to be produced during the final age period (4;7 to 6;0). Category 6 was twice as frequent as category 2 during this age period.

To sum up the analyses discussed to this point, Abe produced category 6 stories throughout the 2½-year period in which he was studied. Category 1 stories, seemingly the direct opposite of category 6 stories in terms of organizational structure, were evident from 2;5 to 4;6. Category 2 stories were also evident throughout the age range of concern, although they were absent from 3;7 to 4;0. Category 3 stories were rare in the speech samples, only occurring from 3;1 to 3;6 and 4;1 to 5;6. Category 4 stories were observed only in the later samples, making their first appearance at 3;7. Category 5 stories were not observed.

Consider the following two stories. The first is an example of a Category 1 story.

> (4;1) One time there was a dog and a cow and a man that had poisonous medicine and the dog was sick. And the man got his poisonous medicine 'cept the dog didn't get killed. And, and he told the queen "Why shouldn't I keep a nice dragon?" And know what? The prince said "Why? Why should you?" "Because the dragon was nice." And that's the end. Wasn't that a nice story?

Contrast this with the following Category 6 story produced at 4;2.

> Once a boy bear was playing. He saw a fire and crawled up a tree. He sat in the tree and smoke was getting in his eyes. And he cried. And then he saw a ___.

M: A what?

> A eagle. And he yelled to the eagle. And the eagle saw him and flew down. He got the bear and ___.

> And they they flied, flew, flied to the ground. And the bear thanked the eagle and gave him a fish. And then a fox asked the eagle for a ride. The eagle said "No, I'm too tired."

> And the bear and the eagle killed
> the fox. And the eagle ate the fox,
> but, but he saved some for the bear.
> The bear ate the fox. The eagle
> goed home. And the bear went to
> his cave.

These two examples illustrate the difference between category 1 and category 6 stories. Category 1 stories are characterized by "chain-complex" associations, one thought leading to another without any overall theme or organization (see Vygotsky, 1962, and Maratsos, 1977, for discussions of the implications of "chain-complex" thinking). Category 6 stories, on the other hand, are cohesive and involve mutual interactions among the central character and at least one secondary character. In between these two extremes are stories that contain only one character (category 2), and stories in which there is only one-way interaction between the main character and the secondary character(s) (categories 3 and 4). One might have expected a developmental pattern in which category 1 stories emerge before any others, category 2 stories before categories 3-6, and categories 3 and 4 before categories 5 and 6. The data, however, do not support this pattern. Although category 3 and 4 stories did seem to emerge after category 1 and 2 stories, category 6 stories were observed prior to category 3 and 4 stories. Thus, there was not a straightforward progression from least advanced to more advanced stories, but instead a mixture of story types at most ages. Although children do seem to produce more coherent and organized stories with increasing age (Applebee, 1978; Botvin & Sutton-Smith, 1977; Sutton-Smith, 1979; Sutton-Smith, et al., 1976), Abe's stories demonstrate that there is not a perfect relation between age and story complexity. At the same time, however, it is true that Abe's stories did tend to become more advanced as he got older. Interestingly, he failed to produce any category 5 stories, these being stories in which secondary characters interact with one another but not the main character. This sort of interaction among characters may be a more advanced type than that in any of the other story types. In order to have the secondary characters interact among themselves but not with the main character, the narrator must temporarily omit the main character from the story. Young children may find it difficult to do so. The ability to create interactions among secondary characters is necessary if one wishes to employ subplots in one's stories, and so may be a critical aspect of the development of the ability to create truly intricate story structures.

Table 6-4 summarizes the data concerning the types of characters that Abe used in his fantasy narratives. Overall, fantasy characters were the most frequent, real people the next most frequent, real toys the next most frequent, real objects quite rare, and real animals even rarer. From a developmental perspective, Table 6-4 reveals that fantasy characters and real people were the two types of characters used in Abe's earliest stories, and that with increasing age, he came to use a wider range of characters (real toys first, real objects later, and real animals still later). Somewhat surprisingly, the use of fantasy characters decreased with increasing age. These findings may reflect a general developing ability that enables children to

Table 6-4. Percentage (and number in parentheses) of Each Type of Character Found in Abe's Fantasy Narratives During Each Age Period

Age Period	Type of Character				
	Fantasy	Real People	Real Toys	Real Object(s)	Real Animal(s)
2;5–3;0	56(5)	44(4)	0	0	0
3;1–3;6	53(9)	35(6)	12(2)	0	0
3;7–4;0	62(8)	0	23(3)	15(2)	0
4;1–4;6	38(5)	0	62(8)	0	0
4;7–5;0	17(1)	67(4)	0	0	17(1)
Overall	48(28)	24(14)	22(13)	3(2)	2(1)

consider actual entities in fantasy contexts. In previous work on children's hypothetical reference, the first author has found that children find it more difficult to contrast actual events and objects with unactual ones than to contrast unactual events with other unactual ones (Kuczaj & Daly, 1979; Kuczaj, 1981). Children may also find it easier to create fantasy narratives if they involve fantasy characters rather than actual ones, although the data are less clear on this latter point. However, parents may contribute to this tendency by their use of fantasy in the speech they direct to their children (Kavanaugh & Graves, 1983; Kavanaugh, Whittington, & Cerbone, 1983). Parents who employ more fantasy in their speech to their children may have children who are more likely to use fantasy characters in their stories than will parents who use less fantasy in their child-directed speech. Parents who expose their children to fantasy when talking to them may also contribute to a general ability on the part of their children to use fantasy.

As shown in Table 6-5, even at the earliest ages, Abe's stories tended to contain both a beginning and an ending. However, the percentage of stories containing both a beginning and an ending tended to increase with age (with slight dips at 3;1 to

Table 6-5. Percentage (and number in parentheses) of Abe's Fantasy Narratives That Contained Neither a Beginning Nor an Ending, Contained Only a Beginning, Contained Only an Ending, or Contained Both a Beginning and an Ending During Each Age Period

Age Period	No Beginning or Ending	Beginning but No Ending	Ending but No Beginning	Beginning and Ending
2;5–3;0	0	44(4)	11(1)	44(4)
3;1–3;6	29(5)	23(4)	12(2)	29(5)
3;7–4;0	8(1)	15(2)	8(1)	69(9)
4;1–4;6	8(1)	31(4)	0	62(8)
4;7–5;0	0	0	0	100(6)
Overall	12(7)	24(14)	8(4)	57(32)

Table 6-6. Percentage (and number in parentheses) of Abe's Fantasy Narratives Initiated by Abe or by Another Person During Each Age Period

	Initiator	
Age Period	Abe	Another Person
2;5–3;0	55(5)	44(4)
3;1–3;6	65(10)	35(6)
3;7–4;0	69(9)	31(4)
4;1–4;6	85(1)	15(2)
4;7–5;0	4(67)	33( )
Overall	67(39)	33(19)

3;6 and 4;1 to 4;6). The percentage of stories that contained neither a beginning nor an ending decreased with age. Considerably more stories contained a beginning and no ending rather than an ending and no beginning. Stories lacking a beginning or an ending also decreased in frequency with increasing age.

Table 6-6 summarizes the data concerning who initiated the story—Abe or another person (by asking Abe a question or commenting to Abe about something). The majority of Abe's stories were self-initiated, and the percentage of self-initiated stories tended to increase with age. Nonetheless, it seems clear that Abe's parents contributed to his storytelling by initiating a fair number of his stories. Moreover, even though Abe initiated 39 of his 58 fantasy narratives, only 9 of these stories were told without any parental input. That is, even when Abe initiated a fantasy narrative, his parents were likely to contribute by asking questions or making comments while Abe was telling the story (see above examples). In this sense, there was a fair amount of audience participation.

Summary and Conclusions

In the above, we have presented the data concerned with Abe's fantasy narratives. Abe preferred the past temporal framework to other temporal frameworks when producing fantasy narratives, this most likely reflecting the fact that the vast majority of the stories that he was told were in the past temporal framework, but possibly also influenced by the relative ease of producing past fantasy narratives as compared to present or future ones.

Abe was also most likely to produce fantasy narratives in which the main character and the peripheral characters interacted with one another, but was next most likely to produce fantasy narratives in which there was no consistent character or theme. He also produced fantasy narratives in between these two extremes, some containing only one character, others containing both main and peripheral characters, but in which either the main character acted upon the peripheral character(s) *or* was acted upon by the peripheral character(s). He did not produce any stories in which the peripheral characters interacted with one another but not with the main character. Abe's stories did tend to become more advanced and more complex as he grew older, which fits well with the findings of previous investigators (Applebee, 1978; Botvin & Sutton-Smith, 1977; Kemper, Chapter 5, Sutton-Smith, 1979; Sutton-Smith, et al., 1976; Umiker-Sebeok, 1979). However, Abe's data demonstrate that the correlation between age and story complexity/sophistication is not perfect. Some of his early stories were as complex as his later ones. These findings suggest that the cognitive abilities necessary to produce complex stories are available to young children. This in turn suggests that the failure to do so is more of a performance problem than a competence one. Although more young children need to be studied in order to better determine the generality of this possibility, it seems reasonable to suggest that investigators address the issue of whether they are studying the children's performance or competence. Both are important, but must be distinguished for theoretical purposes.

Abe was most likely to use fantasy characters in his narratives, and was next most likely to use real (familiar) people in his fantasy narratives (the familiar others engaging in fantasy behaviors). As suggested earlier, Abe's tendency to use fantasy characters may reflect the relative ease of using fantasy characters rather than familiar ones in fantasy contexts. Previous investigators have found that familiar others and the self emerge in children's stories prior to fantasy characters (Abrahms, 1977; Ames, 1966; Pitcher & Prelinger, 1963). This, it has been suggested, reflects a tendency on young children's parts to orient their stories around the immediate context (Applebee, 1978; see also Umiker-Sebeok, 1979). It is possible, then, that Abe is somewhat unique in his preference for fantasy characters. However, he also produced many stories containing familiar others (including himself) or other real objects. It may be that the discrepancy between his data and those reported by other investigators reflects relatively minor differences in children's preferences for the characters in their first stories rather than major differences in developmental tendencies. Additional longitudinal data is needed to determine which of these possibilities is correct.

Abe was most likely to produce stories that contained both a beginning and an ending. He was much more likely to produce stories that contained a beginning but no ending than to produce stories that contained an ending but no beginning. He also occasionally produced stories that had neither a beginning nor an ending. These findings are in general accord with those of previous investigators. Well-formed narratives (fantasy or actual) produced by adults usually begin with orienting statements that inform the listener about the person, place, time, and behavioral situation (Labov & Waletzky, 1967). Early research suggested that young children were unlikely to provide listeners with such orienting information (Labov & Waletzky, 1967), the reason for their failure to do so being their egocentrism (i.e., their inability or unwillingness to recognize that listeners may lack critical information, Piaget, 1926). Subsequent research has revealed that young children are not as egocentric as was once believed (Maratsos, 1973; Shatz & Gelman, 1973), and that young children do provide orienting information in their narratives (Menig-Peterson & McCabe, 1978; Umiker-Sebeok, 1979). Abe's data fit well with those of Menig-Peterson and McCabe (1978) and Umiker-Sebeok (1979) in that he used his beginnings to orient his listeners about who the characters were, where the events took place and why, and when the events occurred. He did not always provide all of this information, but did provide each type of information throughout the age range in which his fantasy narratives were sampled.

Abe also exhibited a strong tendency to provide an ending for his stories. However, he was more likely to omit endings than beginnings. We suspect that this was due to his losing interest in a story once he had begun it: rather than completing it, he simply changed the topic or quit telling the story.

Abe initiated two-thirds of his fantasy narratives, the remaining being initiated by another present person. The listeners also contributed to Abe's stories by asking questions and encouraging him to continue with the story. The interchange of story-teller and listener is but a small subset of the more general types of interchanges involved in conversation to which young children have been found to be sensitive (Bloom, Rocissano, & Hood, 1976; Dore, Gearhart, & Newman, 1978; Shatz, 1983). Abe typically responded in an appropriate fashion to his listeners' queries. It seems likely that the listeners' queries may have alerted Abe to the types of content that he was omitting in his fantasy narratives, and so may have contributed to his later tendency to include such information in the absence of direct requests for it by the listeners.

At the beginning of this chapter, we specified three cognitive prerequisites for the telling of fantasy narratives. These prerequisites are the ability to separate the present from the nonpresent, the ability to distinguish reality and fantasy, and the intention to tell a story. The data that we have presented make it clear that these abilities were present in Abe at the youngest age (2;5) at which his spontaneous speech was sampled, even though his storytelling skills improved with age. The emergence of these three cognitive prerequisites is in need of further investigation, for only by combining the study of the development of these three cognitive capabilities with the study of the development of *how* to tell a story and the study of development of children's concept of a story will we come to truly understand the emergence of the uniquely human capability to create and enjoy fantasy.

References

Abrahms, D. (1977). *Conflict resolution in children's storytelling: An application of Erikson's theory and the conflict enculturation model.* Unpublished doctoral dissertation, Columbia University.

Ames, L. (1966). Children's stories. *Genetic Psychology Monographs, 73,* 337–396.

Applebee, A. (1978). *The child's concept of story*. Chicago: University of Chicago Press.

Bloom, L., Rocissano, L., & Hood, L. (1976). Adult-child discourse: Developmental interaction between information processing and linguistic knowledge. *Cognitive Psychology, 8,* 521–552.

Botvin, G., & Sutton-Smith, B. (1977). The development of structural complexity in children's fantasy narratives. *Developmental Psychology, 13,* 377–388.

Dore, J., Gearhart, M., & Newman, D. (1978). The structure of nursery school conversation. In K. Nelson (Ed.), *Language development*. New York: Wiley.

Garvey, C. (1977). *Play*. Cambridge, MA: Harvard University Press.

Kavanaugh, R., & Graves, T. (April 1983). *Mother's pretense interactions with young children*. Paper presented at the biennial meeting of the Society for Research in Child Development, Detroit.

Kavanaugh, R., Whittington, S., & Cerbone, M. (1983). Mother's use of fantasy in speech to young children. *Journal of Child Language, 10,* 45–55.

Kernan, K. (1977). Semantic and expressive elaboration in children's narratives. In S. Ervin-Tripp & C. Mitchell-Kernan (Eds.), *Child Discourse*. New York: Academic Press.

Kuczaj, S. (1977). The acquisition of regular and irregular past tense forms. *Journal of Verbal Learning and Verbal Behavior, 16,* 589–600.

Kuczaj, S. (1981). Factors influencing children's hypothetical reference. *Journal of Child Language, 8,* 131–138.

Kuczaj, S. (1983). Language play and language acquisition. In H. Reese (Ed.), *Advances in child development and behavior* (pp. 197–232). New York: Academic Press.

Kuczaj, S., & Boston. R. (1982). The nature and development of temporal reference systems. In S. Kuczaj (Ed.), *Language development: Language, thought, and culture* (pp. 365–396). Hillsdale, NJ: Lawrence Erlbaum.

Kuczaj, S., & Daly, M. (1979). The development of hypothetical reference in young children. *Journal of Child Language, 6,* 563–580.

Labov, W., & Waletzky, J. (1967). Narrative analysis: Oral versions of personal experience. In J. Helen (Ed.), *Essays on the verbal and visual arts*. Seattle: University of Washington Press.

Mandler, J. M., and Johnson N. J. (1974). Remembrance of things parsed: Story structure and recall. *Cognitive Psychology, 9,* 111–151.

Maratsos, M. (1973). Nonegocentric communication abilities in preschool children. *Child Development, 44,* 697–700.

Maratsos, M. (1977). Disorganization in thought and word. In R. Shaw & J. Bransford (Eds.), *Perceiving, knowing, and acting*. Hillsdale, NJ: Lawrence Erlbaum.

Menig-Peterson, C., & McCabe, A. (1978). Children's orientation of a listener to the context of their narratives. *Developmental Psychology, 14,* 582–592.

Miller, L. (1979). The idea of conflict: A study of the development of story understanding. In E. Winner & H. Gardner (Eds.), *Fact, fiction, and fantasy in childhood*. San Francisco: Jossey-Bass.

Piaget, J. (1926). *The language and thought of the child*. New York: Harcourt, Brace.

Pitcher, E., & Prelinger, E. (1968). Children tell stories: *An analysis of fantasy*. New York: International Universities Press.

Scarlett, W., & Wolf, D. (1979). When it's only make-believe: The construction of a boundary between fantasy and reality in storytelling. In E. Winner & H. Gardner (Eds.), *Fact, fiction, and fantasy in childhood.* San Francisco: Jossey-Bass.

Shatz, M. (1983). Communication. In J. Flavell & E. Markman (Eds.), *Cognitive development.* P. Mussen (Gen. Ed.), *Carmichael's manual of child psychology* (4th ed.). New York: Wiley.

Shatz, M., & Gelman, R. (1973). The development of communication skills: Modifications in the speech of young children as a function of listener. *Monographs of the Society for Research in Child Development, 38* (5, Serial No. 152).

Stein, N. (1979). How children understand stories. In L. Katz (Ed.), *Current topics in early childhood education* (Vol. 2). Norwood, NJ: Ablex.

Stein, N. (1982). The definition of a story. *Pragmatics, 6,* 110-117.

Stein, N. & Glenn, C. (1979). An analysis of story comprehension in elementary school children. In R. Freedle (Ed.), *New directions in discourse processing* (Vol. 2). Norwood: Ablex.

Stein, N., & Policastro, M. (1983). The concept of a story: A comparison between children's and teachers' viewpoints. In H. Mandl, N. Stein, & T. Trabasso (Eds.), *Learning and comprehension of text.* Hillsdale, NJ: Lawrence Erlbaum.

Sutton-Smith, B. (1979). Presentation and representation in fictional narrative. In E. Winner & H. Gardner (Eds.), *Fact, fiction, and fantasy in childhood.* San Francisco: Jossey-Bass.

Sutton-Smith, B., Botvin, G., & Mahoney, D. (1976). Developmental structures in fantasy narratives. *Human Development, 19,* 1-13.

Trabasso, T., Stein, N., & Johnson, L. (1981). Children's knowledge of events: A causal analysis of story structure. *The Psychology of Learning and Motivation, 15,* 237-282.

Umiker-Sebeok, D. (1979). Preschool children's intraconversational narratives. *Journal of Child Language, 6,* 91-109.

Vygotsky, L. (1982). *Thought and language.* Cambridge: MIT Press.

Weir, R. (1962). *Language in the crib.* The Hague: Mouton.

7. Children's Deictic Reference: The Role of Space and Animacy

Roger Wales

To say that language is used primarily for communication is self-evident. For such a statement to be trivially true would require that we were easily able to give theoretical and empirical content to such a claim. In fact the opposite is largely the case. That is, the way language is used for communication is still one of the most perplexing and challenging issues facing anyone interested in questions of language. In order to approach the issue, it must be addressed through reference, and in particular to how reference is embedded in linguistic expression. It seems a sine qua non for normal communication that contact is made through the devices provided by linguistic reference between the sense of an utterance and the intended context of the communication (see Lyons 1977, Ch. 7, for discussion).

There have been attempts to argue for the centrality of deixis as a device for providing a mechanism for reference (see e.g., Lyons 1975, 1977; McGinn, 1981). The argument in brief is that deixis does so by directing the learner's attention to the appropriate spatial and/or temporal domain in which to locate the intended referent. Thus the latter is introduced, or indexed, by the attention-directing function of deictic expressions such as the demonstratives, pronouns, tense, and so on. In fact, so the argument goes, no other linguistic devices are essential to the linguistic expression of reference, although of course names of various sorts often elaborate and specify the referent more precisely. That is, what the speaker prototypically uses deictic expressions to do is to direct the listener to that part of the domain of the context which is being talked about. In order to account for the ability of the speaker and hearer to focus jointly on the relevant aspects or features of the con-

I am grateful to ARGS for support; and to Vivian Bainbridge, Jane Breekveldt, Anne Mundie, and Libby Nottle for their assistance in many aspects of these studies. In my view (and I hope theirs) this paper has been significantly improved by criticisms and suggestions by Suzanne Romaine and Eve Clark.

text being referred to, does not require a fully specified theory of physical and/or social contexts. Rather one can still relatively unproblematically make the assumption that communication proceeds in such contexts in such a manner that reference may be made to them in a minimal way. From the perspective of a contextually situated theory of interaction within which reference takes place, deixis functions as a linguistic means of focussing attention on salient aspects of the contexts in which speakers communicate with their hearers. With such a contextual theory of reference it is clearly of interest to observe how the spatial and temporal contexts of children's utterances may be related to the ontogenesis of language, and in particular to the ontogenesis of deictic expression.

Deictic expressions are of particular interest because they involve not only semantic and syntactic considerations but also spatial or temporal aspects of the situation of utterance. Thus they are an obvious focus for any attempt to see how the different levels of representation of syntax, semantics, and pragmatics interact with each other and with definable pragmatic issues—usually having to do with the speaker's location at the time of utterance. In recent years, many studies have shown the utility of looking at deictic expressions for an understanding of language acquisition (e.g., Bruner, 1974, Clark, 1978, Tanz, 1980, Wales, 1979). A characteristic finding is that certain key deictic expressions (e.g., that or there) are among the earliest words acquired, and more importantly, are prominent in children's earliest two- and three-word utterances.

It is also true that many instances of these expressions occur in the speech addressed to young children. In a detailed study of mother-child dyads, Wales (1979) reported that most of both the maternal and child deictic utterances (about 80%) are associated with very clear gestural support. The attention-directing function of these expressions is an early acquisition and the provision of precise locational information is usually accomplished via the concomitant gesture. Given these findings, it is not surprising that there is something of a developmental lag before children are able, in the absence of gesture, to use the contrastive spatial feature of the words themselves to reliably convey or comprehend spatial information (e.g., here vs. there or that vs. this). de Villiers and de Villiers (1974) and Wales (1979) have noted that a number of contextual cues can facilitate performance in the absence of gesture, for example, the presence of a small screen between the relatively proximal or remote referents, or whether the child is facing his or her hearer. However, despite these means whereby the child's performance may be improved, the overall tenor of the studies to date suggests that the developmental lag between the two modes of use (i.e., with and without gestural support) is upwards of 6 years (Clark, 1978; Wales, 1979). Something is clearly deflecting the development of the "well formed" use of these deictic expressions in the absence of gestural support.

Simple Comprehension and Production Studies

A possible clue is provided by Kirsner (1979), who proposed that the adult grammar of Dutch demonstratives is changing such that traditional spatial distinctions of proximity and remoteness to speaker are being replaced by distinctions

involving differences of animacy. Thus "this" might be expected to introduce animate and in particular human referents (Kirsner's "high deixis") and "that" to refer
to inanimate referents ("low deixis"). Kirsner's reasons for expecting this shift in
use follows from his use of "deixis" as having to do with the force with which a
hearer is instructed to find a referent. "This" would be seen as suggesting more
forcefully than "that," that a specific referent exists (and the choice of a demonstrative rather than a definite article as suggesting more urging). This view fits with
the current zeitgeist, in which the salience of animacy for other aspects of early
language development is asserted, for example the organization of lexical categories
into actors, actions, and objects (see, e.g., Slobin, 1980). This suggests a reasonable
working hypothesis: The developmental lag in the use of the spatial contrasts
carried by the demonstratives is in fact a consequence of a confounding of that
locational information with the animacy of the referent. This possibility was the
first to be explored in the studies to be reported.

It was approached in the first instance in as simple and direct a manner as possible. Hence there were three basic *comprehension* tasks that were modeled on
those used in the past to study the spatial contrasts without benefit of gesture. The
first was "open ended," in that six toys were placed randomly on a table (a boy,
girl, lion, zebra, truck, and umbrella). The child was asked "which would you call
this?" (or "that"), "which would you say is here?" (or "there"). The other two
comprehension tasks involved one each of the human, animal, and objects being at
either end of the table, with the experimenter either next to the child (same perspective) or opposite the child (opposite perspective). The child's responses to the
questions "Which one would I call this one?" (or "that") "which one would I say is
here?" (or "there") were noted. The order of questions and tasks was randomly
varied across four groups with 20 children in each (approximately equal numbers of
boys and girls), ages being 4, 5, 6, and 7 years, respectively. The layout of the tasks
is shown in Figure 7-1.

Two production tasks were developed using stories in which questions were
based on pictures in such a way as to elicit the deictic terms used with either human,
animal, or inanimate referents. For each of these the aim was to elicit two demonstrative and two locative expressions for each story. The questions for one of the
stories are given below, where the code is H = human, A = animal, O = object,
D = demonstrative, and L = locative.

Picture	Question	Code
I	Which girl is blowing the thistle?	H, D
	Where is the thistle?	O, L
II	Where is the girl?	H, L
	Which frog is watching?	A, D
III	Where is the frog?	A, L
	Which turtle is watching?	A, D
I	Which thistle is blowing away?	O, D
	Where is the girl?	H, L
II	Which girl is sitting down?	H, D
	Where is the flower?	O, L
III	Where is the turtle?	A, L
	Which flower is growing?	O, D

TASK A:

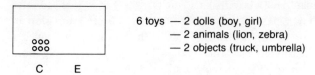

6 toys — 2 dolls (boy, girl)
        — 2 animals (lion, zebra)
        — 2 objects (truck, umbrella)

C   E

E: If you were to call one toy <u>this</u> toy, and one toy <u>that</u> toy, which one would you call <u>this</u> toy? Which one would you call <u>that</u> toy?

E: If you were to say one toy is <u>here</u> and one toy <u>there</u>, which toy would you say is <u>here</u>? Which toy would you say is <u>there</u>?

TASK B:

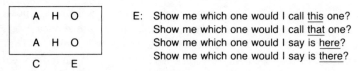

E: Show me which one would I call <u>this</u> one?
    Show me which one would I call <u>that</u> one?
    Show me which one would I say is <u>here</u>?
    Show me which one would I say is <u>there</u>?

(Toys are shuffled and some swap ends after each trial, but always so that there is one human, one animal, and one object at each end.)

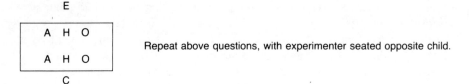

Repeat above questions, with experimenter seated opposite child.

Figure 7-1. The format for the comprehension tasks.

The groups of children were the same as those studied in the comprehension tasks, but they were tested with at least two days between the two types of task. Again, the order of presentation of the tasks was counterbalanced.

Results—Comprehension Study

In this study, interest lay in the form of the responses—whether there was any relation between the markedness of the deictic expression and the animacy (or humanness) of the referent chosen by the children. The results of the open-ended task A were straight forward. There were no differences in the distribution of responses to demonstratives and locatives and so they were pooled for subsequent discussion. If the category of "high" deixis is reserved for "human" referents then there were uniformly 35% "correct" high deixis choices at each age; and low deixis choices rose from 52.5% at age 4 to 62.5% at age 7. The latter result was the closest to an age effect on this task. If animacy (human and animal) was used as the defin-

Table 7-1. Percentage Choices of Referents of High and Low Deixis in Task B

Age	Human[a]		Animacy[b]	
	High	Low	High	Low
4	30.8	61.7	60.8	37.5
5	35.8	60.0	70.0	36.7
6	37.7	67.5	75.0	40.0
7	32.5	69.2	73.3	53.3

[a] High = this/here, human, and proximal. Low = that/there, nonhuman, and distal.
[b] High = this/here, animate, and proximal. Low = that/there, inanimate, and distal.

ing characteristic of "high" deixis, choices of this kind averaged 60%, and "low" deixis correspondingly fell to 30+%. The results for the two parts of task B were indistinguishable—that is, the change in perspective seemed to make no difference to the choice of toys as a function of their animacy. The distribution of pooled choices is summarized in Table 7-1.

There are a number of interesting aspects of these results. Unlike earlier studies on the spatial contrast alone, there are no discernable age effects. Furthermore, on either categorization the high/low deixis distinction is very clear. On the spatial contrast alone, these results were similar to those reported in Wales (1979); namely that there was little improvement with age on demonstratives (average 62%), but on the locatives the improvement went from 65% for 4 year olds to 80% for 7 year olds. Also the net improvement on the spatial contrast was greater for the same perspective than opposite perspective. No such changes were discernable for the animacy contrasts. What is more interesting is to contrast these distributions with the results on the open-ended (nonspatial) task. It seems that the high/low distinction is more strongly represented in task B than task A. This is particularly so when the distinction is operationalized in terms of animacy. The equation of animacy with high deixis gives a better account of the responses in the perspective task. There is also a trend toward an age effect in low deixis. Also worth noting is the fact that consistently across the age groups, approximately 70% of the errors in distal position for that/there were the result of the choosing of a proximal item of appropriate low deixis category. The opposite trend for this/here was not evident in the data.

Production Study

In the production task we were once again concerned with the way in which the demonstratives and locatives were used in relation to the preferred referents. The data are summarized in Table 7-2. Because the choices of demonstrative and locative were equally distributed they have been pooled in Table 7-2. However, it

Table 7-2. Percentage Uses of This/Here and That/There by Category of Referent

Age, in Years	This/Here			That/There		
	Human	Animal	Object	Human	Animal	Object
4	53.3	50.0	46.3	37.5	53.3	62.0
5	62.0	47.5	45.0	45.0	50.0	73.3
6	65.6	48.0	53.3	48.0	47.5	67.5
7	65.6	53.3	53.3	46.3	50.0	65.0

should be noted that there was a clear age effect in that the 4-year-olds tended to choose either a demonstrative or locative adverbial form and consistently use it thereafter (though split equally between the two forms). By the age of 7, children were more likely to use both forms. For this and here neither the age factor nor the demonstrative/locative factor approached significance. The use of this/here by referent (i.e., that these expressions were used more for human, than for animal, than for object referents) was significant $F(2,152) = 5.794$, $p < .01$. Similarly for that/there only the use-by-referent factor was significant (object more than animal more than human) $F(2,152) = 5.68$, $p < .01$. It is clear that the effect for this/here is coming from the "human" referent, and for that/there from the "object" referents.

Discussion

Although these results are not very strong they are sufficiently compelling to suggest that animacy is an important factor between the age when children can fluently use deictic expressions with gestural support and the time when they can use them to convey spatial contrast without gesture. At first this may seem a strange result, but it is coherent and consistent with the contextual theory of deictic reference. If the latter is seen primarily as providing a mechanism with which to direct the hearers' attention to the intended referent, then the salience of the animacy of the referent seems an entirely plausible candidate for helping to organize the search for that referent. That is, this result is consistent with the emphasis of the contextual theory in treating as the primary force of such expressions "the hearer should concentrate on X." Then the animacy as much as the spatial or temporal distance from the speaker should facilitate locating the referent X. This would help to account for the homogeneity of the category of deictic expressions, which seen from the perspective of their syntax or semantics appear otherwise very heterogeneous. What is of some interest in these data is that there seems no diminution of the animacy effect by age (in fact in the few instances where there is any sign of an age effect the trend is to enhance it). If this trend were maintained through to adulthood then this would suggest that the pattern Kirsner reports for Dutch may be starting to apply for adult English.

There are several points that need to be made about these studies: When the children used the high/low distinction they were doing so with wholly inanimate toys; it might be expected therefore that more real-life situations could serve to enhance the effect of animacy. It is interesting that in the apparently more natural production task the main difference is carried by the contrast between the "human" and "inanimate object." This contrast is clearer here than in the comprehension tasks. This may well be a product of the differences in task demands.

The other point that is worth drawing attention to is the lack of difference between the use of the demonstrative and locative forms. This seems to run counter to Kirsner's expectations about "force," since on the latter view it would seem likely that the high/low deixis distinction would be more evident with the demonstratives. This could well be a function of the simple forms of the present tasks and their analyses. (On the other hand it is perhaps significant that demonstratives and locatives are the same for many languages.) Therefore, these studies were extended to a more complex, and perhaps more natural, format.

A More Complex Descriptive Task: The Doll's House

Since Linde and Labov (1975) there have been several studies concerned with the issue of how complex information is organized in a discourse situation. When we consider the studies presented above it is clear that each statement could be, and was, treated separately. There was no problem of deciding which piece of information to introduce when, or how to do so. The more recent studies have started to tackle the general issues of "linearization in discourse" (Levelt, 1982). Several attempts have been made to get speakers to describe rooms or geographical routes (see Jarvella & Klein, 1982, for a range of examples). The common aim is to try to use a reasonably well-defined situation for description, which nevertheless allows for a variety of perfectly acceptable solutions. For example, it seems that to describe a room, it is often the case that the hearer is taken on a verbal tour of the walls of the room before coming to the contents of the center of the room. If such discourse strategies influence children's verbal descriptions, descriptions of spatial arrays such as rooms might reveal the kind of interaction between spatial location and category of referent observed in the studies reported above.

In this study, 40 children in each of two age groups were used (5 and 6 years, respectively). In this task the child was required to describe to a doll the contents in a toy house with a variety of rooms (either four or two) and contents. Specifically, the child was asked to take the doll through the house and tell her about everything and everyone in the house. In each room of the four-room house for example, was a human, an animal, a natural kind object (e.g., fruit), and an artefact (e.g., furniture). (The natural kind category was introduced to try to further specify the contrast between animate and inanimate.) These were varied systematically so that one of each was in the center of each room, one against the wall, and two in corners. A typical layout for the four-room house is shown in Figure 7-2.

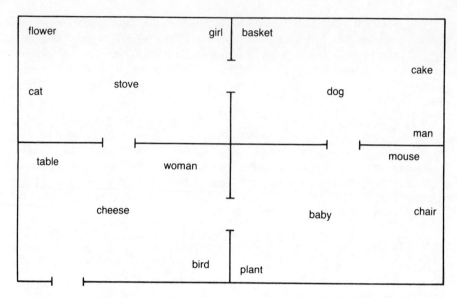

Figure 7-2. Diagram of the contents of a typical instance of a four-room layout.

The positions of the contents of the two-room house were similar to those of the four-room house without either the horizontal or vertical "walls." The toys were of approximately equal size (i.e., they did not vary in size in scale with their normal counterparts). The size of the house was 1 m², and it did not have a roof. The actual contents of the house were varied systematically across all subjects, and between trials on the two-room and four-room layout. The order of the trials on the two layouts was counterbalanced across subjects, as was the configuration of the two-room house between 'horizontal' and 'vertical' forms. The order and position of reference for each room was recorded, as was the way in which the child described the contents to the doll during the tour of the house.

Results

In general, the preferred order of mention was inanimate before animate, with human last; but this interacted with a significant tendency to refer first to items in the middle of each room. Thus there is an interaction between spatial location and animacy in the children's referents.

The details of these results now follow. Because the data from such a study are rich and complex, some attention will have to be given to the detailed form of analyses. These were on the order in which objects were visited within a room/quarter. The object visited initially was given a rank of 1. Objects that were not visited after completion of the house tour were given a rank of 5 (4 + 1) or 9 (8 + 1). Objects were deemed missed only if left unvisited after completion of the house tour, that is, objects visited during a second sojourn in a particular room were not penalized.

Two classes of analyses were run, and within each class there were four subject cases. The classes are:

I: Overall—the data used were from all subjects in which four of each object type occurred within the house regardless of the balance between object type and middle position. The results from this analysis did not differ importantly from the analysis of data from subjects where the object type was balanced around the house for middle position in the room. (Because of occasional errors in experimenter execution and/or subject idiosyncracy of response the former data were often unbalanced, and thus ANOVAs will vary in the degrees of freedom reported.)

II: Middles—the analyses were based on the rank of the object in the middle position of each room (wall and corner objects were ignored). Data used were from subjects in which object type and middle position were balanced within the house.

The four cases of analyses were:

A: Four-room—only four-room array data were used.

B: Two-room—only two-room array data were used.

C: Two-room versus four-room—four-room and two-room data were used, and two-room ranks were reassessed with reference to each quarter of the house, that is, the rooms were divided in half for ranking purposes. This division was somewhat arbitrary with respect to the way in which children toured the house but analytically necessary to make four-room versus two-room comparisons compatible.

D: Two-room one-quarter-house rank data were used. This type of analysis was chiefly run to determine whether differences in effects in (C) were evident as a result of interpreting two-room data in a one-quarter-house set up. They will be reported where relevant.

Analyses were made using Alice ANOVAs for unequal sample sizes. The number of factors varied with the class and case of the analysis but all eight analyses were based on a mixed design with the two factors age and sex as nested dimensions. For a key to the abbreviations used see Table 7-3.

Table 7-3. Key to Dimension/Factor Abbreviations

AG	age	1. prep grade (5)	2. first grade (6)
Sx	sex	1. male (M)	2. female (F)
SS	subjects	number varied with class and case of analysis	
RM	house room array	1. 4 room (4)	2. 2 room (2)
AN	animation	1. inanimate (In)	2. animate (An)
DG	division of animation *not* a real world factor but necessary in the analyses to partition animation effects from object effects		
		1. artificial and beast	2. natural and human
OB	object type following	1. object (O)	2. natural (N)
	AN × DG cross	3. animal (A)	4. human (H)

Table 7-4. Overall: Significant Main Effects and Interactions

Four-room
  AN: $F(1,69) = 9.58, p < .01$ (In, An)
  AG × Sx: $F(1,69) = 4.34, p < .05$ (6 M, 5 F, 6 M, 5 M)
  OB: $F(3,207) = 7.69, p < .001$ (O, N, A, H)

Two-room
  AN: $F(1,70) = 5.63, p < .005$ (MI, EA, FI, M)
  OB: $F(3,210) = 5.98, p < .001$ O, A, N, H)
  AG × OB: $F(3,210) = 3.39, p < .05$ (5 O, 5 A, 6 O, 5 N,
                                                                6 A, 6 H, 6 N, 5 H)
  Sx × OB: $F(3,210) = 4.77, p < .01$ (MO, MN, MA, FO,
                                                                FA, FH, FN, MH)

Two-room vs. four-room   there are no significant effects by
                                              room differences

Two-room as if four-room
  AN: $F(1,70) = 4.04, p < .05$ (In, An)
  AG × AN: $F(1,70) = 4.06, p < .05$ (5 IN (6 In, An) 5 An)
  Sx × AN: $F(1,70) = 6.94, p < .01$ (MIn, FAn, FIn, MAn)
  AG × OB: $F(3,210) = 3.12, p < .05$ (5 O, 5 N, 6 O, 6 H,
                                                                5 A, 6 A, 6 N, 5 H)
  Sx × OB: $F(3,210) = 3.23, p < .05$ (MO, MN, FO, FH,
                                                                FA, MA, FN, MH)

For reasons of space only significant effects will be reported, and these are presented in Table 7-4 (overall) and Table 7-5 (middles). (After each significant F value the order of the levels in the factor will be summarized, from the most to the least preferred.)

Table 7-5. Middles: Significant Main Effects and Interactions

Four-room
  OB: $F(3,159) = 3.55, p < .05$ (A, O, N, H)

Two-room
  Sx × AN: $F(1,52) = 6.07, p < .02$ (MIn, An, FIn, MAn)
  Sx × OB: $F(3,156) = 2,8, p < .05$ (FH, MO, MN, MA,
                                                                FO, FN, FA, MH)

Two-room vs. four-room
  Sx × RM: $F(1,40) = 4.14, p < .05$ (F 4, M 2, F 2, M 4)
  Sx × OB: $F(3,120) = 2.96, p < .05$ (FH, FO, MO, MA,
                                                                FN, FA, MN, MH)

Two-room as four-room
  Sx × OB: $F(3,156) = 2.74, p < .05$ (MO, FH, FO, MN,
                                                                MA, FN, FA, MH)

There were reliable preferences shown by the children for the order in which particular types of objects were introduced. Their preference was generally for artificial objects first, then natural objects, the animals, and finally humans. There were some interactions with age, where the younger children were stronger in their preferences for inanimate objects; and also an interaction in the two-room situation with sex of child, where the boys were markedly stronger in their preference for inanimate objects. Inanimate objects were given preferential attention in both the two-room and the four-room house and the object type preference order was not significantly affected by the house structure. There were also no differences in the relative strengths of these effects for the two house arrays. However, the object preferences of the boys and girls and the 5- and 6-year-olds were influenced in a complex manner by the house arrangement.

The children responded differently to the object placed in the middle position. The children tended to introduce the doll to the object in the middle before those placed by the walls or in the corner. The preferences for inanimate objects over animate objects were not present for all the children. Different preferences were exhibited by the two sexes. Girls tended to pay initial attention to the human and artificial objects in middle positions, whereas boys paid more initial attention to artificial objects and tended to introduce the doll to human objects in the final stages of their room tour. In summary then, there were stable though complex patterns of preferences exhibited where spatial position and animacy of object both contributed interactively to the patterns produced.

The Language Used While Conducting the Tour

For convenience of analysis and exposition, the language that the children used while conducting the tour was divided into five different categories:

1. Deictic expressions used to introduce an object. The alternatives were: this, that, here, there. Also included in this category were uses of "it" where used to introduce an object.
2. The type of articles used to introduce the object: alternatives being a, the, some, (an) other, a possessive pronoun, or complete absence of an article.
3. Descriptions of the room itself and the relationships between objects within a room. The alternatives considered were:
   a. description relating to the function of the room, for example, kitchen.
   b. description relating to the physical structure of the room, for example, the middle of the room, the corner of the room, and so on.
   c. description in relation to the door.
   d. description in relation to other objects within the room.
   e. here and there, when used as a position marker—for example, "the doll is over here."
4. "Transition" language in which the child indicated an awareness of progression from one object to another and "temporal" language where an indication was

given of a temporal sequence within the tour. Within the tokens of transitional language distinctions were made between the type of subject marker used. The alternatives used predominantly here were: you, I, she, and it.

5. The final category was that of "secondary naming." This was defined as instances of a previously named object being rereferred to, either in relation to a description of another object or simply as a second mention of a single object. The alternatives used by the children here were: you, she, it, this, that, the, and a. It is often difficult to determine except by prescriptive adult criteria whether these uses are strictly anaphoric.

At this stage it makes best sense to look for the main trends in the data.

Deixis

The frequency data are summarized in Table 7-6. When describing the four-room arrangement of the doll's house six-year-old females showed an overall preference for "there" as a deictic expression. This was particularly so when the object to which they were referring was animate but not human. The other deictic expressions—"this," "that," "here," and "it"—were all used much less frequently than "there," although within this group individual expressions were used with similar frequency. The 6-year-old males on the other hand, by and large ignored "that" as a

Table 7-6. Deictic Expressions Used to Introduce an Object

Age	Category[a]	This		That		Here		There		It	
		M	F	M	F	M	F	M	F	M	F
Four-room											
5	O	0	5	6	1	3	7	7	8	0	4
	N	3	4	5	0	2	9	6	11	0	5
	A	1	5	5	0	2	7	10	9	0	7
	H	0	4	9	0	4	11	8	9	0	5
6	O	15	5	1	5	10	6	15	17	12	4
	N	11	11	1	3	14	1	17	15	8	6
	A	17	7	1	7	10	1	14	26	11	4
	H	16	6	2	6	15	4	12	18	12	3
Two-room											
5	O	0	6	2	0	4	2	5	9	1	6
	N	1	6	3	2	3	2	7	12	2	5
	A	3	4	1	0	5	0	5	8	1	7
	H	0	8	2	1	5	2	7	12	1	5
6	O	15	17	4	1	11	4	8	26	15	2
	N	11	16	4	2	14	4	12	24	14	2
	A	14	17	4	1	11	3	12	26	10	2
	H	11	17	5	1	11	4	16	29	14	1

[a] O = object; N = natural kind; A = animal; H = human.

deictic expression, while using "this," "there," "here," and "it," with equivalent frequency. The five-year-old females did not use "that," while their male counterparts did not use "this" or "it." All the other expressions were used with much the same frequency.

When the design of the doll's house was changed to two rooms, the use of "this" and "there" by 6-year-old females increased, while the 6-year-old boys employed a similar pattern of usage to describe both arrangements of the house. With the two-room design, 5-year-old females showed a marked drop in the use of "here," while their male counterparts decreased their use of "that," while slightly increasing the use of "here." The variation across object types—animate/inanimate —appears to be minimal within each age and sex group.

Articles

The data are summarized in Table 7-7. The absence of an article was most marked for 5-year-old children, in particular the males. When 6-year-old children failed to use an article it was more likely to be when they were describing the four-room arrangement of the doll's house, than when describing the two-room one.

The use of "some" was primarily retained for the description of inanimate, natural objects (e.g., oranges). This observation held for all the children. Although

Table 7-7. Types of Articles Used to Introduce an Object

Age	Category	A		The		Some		An (other)		Possessive		No Article	
		M	F	M	F	M	F	M	F	M	F	M	F
Four-room													
5	O	40	28	18	28	0	0	0	0	0	0	19	9
	N	24	33	23	16	6	7	3	2	0	0	17	10
	A	41	37	11	24	0	0	1	2	0	0	11	10
	H	40	42	11	18	1	0	4	4	0	0	11	6
6	O	66	53	15	21	0	0	0	0	1	3	7	2
	N	53	40	13	17	14	8	1	1	0	3	4	3
	A	65	57	14	13	0	0	4	1	0	5	6	2
	H	63	49	6	9	0	0	7	5	1	12	10	1
Two-room													
5	O	38	35	27	28	0	0	0	0	0	0	15	5
	N	33	24	22	21	3	4	3	3	0	0	19	8
	A	39	30	18	21	2	0	2	3	0	0	18	11
	H	35	34	14	23	0	1	9	3	1	1	12	3
6	O	62	57	23	17	0	0	0	0	1	3	0	2
	N	48	37	14	9	17	15	4	3	0	4	0	7
	A	59	58	16	17	0	0	6	1	0	3	0	0
	H	57	53	14	12	0	0	5	5	4	8	0	1

one or two younger children did use "some" to describe animate objects, this was not typical. Likewise, "other" and its variants were never used to describe inanimate, artificial objects in either the two-room or four-room arrangement of house. The most frequently used article was "a"; the use of this article being two to three times more frequent than the next most popular article, which was "the."

The five-year-old children tended not to use a possessive pronoun in either arrangement of the house. On the other hand, the six-year-old children, in particular the females, used these pronouns with a frequency similar to most other articles, but not "the" and "a."

Description

The data are summarized in Table 7-8. Each group of children tended to describe objects in relation to the major structures of the room—middle, wall, and corner—but the door proved an exception to this. The door was mainly used as a reference point in the two-room design. Only the 6-year-old children used the door as a reference point in the four-room designs.

The older children were much more likely than the 5-year-olds to orient them-

Table 7-8. Descriptions of the Room Itself and Relationships Within the Room[a]

Age	Category	Room M	Room F	MCW M	MCW F	D M	D F	Object M	Object F	Other M	Other F	Here M	Here F	There M	There F
Four-room															
5	O	6	1	35	41	0	0	1	1	0	1	14	1	10	4
	N	3	2	28	39	2	1	0	3	1	1	12	1	6	5
	A	1	1	35	42	0	0	1	1	4	0	5	2	7	3
	H	1	2	34	41	0	0	1	1	2	2	6	2	6	1
6	O	8	15	80	56	2	6	1	1	4	0	3	7	10	5
	N	8	9	74	58	5	1	2	0	3	0	2	0	6	4
	A	7	14	82	60	3	0	0	0	1	1	0	4	5	4
	H	8	12	78	59	3	1	2	1	1	2	1	8	9	5
Two-room															
5	O	3	0	28	33	4	4	2	1	2	0	11	0	14	3
	N	1	1	29	32	1	7	0	3	1	0	5	3	10	1
	A	2	1	27	33	4	8	2	0	1	1	11	3	7	5
	H	0	2	27	32	2	5	2	1	1	3	7	1	6	2
6	O	16	9	69	56	6	3	4	3	0	3	4	1	0	1
	N	15	8	64	55	6	3	4	1	6	4	2	3	3	1
	A	11	8	68	55	6	4	6	3	0	2	2	2	1	3
	H	14	9	61	56	3	6	6	3	5	8	6	2	1	1

[a] Room = room function, for example, kitchen, bedroom. MCW = in middle, corner, wall. D = in relation to doorway. Object = in relation to other objects. Other = miscellaneous category. Here/There = for example, "the doll is over here."

selves with reference to the use to which a room might be put—for example, kitchen. This occurred with both two- and four-room designs. While the 6-year-old children showed a tendency to describe objects in relation to each other in the two-room doll's house, this tendency disappeared when the room became smaller (i.e., four-room house) and was not apparent for either house arrangement being described by the 5-year-olds.

Transition and Temporal Language

The data are summarized in Table 7-9. All the children tended to use a "running commentary" type of description. That is, they made an explicit transition from one object to another. It was noted that 6-year-old children, and 5-year-old females, had a tendency to relate this with a time-awareness such as "*now* we are going to . . . ." This tendency was absent in the descriptions given by 5-year-old boys.

The principal subject forms employed in the transition between objects was "she," although 5-year-old children, but not 6-year-olds, were also liable to use

Table 7-9. Descriptions Showing Awareness of Progression

						Transition Subject							
		Transition[a]		Temporal[b]		You		I		She		It	
Age	Category	M	F	M	F	M	F	M	F	M	F	M	F
Four-room													
5	O	23	31	3	11	0	0	4	1	12	5	0	7
	N	21	23	4	11	0	0	5	5	9	3	0	4
	A	17	29	1	15	0	1	4	6	5	3	0	7
	H	16	24	3	14	0	0	3	7	7	0	0	7
6	O	18	22	9	7	8	4	0	0	2	8	0	0
	N	15	19	6	11	8	4	0	0	2	9	0	0
	A	15	19	14	8	8	3	1	0	3	9	0	0
	H	15	21	9	12	7	4	1	0	3	9	0	0
Two-room													
5	O	14	25	4	10	0	0	1	5	4	10	0	0
	N	23	24	6	11	0	0	4	5	4	7	0	0
	A	16	19	3	11	0	0	5	6	3	8	0	0
	H	15	25	3	13	0	0	4	3	2	12	0	0
6	O	19	15	6	7	7	0	2	3	3	8	4	0
	N	18	11	7	6	8	0	0	2	3	7	5	0
	A	20	13	12	9	8	0	0	3	3	8	4	0
	H	15	11	7	7	8	0	0	1	1	9	2	3

[a] Transition = Comments on progress between objects, for example, from the hat she is going to the chair.
[b] Temporal = Either "now we are going to the chair," "and then we go . . . ," or "past the chair she went to before," and so on.

"I." "It" was used occasionally, and "you" was only used in the four-room house by 6-year-old children, and by 6-year-old boys in the two-room house.

Secondary Reference

The data are summarized in Table 7-10. The predominant term used by all children for second reference to an object was "it." Although "you," "she," "this," "that," "the," and "a" were recorded, the incidence of these forms was limited. Such forms were restricted in their use to a few particular children, rather than being occasionally employed by all the children.

Table 7-10. Secondary Naming/Anaphora

Age	Category	You M	You F	She M	She F	It M	It F	This M	This F	That M	That F	The M	The F	A M	A F
Four-room															
5	O	0	0	0	0	2	8	0	0	1	0	3	7	0	0
	N	0	0	2	0	5	6	0	0	1	0	2	7	1	0
	A	1	0	0	0	4	9	0	0	4	0	3	6	0	1
	H	1	0	1	1	1	6	1	1	2	0	1	4	0	0
6	O	5	0	0	1	28	25	1	0	9	1	2	2	0	0
	N	4	0	0	2	31	26	1	0	1	3	2	1	1	0
	A	3	0	0	4	26	23	1	2	3	2	3	2	1	1
	H	3	0	11	8	20	19	1	1	1	3	0	1	0	0
Two-room															
5	O	0	0	1	0	1	8	0	0	0	1	7	10	0	0
	N	0	0	0	1	5	4	0	0	2	1	2	3	1	2
	A	0	0	1	2	2	7	0	0	3	1	2	6	0	0
	H	0	0	0	5	0	7	0	0	0	2	2	4	0	0
6	O	4	1	1	1	33	36	1	0	1	1	6	5	4	1
	N	4	0	1	0	33	32	0	0	3	1	4	1	6	0
	A	4	0	8	11	23	29	2	0	0	4	3	4	6	0
	H	4	0	13	20	21	18	1	0	1	0	3	5	5	0

General Discussion

Within the broad outlines described, children did not tend to discriminate between the type of objects they were describing. Therefore, although children are selective in type of terms they employ, by and large this selectivity does not extend to distinctions about the animacy or "naturalness" of the forms they are describing. This fact would seem at first glance to run counter to earlier claims, and to the expectations following from them. However, it seems clear that in general the children are employing complex and often appropriate (some might say sophisticated) discourse devices to convey the necessary information.

There appears in general to be a lack of correspondence in the use of the linguistic expression in relation to the preferences in the choice of items. This may suggest that with the latter carrying effective ostensive definition the need to make linguistic adjustments to the category of object described is lost. That is, the status of the object being referred to is made clear by moving the doll to it. On this interpretation the children seem to use a pragmatic operating principle in doing this descriptive task which says something like: tend to pick referents in the middle of the room first, especially the inanimate ones and don't worry about the referring expressions you use to refer to them for the hearer (since she can see the referents next to the doll anyway). This seems to reduce, if not eliminate, the need to vary the linguistic means available to place the referent in context, given that the status of the referent is already clear and certain. This in turn casts doubt on the need to contrast high/low deixis with spatial deixis. Rather it fits the pattern of the earlier argument that what animacy in association with spatial deixis is doing is reinforcing in certain contexts the direction of the hearer's search for an appropriate candidate referent. What the structure of these "certain contexts" might be is still unclear although it would seem that uncertainty and lack of gestural information are likely to be important components. We would also expect (as in most discourse situations) that the possibility of error in interpreting the referring expression would play a part. In particular it could be expected that there might, on occasion, be a conflict in interpreting the available spatial and animacy cues. Can the latter be placed in opposition? Possibly not, in the normal way of discourse. It may be that there is a saliency hierarchy that focuses the hearer on one parameter rather than another. (For some discussion of a "hierarchy of animacy" and its interaction with other parameters such as definiteness, see Comrie, 1981). As implied earlier, a candidate for the organizing basis of such a hierarchy could be the degree of uncertainty as to the speaker's intended referent. If so, we might expect it to interact with the modality of the utterance, that is the expression to the hearer of the degree of certainty and commitment of the speaker to the content of the utterance. Compare, for example, the difference in likelihood of the hearer attending to the spatial or animacy cues in interpreting "this" in the following two questions: "What must I call this?" versus "What might I call this?" Informal observations with adults suggest that they are more likely to respond to the former using animacy cues and to the latter using spatial ones. At best these are speculative observations, but they do at least suggest that there is more of interest to explore in such data.

A question arises from the results reported here: Are they purely linguistic processes or are they dependent on more general cognitive ones? In order to refer to an object it is clearly necessary to have some conception of the possible continued existence of that object. That is, for linguistic reference to be more than a labeling response to a present stimulus, out of sight must not be out of mind. Most of the cognitive discussions of such object permanence have been couched in spatial terms (cf. Bower, 1979; Piaget, 1955). Gelman and Spelke (1981) provide an interesting discussion of the possibility of using the distinction between animate and inanimate objects as the basis for the development of object permanence. Their suggestions would certainly be consistent with the view advanced here that the young child coming to early language use, and hence deixis, will be likely first to focus on animate properties of the referent. Gelman and Spelke's arguments would suggest that the results reported here have their genesis in more general cognitive strategies, and not purely linguistic ones. They also indicate a need to study further exactly which animacy cues are being used when, much as earlier studies have done for spatial cues.

One final point arising out of these results justifies brief comment. Despite the qualifications properly advanced by Atkinson (1982), there seems to be a very widely held assumption in discussions of language acquisition that children do not confuse major semantic categories (see Bowerman, 1981, for some fascinating qualifications to this view). This amounts to a tacit belief that children do not need to unlearn any significant part of their semantic acquisition. Of course talking of "unlearning" seems to presuppose a view of the developmental process which is defined in terms of the adult endpoint; in itself a debatable view unless severely qualified. More pointedly still, such otherwise diverse positions as those held by Bever (1970), McNamara (1972), Slobin (1980), and Wexler and Culicover (1980) all seem to assume that there is some mechanism whereby basic conceptual/perceptual categories get mapped into semantic ones. These in turn form the foundation for their (different) views of the mechanism of syntactic development. These accounts do not make clear what would count as "the confusing of major semantic categories." It would obviously be possible to interpret results of developmental strategies where the categories of animacy and space overlap as showing that such confusion has taken place. If so, then this shared assumption would appear incorrect. However, given that such "confusion" is likely to be rare if restricted to the domain of normal deixis, when other contextual features such as concomitant gesture is taken into account, the basic assumption is less threatened. On this view, normal deixis is more likely to "fuse" than "confuse" such semantic categories as space and animacy.

As for whether any unlearning is seen to be necessary, it is currently a moot point. One possibility is that the interaction of categories is conditioning language change. Another possibility, not necessarily opposed to the latter, is that the mechanism by which both are used in a deitic manner may in turn be conditioned by the interaction with linguistic mood. Rather than unlearning then, this suggests that more learning—of the more complex contextualizing system—is the appropriate developmental expectation. This expectation is consistent with the findings of Karmiloff-Smith (1979) and Hickmann (1980) that there is a progression across age in the discourse functions that the same linguistic form (e.g., definite article or demonstrative) may have. They show that intralinguistic uses of such expressions in the creation of referents (i.e., using them anaphorically, not just deictically) are a relatively late development. Hickmann in particular presents data relevant to the content of the present paper in showing that both animacy, and participation in speech events, play a role in the cohesive properties of children's narrative discourse. Karmiloff-Smith and Hickmann present their evidence of old words learning new tricks over an age range which is similar to that addressed in the present paper. If this parallelism is not an accident then perhaps the new tricks do not so much involve new, or at least more involved, linguistic properties (e.g., controlling distinctions of space, animacy, and class membership), as learning to control these properties in contexts whose functions are socially different and perhaps more complex. For instance the idea that deixis might be interpreted as 'the force with which the listener is asked to attend to the referent' might be reinterpreted as having to do with social distance involving intimacy/solidarity, e.g., 'get *that* cat out of here' said in reference to a proximal cat, where the spatial deictic import is overridden by the speaker's 'attitude' toward the cat. Does this shift in interpretation from a more psycholinguistic to a more sociolinguistic principle have ontogenetic consequences and, if so, how and where? Learning how to determine which are the prior organizing principles and how they interact in such instances may be the key to deeper understanding of children's discourse.

Conclusion

The results of this study support the notion that children's communicative use of language is rooted in the situation of the utterance. Nevertheless, as suggested in the introduction it is not necessarily the case that we have to have an independent theory of context in order to understand the process of development. Rather what we can study with profit is the acquisition and use of the devices that language provides through deixis of focusing the hearer's attention on the intended referent. We have seen here that children do use the traditional deictic devices of ostensive gesture and spatial contrast, and that these interact with their use of animacy. The implications of these findings, as discussed above, are that instead of acquiring language in terms of discrete "pure" semantic categories, the child's organizing framework is provided by the functional interaction in natural communicative contexts between the child's available cognitive structures and the syntactic devices (e.g., deictic ones) that the language provides.

References

Atkinson, M. (1982). *Explanations in the study of child language development.* Cambridge: Cambridge University Press.
Bever, T. G. (1970). The cognitive basis of linguistic structures. In J. R. Hayes (Ed.), *Cognition and the development of language.* New York.
Bower, T. G. R. (1979). *Human development.* San Francisco: Freeman.
Bowerman, M. (1981). The child's expression of meaning: Expanding relationships

among lexicon, syntax and morphology. *Annual of the New York Academy of Sciences, 379,* 172–189.

Bruner, J. S. (1974). From communication to language—A psychological perspective. *Cognition, 3,* 255–287.

Clark, E. V. (1978). From gesture to word: On the natural history of deixis in language acquisition. In J. S. Bruner & A. Garton (Eds.), *Human growth and development.* Oxford: Oxford University Press.

Comrie, B. (1981). *Language universals and linguistic typology.* Oxford: Blackwell.

de Villers, P. A., & de Villers, J. G. (1974). On this, that and the other: Nonegocentrism in very young children. *Journal of Experimental Child Psychology, 18,* 438–447.

Gelman, R., & Spelke, E. (1981). The development of thoughts about animate and inanimate objects: Implications for research on social cognition. In J. H. Flavell & L. Ross (Eds.), *Social cognitive development.* Cambridge: Cambridge University Press.

Hickmann, M. (1980). Creating referents in discourse: A developmental analysis of linguistic cohesion. *Papers from the 16th meeting of the Chicago Linguistic Society.* Chicago: Chicago Linguistic Society.

Jarvella, R. J., & Klein, W. (Eds.). (1982). *Speech, place and action: Studies in deixis and related topics.* New York: Wiley.

Karmiloff-Smith, A. (1979). *A functional approach to child language: A study of determiners and reference.* Cambridge: Cambridge University Press.

Kirsner, R. S. (1979). Deixis in discourse: An exploratory quantitative study of the modern Dutch demonstrative adjectives. In T. Givon (Ed.), *Syntax and semantics Vol. 12: Discourse and syntax.* New York: Academic Press.

Levelt, W. J. M. (1982). Linearization in describing spatial networks. In S. Peters & E. Saarinen (Eds.), *Processes, beliefs and questions.* Amsterdam: Reidel.

Linde, C., & Labov, W. (1975). Spatial networks as a site for the study of language and thought. *Language, 51,* 924–939.

Lyons, J. (1975). Deixis as a source of reference. In E. Keeman (Ed.), *Formal semantics and natural language.* Cambridge: Cambridge University Press.

Lyons, J. (1977). *Semantics* (Vol. 2). Cambridge: Cambridge University Press.

McGinn, C. (1981). The mechanism of reference. *Synthese, 49,* 157–186.

McNamara, J. (1972). Cognitive basis of language learning in infants. *Psychological Review, 79,* 1–13.

Piaget, J. (1955). *The construction of reality in the child.* London: Routledge & Kegan Paul.

Slobin, D. (1980). The repeated path between transparency and opacity in language. In U. Bellugi & M. Studdert-Kenedy (Eds.), *Signed and spoken language: Biological constraints on linguistic form.* Weinheim: Verlag Chamie.

Tanz, C. (1980). *Studies in the acquisition of deictic terms.* Cambridge: Cambridge University Press.

Wales, R. J. (1979). Deixis. In P. Fletcher & M. Garman (Eds.), *Language acquisition.* Cambridge: Cambridge University Press.

Wexler, K., & Culicover, P. (1980). *Formal principles of language acquisition.* Cambridge, MA: MIT Press.

8. Discourse Development in Atypical Language Learners

Sandy Friel-Patti and Gina Conti-Ramsden

The observation and analyses of pathological phenomena often yield greater insight into the processes of the organism than that of the normal. (Goldstein, 1939)

During the last two decades, the study of language development in children has experienced a broadening of perspective from an emphasis on form to a concern with function. There has also been a move from the analysis of the speaker to the analysis of the communicative dyad. This change in focus has brought about new methodologies, issues, and problems that are the current concern of both psychologists and linguists alike.

One area of potential impact for the study of the development of language use is conversational discourse. We have chosen to focus on the atypical population of language-impaired children because the information provided by such an approach not only has clinical relevance for the assessment and remediation of language impairment, but also has broader implications for the nature of normally developing processes and language systems in general. This chapter is divided into four major topic areas: (a) The population of language-impaired children is defined and the characteristics of this group are discussed; (b) the available research on the discourse abilities of preschool and school-aged language-impaired children is discussed from a methodological as well as a developmental perspective; (c) the discourse skills of language-impaired children are considered with particular emphasis on the segmentation of the verbal/nonverbal stream of behavior; and (d) the chapter concludes with a discussion of directions for future research.

Description of the Language-Impaired Population

The population of language-impaired children is a heterogeneous one, generally described as demonstrating a linguistic system which, in certain significant aspects, is different from that of their normal language-learning peers. The clinical entity of language impairment in children is most often defined by exclusion: that is, language impairment is a developmental disorder characterized by the late appearance and/or slow development of comprehension and/or expression of spoken language in a group of children who do *not* have hearing loss, mental retardation, or emotional disorder (Leonard, 1979; Stark & Tallal, 1981). Historically, various terms have been used to refer to this group of children, including "congenital aphasia" (Eisenson, 1972), "delayed language" (Lee, 1966), "language disordered" (Rees, 1973), "deviant language" (Leonard, 1972), and "specific language deficit" (Stark & Tallal, 1981) (for a review of the nomenclature see Bloom & Lahey, 1978). In keeping with the more recent work in this area, the term "language impairment" will be used throughout this chapter.

Further complication arises when one attempts to transform both the exclusion and inclusion factors for the population of language-impaired children into a set of measurement criteria. Particularly problematic is the measurement of severity, in that there is no single commonly accepted measure or battery of measures for assessing language delay. Moreover, there is no consensus concerning the descriptive labels of mild, moderate, and severe language impairment. As a result, some researchers have included in their experimental population children with either expressive or receptive delays (Gallagher & Darnton, 1978), while others have included only children with delayed expressive language (Conti, 1982; Rosenblum & Stephens, 1981; Friel-Patti, 1976, 1977, 1980). Still others have required that each child have both receptive and expressive language delays (Prinz & Ferrier, 1983; Van Kleeck & Frankel, 1981), while a few have not specified the nature of the delay (Snyder, 1976, 1978; Nettelbladt, 1982). It is not surprising that different and oftentimes conflicting results have been reported for this mixed population.

Traditionally, the criterial attribute of language impairment has been a delay in the production of age-appropriate syntax, thereby defining the population on one aspect of expressive language skills exclusively. Recently, Rizzo and Stephens (1981) found that their subject group originally defined by expressive delay only had varying degrees of delay in the comprehension of language in addition to the lack of age-appropriate syntax. In a recent effort to devise a standard approach to the selection of language-impaired children for a rather large research project examining sensory and perceptual functioning of the language-impaired subjects, Stark and Tallal (1981) developed a strict set of criteria to define "specific language impairment" that involved set levels of receptive and expressive language, hearing, intellectual ability, and neurological, behavioral, and emotional status as well as reading ability. The intention was to select children who would be most representative of the clinical population of language-impaired school children who did not have any accompanying deficits. A total of 132 children was referred by speech-language clinicians as appropriate for enrollment in the project based on broadly defined criteria made available to the clinicians. After further evaluation by the investigators, less than one-third of these children met the more precisely defined criteria employed in the project. Therefore, the criteria used by Stark and Tallal described a tightly specified subgroup of children with language impairment rather than a representative sample of language-impaired children enrolled for treatment. Stark and Tallal reported difficulty in implementing a set of criteria related to severity of the language impairment because different expressive and receptive tests assess aspects of different language functioning. As a result, the group of children selected for the study was not homogeneous with respect to the manifestation of language impairment. Thus, the results are severely limited in generality.

What we have then, is a double-edged sword. Studies with either loose or different criteria of language impairment often produce conflicting results. Studies with strictly defined criteria may yield results that are not easily generalized to the population of language-impaired children. Given the heterogeneity of the population it may be misleading then to have an all-encompassing classificatory term such as "language impairment." Leonard (1979, p. 229) proposed that language impairment "should no longer be viewed as a strictly linguistic deficit, but rather as a deficit associated with a delay in the development of a number of representational abilities." Leonard based this conclusion on findings that indicate that language-impaired children manifest deficits in nonlinguistic representational skills including symbolic play (Brown, Redmond, Bass, Liebergott, & Swope, 1975; Lovell, Hoyle, & Siddall, 1968) and imagery (deAjuriaguerra, Jaeggi, Guignard, Kocher, Marquard, Roth, & Schmid, 1965; Inhelder, 1966).

Once the criteria for the group of children to be studied have been set, the question of with whom the language-impaired child should be compared arises. In the 1960s, comparison studies of normal and language-impaired children of equivalent age were prevalent. In two early studies of the syntax of language-impaired and normally developing children, both investigators interpreted their findings to suggest that language-impaired children were qualitatively different from normal language-learning children of the same chronological age (Lee, 1966; Menyuk, 1964). That is, language-impaired children were found to employ syntactic features in their speech that were thought to be unique to that population. However, subsequent reanalysis of these data has led Leonard (1979, p. 208) to conclude that "even on a nonstatistical, descriptive basis it is difficult to find support for a qualitative difference between the two groups of children." Indeed, the overwhelming conclusion is that language-impaired children's syntactic usage is similar to that of younger normal children (Leonard, 1979).

The comparison of language-impaired children with normal language-learning children of the same language stage as measured by mean length of utterance (MLU) represented an important methodological refinement. The findings of the studies that made use of this comparison revealed on a number of dimensions (phonologically, syntactically, semantically, and in play interaction) language-impaired children performed similarly to younger, normally developing children of the same MLU level (Folger & Leonard, 1978; Leonard, Bolders, & Miller, 1976;

Leonard, Steckol, & Schwartz, 1978; Lovell et al., 1968). The pragmatic skills employed by language-impaired children are also found in the repertoire of normally
developing children. However, the language-impaired children have been found to
use these pragmatic skills less frequently and with somewhat less flexibility than
their normal counterparts (Snyder, 1976). In addition, for many language-impaired
children these skills have been acquired at a later stage of development. That is,
in some instances the language-impaired children failed to use pragmatic features
employed by normal language-learning children at a comparable MLU level (Conti,
1982; Conti-Ramsden & Friel-Patti, 1983, in press; Gallagher, 1977). Furthermore,
the language-impaired children lacked "linguistic creativity," in that they appeared
restricted in the use of syntactic forms and semantic notions for communicative
purposes.

A few recent studies have contributed support to the idea that language impairment is more than a general delay in linguistic abilities. Friel-Patti and Harris (1982)
compared language-impaired children with both their chronological age-mates and
their MLU matches. They found that the social interaction of language-impaired
children was neither like that of their chronological age-mates nor like that of
their MLU matches, but fell between the two groups. Thus, though the two groups
of children were matched for productive language ability, their social interaction
was different. Van Kleeck and Frankel (1981) studied the revision behaviors of a
group of language-impaired children and then identified a point in normal language development where such behaviors begin to occur. Kamhi (1981) compared
language-impaired children with both their MLU-matched controls and mental-
age- (MA) matched peers. He found that the nonlinguistic symbolic and conceptual
abilities of language-impaired children were better than those of their MLU-matched
controls but poorer than those of their MA-matched peers.

Current Level of Knowledge Concerning Discourse Development
in Atypical Language Learners

Research with language-impaired children has typically lagged behind that of
normally developing children and has often been fragmentary. This resulted from
the fact that investigations with atypical language learners tend to look at skills
in particular tasks at a particular moment in time rather than looking at patterns
of behaviors and development over time.

At the one-word stage of development, the focus of study has been the performative and presuppositional skills of language-impaired children as they compare
with those of normal language-learning children of the same linguistic ability.
Snyder (1976, 1978) developed a task to elicit declarative performatives, imperative
performatives, and encoding of the most informative element in the context. She
found that language-impaired children were different from normal language-learning
children of the same language stage in their pragmatic use of language. The language-impaired children appeared deficient in that they had difficulty generating

linguistic performatives, encoding the most informative contextual element, and disengaging themselves from the immediate context. Thus, despite the fact that the groups of language-impaired and normal language-learning children were matched for level of linguistic performance and vocabulary development, and despite the fact that the two groups were similar in their nonverbal use of communicative behaviors expressing declarative and imperative functions, the language-impaired children were far less likely to express these intentions linguistically. However, Rowan and Leonard (1981) repeated Snyder's task but failed to replicate her findings. In their study, Rowan and Leonard (1981) found that the language-impaired children's presuppositional and performative skills were highly similar to those of normal language-learning children of the same language stage. They explain the discrepancy between their results and Snyder's in terms of the different characteristics of the subjects used in the two studies. Once again then, methodological considerations concerning subject description have clouded our knowledge in this area.

Beyond the one-word stage there has been little developmental emphasis to the research with language-impaired children. The approach to the study of discourse abilities of preschool language-impaired children has been to select a group of language-impaired children and compare them with their chronological age-mates and/or MLU matches. No systematic attempt has been made to discover developmental patterns in the language-impaired population. In addition, research with this population has been limited in scope (only a few aspects of discourse have been examined) and limited by the methodological problems previously discussed.

Gallagher and Darnton (1978) examined the abilities of language-impaired children and normal language-learning children of the same language stage to revise messages for their listener. They found that although the language-impaired children revised their utterances in response to listener misunderstanding, the revision strategies they used were different from those found in normal children and were not systematically related to their levels of structural knowledge. That is, the forms of the repairs produced by the two groups of children differed significantly. The language-impaired children were sensitive to the listener requests for clarification, but there were nonetheless qualitative differences in the nature of language-impaired children's response strategies when compared to those of normal language-learning children of the same language stage. Unlike normal language-learning children of the same language stage, language-impaired children responded primarily by revising the linguistic form of their message. Similarly, Gale, Liebergott, and Griffin (1981) found that language-impaired children's request for clarification patterns were qualitatively different from those of normal language-learning children of the same language stage. Not only did language-impaired children use significantly more nonverbal requests for clarification, but when using verbal requests, employed a restricted number of linguistic forms. Since requests for clarification interrupt the flow of the conversation and place constraints on the speaker's response, it would seem that the language-impaired children are less assertive in conversation than their counterparts (Fey & Leonard, 1983).

In contrast, Van Kleeck and Frankel (1981) found that language-impaired children's focus and substitution operations used to relate their utterances to antecedent discourse were not different from those used by younger normally developing children. Similarly, Rom and Bliss (1981) found no qualitative differences in the use of speech acts in discourse by language-impaired and normal language-learning children of the same language stage. Both groups of children appeared to have highly similar repertoires of speech acts.

Recently, in examining mother-child dialogues, Conti (1982) and Conti-Ramsden and Friel-Patti (1983, in press) have found both qualitative and quantitative differences in the discourse abilities of language-impaired children. Conti (1982) and Conti-Ramsden and Friel Patti (1983) found quantitative differences in the amount of dialogue participation of language-impaired children and normal language-learning children of the same language stage. Specifically, the language-impaired children initiated dialogue and introduced topics less often than did the normal control children. Conti (1982) and Conti-Ramsden and Friel-Patti (in press) also found qualitative differences in the type of responses language-impaired children use in dialogues with their mothers. Language-impaired children had more inadequate and ambiguous responses to mothers' initiations than did the normal language-learning children of the same language stage. Similar results were found by Brinton and Fujiki (1982) in child-to-child interaction. In addition, Geller and Wollner (1976) compared the speech act repertoires of three language-impaired children with those of age-matched subjects reported by Dore (1977). The language-impaired subjects were markedly deficient in the range of speech acts they employed.

These findings suggest that language-impaired children may well be not only quantitatively and qualitatively different from normal language-learning children of the same language stage, but differentially delayed in both the acquisition of structural aspects of language as well as the development of communicative intention. These findings have two major implications for our conceptualization of different language subsystems. First, it would appear that structural aspects of language such as syntax and phonology may be based upon different sets of skills than communicative aspects of language such as pragmatics and discourse. Thus, children may acquire the rules of English grammar but fail to participate successfully in dialogue with their mothers. Indeed, this is the sort of children described by Blank, Gessner, and Esposito (1979), Conti (1982), and Conti-Ramsden and Friel-Patti (1983, in press). Second, it appears that at least for the subsystems of pragmatics and discourse there may be a need to point to the possible heterogeneity as well as independence of the various skills comprising the subsystems. Thus, quantitative as well as qualitative differences may be found in language-impaired children's abilities to participate in discourse (Conti, 1982; Conti-Ramsden & Friel-Patti, 1981, in press). In addition, depending on which pragmatic skill is under consideration, one may find qualitative differences (Gallagher & Darnton, 1978) or one may not (Rom & Bliss, 1981; Van Kleeck & Frankel, 1981). Consequently, the results obtained for a particular skill within the subsystem may not be generalized to the rest.

Donahue, Pearl, and Bryan (1980) investigated school-age language-impaired/

learning-disabled children's understanding of conversational rules for initiating the repair of a communicative breakdown. The language-impaired and normal children, enrolled in grades 1 through 8 assumed the listener role in a referential communication task based on varying degrees of informational adequacy. The language-impaired children were less likely to request clarification of inadequate messages. Although the language-impaired children produced fewer requests, an examination of the types of requests they did produce indicated that the linguistic skills needed to appropriately request clarification were well within the children's productive language abilities. Donahue et al. interpreted this finding as evidence of a deficit in the development of pragmatic competence rather than a limitation of linguistic structure. In other words, cooperative listeners are expected to indicate when a topic has been inadequately specified and the language-impaired/learning-disabled children in this study did not do so. These results suggest that the development of pragmatic competence involves social knowledge at least as much as knowledge of linguistic structure. In a follow-up investigation, Donahue (1981) examined the pragmatic competence of language-impaired children on a task that permitted the separate assessment of linguistic and social knowledge. Language-impaired and normal children made requests of four imaginary listeners varying in the dimensions of intimacy and power/social status. The data corroborated previous studies reporting that school-age children vary politeness of their requests according to the social status and familiarity of their listener (Ervin-Tripp, 1977; James, 1978; Mitchell-Kernan & Kernan, 1977; Piche, Rubin, & Michlin, 1978). The language-impaired children did not differ from the normal group on the number of different request forms produced indicating an adequate linguistic repertoire for the task. The major finding of this study was that the language-impaired boys produced a smaller variety of persuasive appeals and fewer appropriate request strategies even though their linguistic repertoire was not deficient. Donahue hypothesized that the language-impaired boys were less likely to use their full potential of persuasive skills when interacting with familiar listeners because of the social rejection these children experience. That is, their unpopularity with peers contributes to a lack of social knowledge, which in turn inhibits pragmatic development. Thus, the pragmatic deficit seemed attributable to inadequate social knowledge rather than to linguistic performance. Even more recently, however, Donahue, Pearl, and Bryan (1982) presented results that indicate that the productive language deficits may be sufficiently significant to interfere with even the informal and elliptical conversations characteristic of communication among peers and family members. In this study, the researchers examined syntactic proficiency of the language-impaired/learning disabled children during a task requiring them to convey information to a listener. It appears that the acquisition of pragmatic competence does indeed involve the mutual development of social knowledge and linguistic knowledge in school-aged language-impaired children. This in turn suggests that the present techniques for assessing linguistic skills in these children may be too limited.

   Narrative discourse abilities have also been examined in school-age language-impaired children. Graybeal (1981) compared the ability of language-impaired children and their chronological age-mates to recall two stories read to them. She found that despite the fact that both groups of children had the vocabulary and structural linguistic skills necessary to understand the stories, the language-impaired group recalled significantly fewer ideas than the normal controls did. Nonetheless, the two groups of children did not differ in the ordering of the story information, the amount of plausible information added to the story, or the number of errors in recall. It is possible that memory constraints may account for the language observed in these children. Johnston (1982) presented a case study of a language-impaired girl who had patterns of recall and story construction that were not similar to the patterns usually found in children of her age.

These two studies suggest that school-age language-impaired children may have difficulties with other types of discourse aside from conversation. They also suggest that different types of discourse may be interrelated to systems such as memory and cognition in very specific ways. Further research in this area should help us better understand the nature of language impairment as well as discourse development in general.

It appears then that the problems preschool language-impaired children have in conversations persist through the school-age years. Comparisons of the research done with preschool children and that done with school-age children are problematic. Research with preschool language-impaired is usually done by comparing them with younger normal language-learning children of the same linguistic ability, while research with school-age language-impaired children is done by comparing them with their chronological age-mates. Nonetheless, it is evident that the study of language impairment through the school years continues to focus our attention on the kinds of interrelations that exist among the different language subsystems, their internal organization as well as their interaction with other systems such as memory and cognition. As children grow older language becomes more and more important for survival. Language for the school-age child is not only a tool for communication but a social tool as well.

Analyzing Discourse Skills in Atypical Populations: Segmentation of the Verbal/Nonverbal Stream

A conversation encompasses more than what is said in words; the nonverbal accompaniments to the verbal dialogue help to convey much of the intended meaning as well as regulate the flow of listener-speaker exchanges. An examination of children's conversational abilities involves a careful consideration of the relationship between the verbal and nonverbal elements of child discourse. Most researchers interested in nonverbal behaviors now recognize that such a system of communication is simultaneously a biological phenomenon with deep evolutionary roots involving the expression of emotions, and a learned phenomenon that is organized to support and interact with language (Buck, 1982). A central assumption of such a dichotomy is that voluntary and nonvoluntary nonverbal behavior can be distinguished. Ekman (1979), for example, has presented a number of characteristics to differentiate spontaneous and voluntary expression in the distinction between emotional and conversational facial expression. The "spontaneous" nonverbal behavior associated with the expression of emotion is distinct from the "symbolic" nonverbal behavior at the level of intentionality (Dittmann, 1972; Druckman, Rozelle, & Baxter, 1982). Spontaneous communication is based upon a biologically shared signal system, the elements of which are signs that bear a natural relationship to the referent. The signal system is thought to be spontaneous and nonpropositional, in which the content involves motivational/emotional states. Symbolic communication, on the other hand, is based upon a socially defined set of symbols that has an arbitrary but conventional relationship with their referents. Symbolic communication involves the transmission of propositions that are intentional and voluntary, although the use of these symbols need not be at a conscious level. Buck (1982) views human communication as the simultaneous occurrence of the two streams involving different sorts of behavior. The spontaneous stream is commonly associated with "nonverbal communication" or "body language." These complex processes normally have emerged as interdependent functions by the end of the first 18 months of life, if not earlier (Lewis & Rosenblum, 1978) and continue to differentiate throughout childhood and adolescence (Breger, 1974; Saarni, 1982).

The typical data collection methodology used in studies of conversational dialogues includes the observation of naturally occurring behaviors. The goal of observational research is to gather samples of behavior that are representative of the subject's actual response repertoire. The adequacy of these samples depends in part on a series of decisions made by the investigator. The collection of performance speech data necessitates decisions on the means of observing and recording (e.g., live observation or videotape and/or audiotape, hidden camera or camera in view, stationary or mobile camera, wide-angle or zoom lens, etc.). The use of a hidden videotape recorder permits unobtrusive observation and the opportunity for repeated viewings of the behaviors under study. Decisions regarding the conditions under which the data are collected include whether to employ a "play with toys" condition and if so, the type of toys to have available. The introduction of toys affects subsequent interaction and dialogue. Similarly, the decision to record a teaching situation where a challenging toy or game is used also alters the data collected. These effects need to be recognized (Conti, 1982) and more fully explored. Decisions concerning the size of room, the placement of furniture, and the time of day when the recording is made also result in differences in the dialogue. Even though the observational method is intended to record the behavioral stream as it naturally occurs, in making each of these decisions, the researcher necessarily introduces examiner selectivity to the observation (Dunbar, 1976; Sackett, Ruppenthal, & Gluck, 1978; Whiting & Whiting, 1973).

Once the data are recorded, they are further filtered in the transcription process. The transcriptions, in fact, are the researcher's data for studies of conversational performance and the transcription process is a selective one that reflects the theoretical goals of the investigator (Keller-Cohen, 1982; Ochs, 1979; Sacks, Schegloff,

& Jefferson, 1974). That is, what is on the transcript influences and constrains the generalizations that emerge (see Keller-Cohen, 1982, Ochs, 1979, for a detailed discussion of transcription and theory). Of particular importance in the study of children's conversational discourse are the decisions made concerning the children's behavior and contextual notations. One of the major advances in the child language literature in the past 15 years has been the appreciation of the importance of non-verbal behavior among young children. The use of context has served as an interpretive aid for the child-language researcher (Bloom, 1970; Brown, 1973; Keller-Cohen, 1982) as well as for the child (Ervin-Tripp, 1973). Children can use gestures, body orientation, eye gaze, and/or facial expression in combination with verbal behavior to extend or support the meaning of their words. They can also use these nonverbal behaviors as an alternative to verbal expression (Bates, Camaioni, & Volterra, 1975; Carter, 1979).

When studying atypical populations such as language-impaired children, one is confronted, much like the psychologist studying normal language development, with the problems inherent in data collection as well as transcription methodologies. Moreover, researchers interested in atypical language development have had to face an additional set of problems characteristic of the population of language-impaired children. In the data-gathering phase, problems arise given the large range of performance of language-impaired children with changes in the conditions under which their behavior is observed. Conti (1982) found that differences observed in mother-child dialogues with language-impaired children and normal language-learning children of the same language stage would not hold across changes in toy conditions. She studied two experimental conditions: a free play condition where toys appropriate for the children's ages were scattered throughout a playroom and, a teaching condition where only one toy (selected to be somewhat challenging for the children in the study) was placed in the playroom. She found that the number of turns exchanged by the normal dyads did not vary across the two experimental conditions. Conversely, dyads of mothers and their language-impaired children had significantly greater number of turn exchanges in the teaching situation when compared with the free play situation. Thus, the pressure to communicate exerted by the teaching situation differentially affected the two sets of dyads. Consequently, caution must be exercised when interpreting the results of language-impaired dyads in specific situations as they may not be representative of the full repertoire for the dyad. Indeed, the results on one condition alone may seriously underestimate the communicative abilities of these dyads.

Similarly, Conti (1982) found that the stability of the children's style of interaction from situation to situation was also different. It was found that language-impaired children, unlike normal language-learning children of the same linguistic ability, responded differently to mothers' initiations in the two experimental conditions. Language-impaired dyads had significantly fewer instances of communication breakdowns in the teaching condition than in the free play condition. Specifically, language-impaired children had fewer inadequate responses and more adequate responses in the teaching situation. Thus, while normal language-learning children's style of interaction was stable across conditions, the style of interaction of language-impaired children was not. Once again, conflicting results could be easily obtained with the population of language-impaired children when there were slight changes in the conditions under which their behavior was observed.

Probably the most dramatic example of language-impaired children's wide range of performance when compared to normal language-learning children of similar linguistic ability is found in the area of topic shifting. Further analyses of Conti (1982) revealed that normal language-learning children behaviorally shift the focus of the interaction between 0% and 12% of the time, depending on the experimental condition. Comparatively, language-impaired children behaviorally changed the topic of the interaction between 11% and 69% of the time. These are hardly comparable ranges of behavior.

The aforementioned discussion has been limited to one aspect of data collection, namely the choice of the number and type of toys to be placed in the playroom. Nonetheless, it is felt that the effect on language-impaired children's performance will be similar when other aspects of data collection are manipulated. It appears that there are variations in the behavior of normal language-learning children but these do not extend beyond certain limits. As for the language-impaired population we are only beginning to realize how different and varied their performance is and where their limits might be.

In the transcription phase, problems arise given the range of intelligibility of language-impaired children's speech. Many language-impaired children demonstrate severe phonological problems that greatly interfere with the intelligibility of their productive language (Compton, 1970; Oller, 1973, 1975; Haas, 1963; Lorentz, 1974; Ingram, 1976). Thus, transcriptions of language-impaired children's verbal utterances may involve part or whole utterances and/or turns that are unintelligible to the transcriber. But, this also occurs when studying normally developing children. So what is so special about language-impaired children? The answer, once again, lies in the range of performance of atypical language learners.

During subject selection procedures, it became apparent to Conti (1982) that many of the language-impaired children had to be eliminated given the high percentage of unintelligible utterances in their speech. Indeed, a conscious effort was made to try to match the speech intelligibility of normal and language-impaired children. For the 28 children studied, an average of 7.5% (range 0% to 27%) of all utterances from normal language-learning children were unintelligible. Similarly, an average of 6.3% (range 0% to 30%) of all utterances from the language-impaired children were unintelligible. But, this group of language-impaired children was chosen because they were quite intelligible. What about all those other children who had to be eliminated from the study? Our clinical experience with language-impaired children suggests that this group of atypical language learners can range from being completely intelligible to being unintelligible 80% of the time. Thus, unlike research with normal language-learning children, analyses of language-impaired children's discourse may begin with very limited information from the verbal mode.

It is our view that there is a need to document not only what is put into the study of discourse development in atypical language learners, but also what is taken out. Only in this way can the issues of comparability and representativeness be discussed and parallels be drawn between normal and atypical discourse development. We have included the transcription guidelines we have developed for our work in the Appendix in order to make explicit the decisions we make about conversational data. We have found it useful to document unintelligibility making use of two rules. First, an unintelligible utterance or portion of an utterance is indicated by five Xs on our transcripts. The transcriber should give an estimate of the length of the unintelligible utterances by making one or more groupings of Xs.

(1)   (Child is playing with Fisher-Price garage elevator)
       JG: XXXXX it up

(2)   (Mother and child are playing with Fisher-Price garage)
       Mother: What is this wheel? (Mother points to handle of elevator)
       KB: XXXXX
       Mother: Hum?
       KB: XXXXX
       Mother: Hum?
       KB: Me!
                     That car (gives car to mother)

(3)   (Child picks up shape slide of the Etch-a-Sketch Skedoodle toy and then shakes the toy)
       KB: Oh, oh XXXXX XXXXX
       Mother: (Mother helps the child to put the slide in)
                     You just have to put it there and pop it in.

Secondly, whenever the transcriber is unsure about the transcription, this is indicated by marking the relevant portion with a coded sign. (For ease of typing our transcripts, we have chosen for our "questionable" code marker to use a non-alphanumeric character on the typewriter keyboard. In the examples to follow the questionable portion is marked with dollar signs ($).) In this way, when the reliability of the transcription is checked by an independent transcriber, if these portions of the transcription are reliable, they are included as part of the data to be analyzed; otherwise, they are excluded from the analysis. In the study by Conti (1982) both normal and language-impaired children had a similar number of questionable utterances. The normal language-learning children had an average of 7.9% (range 0% to 33%) of questionable utterances and the language-impaired children had an average of 10.7% (range 0% to 33%) of questionable utterances.

(4)   (Child goes to Fisher-Price garage, peers in, and starts playing with the elevator platform)
       JG: $ We want go up $
       Mother: Well, turn it over here, let me see.

(5)   (Child takes Leggos out of a box)
       JY: $ I want hook $
       Mother: You want them to hook together?

This approach allows one to describe the type of verbal behavior that has been included in the analysis, but also serves to caution one's conclusion about children's discourse. Take, for example, these two dialogue sequences:

Child: I like airplanes.
              They fly.
              XXXXX XXXXX
Mother: The trucks are big.

Mother: But why not there?
Child: XXXXX XXXXX
Mother: Oh.

In the first sequence, if the purpose of our analysis is to examine topic change then we are in trouble. Did the mother change the topic or was the topic changed by the child in his or her last utterance that we could not understand? In the second sequence, if the purpose of our analysis is to examine children's response adequacy, then again we are faced with a problem. How do we classify this response? Mother's "Oh" utterance does not help disambiguate the child's response, as one could react to an adequate, inadequate, or ambiguous response in this way. By including in the transcript the unintelligible sequences we are reminded later in the analysis that the child said something that was not understood by the transcriber but could have been understood by the child's mother.

The data base available from language-impaired children's discourse is varied and runs the risk of being quite small, and as a consequence, could be an underestimation of the child's abilities to participate in conversation. In the study of atypical populations the question, "What constitutes the data base?," is of utmost importance.

In the segmentation stage where conversational units are identified the issue of what constitutes a "turn" arises. A turn is defined simply by Kaye and Charney (1980) as a string of one or more utterances followed by a pause of 3 S or more or one or more nonverbal acts strung together without a pause. Here again there are problems. What sorts of nonverbal acts constitute a turn in conversation? Should one only include those nonverbal acts that (a) result in a response from the conversational partner (example 6), or (b) stem from the verbal/nonverbal behaviors of the conversational partner (example 7)?

(6)   Nonverbal acts that constitute a turn are enclosed in + +. (Child is playing with an Etch-a-Sketch Skedoodle toy)
       KB: + Draws a picture on the screen +
       Mother: Oh, good girl.
                    Good girl.

(7)   (Child is playing with Etch-a-Sketch Skedoodle toy)
       Mother: Clean it off.
       JY: + Shakes the toy +

If so, what about those nonverbal acts of which the conversational partner is not aware? For example, should the language-impaired child's unsuccessful non-verbal attempts to attract his or her conversational partner's attention not be considered as turns? The problem is basically one of deciding upon the appropriate behavioral criterion. Should a nonverbal turn be categorized based upon criteria established on the inferred intention of the child or should it be categorized based upon criteria on the conversational partner's response to the behaviors? The more reliable and by far the easier route is the latter. However, one cannot help but wonder how much information is lost by the use of this criterion. Psychologists studying normal discourse development are faced with similar problems, but what makes the study of atypical language learners unique is the degree and frequency of occurrence of these problematic behaviors.

Language-impaired children appear to use nonverbal behaviors in conversation with their mothers more often than normal language-learning children of the same language-learning stage (Conti, 1982). Similarly, Gale et al. (1981) found that language-impaired children, when in structured play activity with one of the investigators, produced significantly more nonverbal/behavioral requests for clarification than did normal language-learning children of similar linguistic ability. Thus, within the body of information about language-impaired children's performance in discourse we have significantly more problematic behaviors that are difficult to segment. It may be particularly relevant then to tighten the criteria for the segmentation of the verbal/nonverbal stream produced by language-impaired children. Thus, segmentation of the verbal/nonverbal stream into turns defined by *both* child-based and conversational partner-based criteria will probably result in a more accurate picture of the turn-taking abilities of language-impaired children.

Future Research Directions

Clearly, there are problems involved in the data collection, transcription, and analyses of language-impaired children's discourse skills; their cumulative effect raises questions specific to the population of atypical language learners. Further research with language-impaired children should aim to tighten the methodological decisions. In this way, we can enhance our knowledge of atypical language learners' discourse abilities at a particular point in time as well as across time.

The lack of longitudinal research makes it difficult to compare the developmental profile of a language-impaired child with that of a normal language-learning child. This type of research is sorely needed. Cross-sectional research involving comparisons of language-impaired children with different groups of normal language-learning children is informative but lacks the developmental perspective that is necessary to understand the origins, nature, and conditions for language impairment. The normally developing child acquires a variety of physical, social, cognitive, and language skills across time. Language-impaired children, on the other hand, are described as progressing satisfactorily in most physical, social, and even cognitive skills, while their language development is disrupted. The finding that language-impaired children are deficient in nonlinguistic behaviors requiring related abilities in mental representation has led Leonard (1979) to speculate that the relationship between these abilities and linguistic development is potentially important and merits further study. The research reviewed by Leonard without exception reported that language-impaired children were less skilled than their normally developing age-mates on a number of representational nonlinguistic abilities. Such evidence suggests that language-impaired children's difficulties are not limited to the processing and use of language. The nature of the relationship between linguistic and other representational nonlinguistic skills needs further elaboration. The population of language-impaired children offers a special lens for viewing the relationship between language and cognition. Descriptions of the characteristics of the language-impaired children under study should include measures of speech, hearing, language, communication skills, representational skills such as symbolic play or imagery, intelligence, motor, and emotional status if future clinical and research endeavors are to contribute the needed information. Much like Stark and Tallal (1981), we advocate the development of profiles that describe groups of children with different types and degrees of speech, language, sensory, perceptual, and motor impairments. In this way, it will eventually be possible to identify those profiles and behavioral clusters descriptive of subgroups of language-impaired children.

Cromer (1981a) has suggested that there are undoubtedly subgroups of language-impaired children. He identified two views of cognitive processes that may well contribute to our understanding of language impairment. Short-term memory is an example of a cognitive mechanism, the impairment of which in some groups of children may account for observed language deficits. An alternative view is to study the development of the child's conceptual knowledge and the effect that development has on the acquisition of syntax and semantics. Cromer concluded that it is necessary to consider the interrelationships among all of the components of language in order to understand normal language development and also to develop insight for specific language impaired subgroups. In our efforts to describe profiles of subgroups of language-impaired children, we must be careful not to overlook the individual differences depicted in the heterogeneity of this population. Carefully conducted case studies of children with language deficits could contribute a much needed developmental perspective as these children progress through an intervention program.

In the field of neurolinguistics, studies with clinical populations have long contributed valuable information, most notably in the understanding of the organization of memory, recall, and storage of linguistic information. Currently in the area of child development, we have used linguistic theories to further our understanding of language development, but such a broad-based approach may not be especially useful for those concerned with language impairment in children. What is needed is a systematic attempt to exploit the evidence obtained from language-impaired populations to derive theories for language development. The prevailing hypotheses about impaired processes that contribute to language impairment include deficits in memory, linguistic processing, auditory processing, phonological processing, sequencing, and hierarchical planning (Cromer, 1981b). Each of these, upon careful examination in language-impaired children, could well contribute to our understanding of the conceptual-linguistic system in normally developing children.

Following Cromer's (1981a) lead about subgroups of language-impaired children, it is possible to consider the differences exhibited by language-impaired children with normal cognitive abilities contrasted with those language-impaired children who are also impaired cognitively. In the former group, it is a frequent clinical observation that these children usually "catch up" with their age-mates. The question that remains is what factor(s) contributed to the delay in the first place. Longitudinal studies with these children would help elucidate the relationship between language and cognition and their possible area of independence. Research with language-impaired children who are also impaired cognitively may help us understand the dependent role of cognition and language learning.

Within the area of language impairment itself, it would be useful to compare the performance profiles of children with different types of language impairment, for example, children with expressive language delay only, children with a phonological disorder only, those with receptive language disorders, and those with pragmatic disorders. Subject specification and description need to be made more explicit so that groups of children can be comparable.

Future research can take advantage of the unique opportunity provided by language-impaired children: This group of children with their slow rate of development gives us a gradual and possibly more detailed picture of the steps involved in acquiring discourse skills, steps that may otherwise be missed if we restrict ourselves to the study of normal language-learning children only. A recent experimental approach has recognized that early child communication must involve a consideration of more than vocal/verbal utterances: It must also view the nonverbal elements of communication as being as intrinsic as the verbal (Foster, 1980). We have found that language-impaired children make use of some nonverbal behaviors in conversation more often than normal language-learning children (Conti, 1982; Gale et al. 1981). Thus, the study of language-impaired populations provides us with the opportunity to explore in more depth the relationship between verbal and nonverbal behaviors in communication as well as the general question of the flexibility and adaptiveness of the human communicative system.

Appendix

The aim of the transcription is threefold: (a) to record all speech produced by mother and child, (b) to record the relevant nonverbal behaviors of both participants, and (c) to record information about the context in which the verbal and nonverbal behaviors occur as they relate to turn-taking. For the purposes of this research project, a turn consists of a string of one or more utterances followed by a string of one or more utterances followed by a pause of 3 s or more with or without accompanying gestures, or one or more nonverbal acts strung together without a pause. Thus, nonverbal behaviors consist primarily of actions and gestures that are part of a turn or constitute a turn. Facial expressions, eye gaze behaviors, and fine body movements are not included in the transcription.

Starting a Transcription

The data base consists of videotapes of mother-child dyads. Each videotape is labeled with the child's name, the date of test (DOT), the experimental conditions attempted (teach, play, no toys), and the start and stop times for each condition. The format is as follows:

John Smith	(1) No toys	08:20:40 to 08:25:50
DOT: 5/7/83	(2) Teach	09:15:20 to 09:20:30
	(3) Play	10:20:30 to 10:25:40
		hr min s

The name of the child and the condition to be transcribed are recorded at the top of the transcription sheet. The videotape is started and the time at which transcription began is recorded. This time is shown at the bottom of the TV screen and may not coincide with the start time appearing in the videotape label. The former refers to the beginning of transcription while the latter refers to the beginning of the videotape session. Often the transcriber begins after a warm-up period. The next 5 min of mother-child dialogue are transcribed. The time at which the transcription ended is recorded at the beginning of the transcription (see example).

Format of the Transcription

1. All speech by the participants is fully transcribed using standard English orthography on the right two-thirds of the transcription sheet. The participants are identified by an initial (M for mother, C for child). Information about the situational context also appears on the right two-thirds of the paper and is enclosed in parentheses. Each new utterance occupies a new line in the transcription sheet. The utterance boundary is determined by length of pause before the next utterance and by its apparent terminal countour, rising or falling. Miller (1981) asserts that 80% of the time pauses greater than 2 s occur between utterances. In addition, turns are separated by a blank line. For example:

Turn #	Utterance #	Speaker	Dialogue
1	1	M	(Mother takes a ball out of toy box) Look what I have here!
2	1	C	A ball.
3	1	M	Yes, a blue ball.

2. An action or event that occurs simultaneously with the child utterance appears on the same line with that utterance. For example:

    C: A kitty! (Points to cat)

3. When an action or event precedes or follows an utterance, the action or event appears on the preceding or succeeding line. For example:

    C: (C throws block)
        All gone.
        (C picks up guitar)

4. When an action or a set of actions compose a turn, that is, when they constitute an initiation or a response in conversation the parentheses are omitted and the action or set of actions are surrounded by plus signs. Following are some examples.

    M: Bring me the baby doll.
    C: +brings the doll to M.+
    M: Thank you.
        You are a nice girl.

    M: This is a nice playroom.
    C: +C gets up, takes guitar out of
        toy box and pokes M with it+.
    M: Do you want me to play it?

In addition, if a participant's turn demands a response from the conversational partner and the conversational partner does not respond within 3 s, the absence of a response is noted. For example:

    M: Bring me the baby doll.
    C: +no response, C is looking at truck+
    M: Johnny, Can you bring me the dolly?
    C: +no response, continues to look
        at truck+
    M: Are you listening?
    C: What?

5. When the two participants speak simultaneously, the overlapping speech is surrounded by slashes. An attempt should be made to indicate precisely which words overlapped. For example:

    M: Put it by this /car/ (Pointing to car)
    C: /Yeah/

6. Questionable transcriptions are surrounded by dollar signs ($). Whenever the transcriber is unsure about the transcription she or he should indicate this with the dollar signs. For example:

C: This is $a toy$

In this way, if these portions of the transcription are reliable they are included as part of the data to be analyzed. Thus, such transcriptions allow one to credit the participant with a turn, that is, an initiation or a response.

7. An unintelligible utterance or portion of an utterance is indicated by five Xs. It is necessary to give an estimate of the length of unintelligible utterances by making one or more groupings by Xs. A group of five Xs represents a word. For example:

C: All gone XXXXX house.

8. On the left one-third of the paper the turn number and number of utterances per turn are recorded. Events and nonverbal behaviors receive a 0 on the utterance column. For example:

Turn #	Utterance #	Speaker	Dialogue
1	1	M	Bring me the ball. (points)
2	0	C	+brings the ball to M.+
3	1	M	Thank you.
	0		(Gets up and picks up doll)
			Look what I have
	3		Isn't it pretty?
4	1	C	Yeah.
5	1	M	What is it's name?
6	0	C	+no response+
7	1	M	Do you know?
8	1	C	No.
	0		(Gets up and brings truck)
9	1	M	Is that a dump truck?
10	1	C	Yeah.

Punctuation

1. The initial letter of each utterance is capitalized.
2. Each new utterance occupies a new line. It is not necessary to enter a period at the end of each utterance. Though an utterance can be identified by the length of the pause before the next utterance and by its apparent terminal contour the judgment is sometimes difficult to make. Thus, the transcriber should judge the verbal behavior as carefully and objectively as possible.
3. Utterances that are exclamatory should be followed by an exclamation mark. For example:

C: A little kitty.
M: A kitty!
    A baby kitty!

4. Questions are indicated by a question mark. For example:

> **M:**   What is that?
> **C:**   A block.

5. Tag questions with rising intonation are followed by a question mark while tag questions with flat intonation are followed by a period. For example:

> **M:**   This is a butterfly, isn't it?
> **C:**   Uh-huh.
>
> **C:**   A pretty baby.
> **M:**   It is a pretty baby, isn't it.
>   You used to be a pretty baby too.

6. A pause within an utterance is indicated by three dots. For example:

> **M:**   I'll . . . bake a cake!
>
> **C:**   These are his . . . my toys.

7. A breath within an utterance is indicated by a comma. For example:

> **M:**   Honey, can you bring me the doll?

Labeling

1. Pages should be numbered with roman numerals in the upper-right-hand corner of the paper.

Transcription Sheets

Name: John Smith	Begin:08:20:20
Task: Teach	End: 08:25:20

Turn #
Utt #
Speaker
Dialogue

1
1
M
Honey, are you going to do anything besides take them out?

2
0
C
(Taking toys out of toy box)
1
Ah

3
1
M
What?

4 .
0
C
+no response, C keeps on taking out toys+

5
0
M
+M picks up Teddy bear and shows it to C+

6
1
C
No!

7
0
M
+M shows bear again+

8
1
C
No!
0
(C continues to take toys out)
2
Look, mommy (C has a ball in his hands)

9
1
M
Yeah
0
(M yawns)
2
Think I'm gonna take a nap

10
1
C
Mom take nap now?

11
1
M
Mm-huh

12
1
C
Take the toys out

13
1
M
Noticed you're taking the toys out
2
What will you do after you take all the toys out?

14
1
C
Dump'em (C dumps box of toys)

15
1
M
Dump'em, huh.
2
$ Well, this is XXXXX $

16
1
C
Look at the toys!

17
1
M
Huh?

18
1
M
House! (C is pointing to doll house)

19
1
M
Mm-huh

20
1
C
Open house

21
1
M
You can open the house

22
1
C
Open house

23
1
M
Mm-huh

24
1
C
Look, truck! (C pushes truck)
2
Truck (C pushes truck again)
3
Fire truck
4
That fire truck get in truck
5
$ Let that get in truck $

25
1
M
Mmm?

26
1
C
$ Let that get in truck $
2
That get in truck

27
1
M
Oh . . . I see
2
Are you lining up all the trucks?

28
1
C
That house (C pushes trailer house on the floor)

29
1
M
That's a house on wheels?
2
Maybe it's a trailer

30
0
C
(C gets an airplane)
1
Fly airplane
2
Fly airplane

31
1
M
Come here

32
1
C
Airplane go up

33
1
M
Yeah
2
Where's it going?

References

Bates, E., Camaioni, L., & Volterra, V. (1975). The acquisition of performatives prior to speech. *Merrill-Palmer Quarterly, 21*, 205–226.

Blank, M., Gessner, M., & Esposito, A. (1979). Language without communication: A case study. *Journal of Child Language, 6*, 329–352.

Bloom, L. (1970). *Language development: Form and function in emerging grammars.* Cambridge, MA: The MIT Press.

Bloom, L., & Lahey, M. (1978). *Language development and language disorders.* New York: John Wiley & Sons.

Breger, L. (1974). *From instinct to identity.* Englewood Cliffs, NJ: Prentice-Hall.

Brinton, B., & Fujiki, M. (1982). A comparison of request-response sequences in the discourse of normal and language-disordered children. *Journal of Speech and Hearing Disorders, 47*, 57–62.

Brown, J., Redmond, A., Bass, K., Liebergott, J., & Swope, S. (1975). *Symbolic play in normal and language-impaired children.* Paper presented to American Speech and Hearing Association Convention, Washington.

Brown, R. (1973). *A first language.* Cambridge, MA: Harvard University Press.

Buck, R. (1982). Spontaneous and symbolic nonverbal behavior and the ontogeny of communication. In R. S. Feldman (Ed.), *Development of nonverbal behavior in children.* New York: Springer-Verlag.

Carter, A. (1979). Prespeech meaning relations: An outline of one infant's sensorimotor morpheme development. In P. Fletcher & M. Garman (Eds.), *Language acquisition.* Cambridge: Cambridge University Press.

Compton, A. J. (1970). Generative studies of children's phonological disorders. *Journal of Speech and Hearing Disorders, 35,* 315–339.

Conti, G. (1982). *Mothers in dialogue: Some discourse features of motherese with normal and language impaired children.* Unpublished doctoral dissertation, University of Texas at Dallas.

Conti-Ramsden, G., & Friel-Patti, S. (1983). Mothers' discourse adjustments to language-impaired and non language-impaired children. *Journal of Speech and Hearing Disorders, 48,* 360–367.

Conti-Ramsden, G., & Friel-Patti, S. (in press). Mother-child dialogues: A comparison of normal and language impaired children. *Journal of Communication Disorders.*

Cromer, R. (1981a). Developmental language disorders: Cognitive processes, semantics, pragmatics, phonology, and syntax. *Journal of Autism and Developmental Disorders, 11,* 57–74.

Cromer, R. (1981b). Reconceptualizing language acquisition and cognitive development. In R. Schiefelsbusch & D. Bricker (Eds.), *Early language: Acquisition and intervention.* Baltimore: University Park Press.

deAjuriaguerra, J., Jaeggi, A., Guignard, F., Kocher, F., Marquard, M., Roth, S., & Schmid, E. (1965). Evolution et prognostic de la dysphasie chez l'enfant. *La Psychiatrie de L'Enfant, 8,* 291–352.

Dittmann, A. T. (1972). *Interpersonal messages of emotion.* New York: Springer-Verlag.

Donahue, M. (1981). Requesting strategies of learning disabled children. *Applied Psycholinguistics, 2,* 213–234.

Donahue, M., Pearl, R., & Bryan, T. (1980). Learning disabled children's conversational competence: Responses to inadequate messages. *Applied Psycholinguistics, 1,* 387–403.

Donahue, M., Pearl, R., & Bryan, T. (1982). Learning disabled children's syntactic proficiency on a communicative task. *Journal of Speech and Hearing Disorders, 47,* 397–403.

Dore, J. (1977). Oh them sheriff: A pragmatic analysis of children's responses to questions. In S. Ervin-Tripp & C. Mitchell-Kernan (Eds.), *Child discourse.* New York: Academic Press.

Druckman, D., Rozelle, R. M., & Baxter, J. C. (1982). *Nonverbal communication: Survey, theory and research.* Beverly Hills, CA: Sage Publications.

Dunbar, R. (1976). Some aspects of research design and their implications in the observational study of behaviour. *Behaviour, 58,* 78–98.

Eisenson, J. (1972). *Aphasia in children.* New York: Harper & Row, Pub.

Ekman, P. (1979). About brows: Emotional and conversational signals. In M. vonCranach, K. Foppa, W. Lepenies, Y. Ploog (Eds.), *Human ethology.* London: Cambridge University Press.

Ervin-Tripp, S. (1973). Some strategies for the first two years. In T. Moore (Ed.), *Cognitive development and the acquisition of language.* New York: Academic Press.

Ervin-Tripp, S. (1977). Wait for one, roller-skate. In S. Ervin-Tripp & C. Mitchell-Kernan (Eds.), *Child discourse.* New York: Academic Press.

Fey, M., & Leonard, L. (1983). Pragmatic skills of children with specific language impairment. In T. Gallagher & C. Prutting (Eds.), *Pragmatic assessment and intervention issues in language.* San Diego, CA: College-Hill Press.

Folger, M., & Leonard, L. (1978). Language and sensorimotor development during the early period of referential speech. *Journal of Speech and Hearing Research, 21,* 519–527.

Foster, S. (1980). Interpreting child discourse. In P. French & M. MacClure (Eds.), *Adult-child conversation.* New York: St. Martin's Press.

Friel-Patti, S. (1976). *Good looking: An analysis of verbal and nonverbal behaviors in a group of language disordered children.* Paper presented at the American Speech-Language-Hearing Association Convention, Houston.

Friel-Patti, S. (1977). *Nonverbal/verbal relationships in mother-child dyads with normal and language disordered children.* Paper presented at the American Speech-Language-Hearing Association Convention.

Friel-Patti, S. (1980). Aspects of mother-child interaction as related to the remediation process. *Annals of Otology, Rhinology and Laryngology, 89,* 171–174.

Friel-Patti, S., & Harris, M. (1982). *Language impaired children's use of play and socially directed behaviors.* Manuscript submitted for publication.

Gale, D. C., Liebergott, J. W., & Griffin, S. (1981). *Getting it: Children's requests for clarification.* Paper presented at the American Speech-Language-Hearing Association Convention, Los Angeles.

Gallagher, T. (1977). Revision behaviors in the speech of normal children developing language. *Journal of Speech and Hearing Research, 20,* 303–318.

Gallagher, T. M., & Darnton, B. A. (1978). Conversational aspects of the speech of language-disordered children: Revision behaviors. *Journal of Speech and Hearing Research, 21,* 118–135.

Geller, E., & Wollner, S. (1976). A preliminary investigation of the communicative competence of three linguistically impaired children. Paper presented to New York State Speech and Hearing Association.

Goldstein, K. (1939). *The organism.* New York: American Books, 1939.

Graybeal, C. M. (1981). Memory for stories in language-impaired children. *Applied Psycholinguistics, 2,* 269–283.

Haas, W. (1963). Phonological analysis of a case of dyslalia. *Journal of Speech and Hearing Disorders, 28,* 239–246.

Ingram, D. (1976). *Phonological disability in children.* London: Edward Arnold.

Inhelder, B. (1976). Cognitive development and its contribution to the diagnosis of some phenomena of mental deficiency. *Merrill-Palmer Quarterly, 12,* 299–319.

James, S. (1978). Effect of listener age on the politeness of children's directives. *Journal of Psycholinguistic Research, 7,* 307–317.

Johnston, J. R. (1982). Narratives: A new look at communication problems in older language-disordered children. *Language, Speech and Hearing Services in Schools, 13,* 144–155.

Kamhi, A. (1981). Nonlinguistic symbolic and conceptual abilities of language-impaired children. *Journal of Speech and Hearing Research, 24,* 446–453.

Kaye, K., & Charney, R. (1980). How mothers maintain "dialogue" with two-year olds. In D. Olson (Ed.), *The social foundations of language and thought*. New York: Norton.

Keller-Cohen, D. (1982). Context in child language. *Annual Review of Anthropology, 7*, 453–482.

Lee, L. (1966). Development of sentence types: A method for comparing normal and deviant syntactic development. *Journal of Speech and Hearing Disorders, 31*, 311–330.

Leonard, L. (1979). Language impairment in children. *Merrill-Palmer Quarterly, 25*, 205–232.

Leonard, L. (1972). What is deviant language? *Journal for Speech and Hearing Disorders, 37*, 427–446.

Leonard, L., Bolders, J., & Miller, J. (1976). An examination of the semantic relations reflected in the language usage of normal and language disordered children. *Journal of Speech and Hearing Research, 19*, 371–392.

Leonard, L., Steckol, K., & Schwartz, R. (1978). Semantic relations and utterance length in child language. In F. Peng & W. Von Raffler-Engel (Eds.), *Language acquisition and developmental kinesis*. Tokyo: Bunka Kyoron.

Lewis, M., & Rosenblum, L. (Eds.). (1978). *The development of affect*. New York: Plenum.

Lorentz, J. (1974). A deviant phonological system of English. *Papers and Reports on Child Language Development, 8*, 55–64.

Lovell, K., Hoyle, H., & Siddall, M. (1968). A study of some aspects of the play and language of young children with delayed speech. *Journal of Child Psychology and Psychiatry, 9*, 41–50.

Menyuk, P. (1964). Comparison of grammar of children with functionally deviant and normal speech. *Journal of Speech and Hearing Research, 7*, 109–121.

Miller, J. (1981). *Assessing language production in children*. Baltimore: University Park Press.

Mitchell-Kernan, C., & Kernan, C. (1977). Pragmatics of directive choice among children. In S. Ervin-Tripp and C. Mitchell-Kernan (Eds.), *Child discourse*. New York: Academic Press.

Nettelbladt, V. (1982). On phonotactic and prosodic development in normal and language disordered Swedish children. *Papers and Reports on Child Language Development, 21*, 125–129.

Ochs, E. (1979). Transcription as theory. In E. Ochs & B. Schieffelin (Eds.), *Developmental pragmatics*. New York: Academic Press.

Oller, D. K. (1973). Regularities in abnormal phonology. *Journal of Speech and Hearing Disorders, 38*, 36–47.

Oller, D. K. (1975). Why are childhood phonological production rules so varied? Paper presented at the American Speech-Language-Hearing Association Convention, Las Vegas.

Piche, G., Rubin, D., & Michlin, M. (1978). Age and social class in children's use of persuasive communicative appeals. *Child Development, 49*, 773–780.

Prinz, P. M., & Ferrier, L. J. (1983). "Can you give me that one": The comprehension, production and judgment of directives in language-impaired children. *Journal of Speech and Hearing Disorders, 48*, 44–54.

Rees, N. (1973). Auditory processing factors in language disorders: The view from Procrustes' bed. *Journal of Speech and Hearing Disorders, 38*, 304–315.

Rizzo, J., & Stephens, M. I. (1981). Performance of children with normal and impaired oral language production on a set of auditory comprehension tests. *Journal of Speech and Hearing Disorders, 46*, 150–159.

Rom, A., & Bliss, L. S. (1981). A comparison of verbal communicative skills of language impaired and normal speaking children. *Journal of Communication Disorders, 4*, 133–140.

Rosenblum, D., & Stephens, M. I. (1981). Correlates of syntactic development in kindergartners: Deficiency vs. proficiency. *Brain and Language, 13*, 103–117.

Rowan, L. E., & Leonard, L. (1981). *Performative and presuppositional skills.* Paper presented at the American Speech-Language-Hearing Association Convention, Los Angeles.

Saarni, C. (1982). Social and affective functions of nonverbal behavior: Developmental concerns. In R. S. Feldman (Ed.), *Development of nonverbal behavior in children.* New York: Springer-Verlag.

Sackett, G., Ruppenthal, G., & Gluck J. (1979). An overview of methodological and statistical problems in observational research. In G. Sackett (Ed.), *Observing behavior Volume II: Data collection and analysis methods.* Baltimore: University Park Press.

Sacks, H., Schegloff, E., & Jefferson, G. (1974). A simplest systematics for the organization of turn-taking for conversation. *Language, 50*, 696–735.

Snyder, L. S. (1976). The early presuppositions and performatives of normal and language disabled children. *Papers and Reports on Child Language Development, 12*, 221–229.

Snyder, L. S. (1978). Communicative and cognitive abilities and disabilities in the sensorimotor period. *Merrill-Palmer Quarterly, 24*, 161–180.

Stark, R. E. & Tallal, P. (1981). Selection of children with specific language deficits. *Journal of Speech and Hearing Disorders, 46*, 114–122.

Van Kleeck, A., & Frankel, T. L. (1981). Discourse devices used by language disordered children: A preliminary investigation. *Journal of Speech and Hearing Research, 46*, 250–257.

Whiting, B., & Whiting, J. (1973). Methods for observing and recording behavior. In R. Norall & R. Cohen (Eds.), *A handbook of method in cultural anthropology.* New York: Columbia University Press.

Author Index

Subject Index